The Cambridge Introductio
English Theatre, 1660–1900

This introduction aims to share with readers the author's enjoyment of the turbulent 240-year history of a theatre that tried, often against the odds, to be 'modern'. In each of its five parts, it deals successively with history and cultural context, and with the plays and the actors who caught the imagination of their era. Peter Thomson's text, always approachable, is enriched by quotations and carefully selected illustrations that capture 'the spirit of the age' under consideration. Beginning with the reopening of the playhouses under licence from Charles II, Thomson introduces the modern English theatre by breaking off at key dates – 1700, 1737, 1789 and 1843 – in order to explore both continuity and innovation. Familiar names and well-known plays feature alongside the forgotten and neglected. This is a reading of dramatic history that keeps constantly in mind the material circumstances that produced, and sometimes oppressed, a supremely popular theatre.

PETER THOMSON is Emeritus Professor of Drama, University of Exeter.

Cambridge Introductions to Literature

This series is designed to introduce students to key topics and authors.
Accessible and lively, these introductions will also appeal to readers who
want to broaden their understanding of the books and authors they enjoy.

- Ideal for students, teachers, and lecturers
- Concise, yet packed with essential information
- Key suggestions for further reading

Titles in this series:

Eric Bulson *The Cambridge Introduction to James Joyce*
John Xiros Cooper *The Cambridge Introduction to T. S. Eliot*
Janette Dillon *The Cambridge Introduction to Early English Theatre*
Jane Goldman *The Cambridge Introduction to Virginia Woolf*
David Holdeman *The Cambridge Introduction to W. B. Yeats*
Ronan McDonald *The Cambridge Introduction to Samuel Beckett*
John Peters *The Cambridge Introduction to Joseph Conrad*
Martin Scofield *The Cambridge Introduction to the American Short Story*
Peter Thomson *The Cambridge Introduction to English Theatre, 1660–1900*
Janet Todd *The Cambridge Introduction to Jane Austen*

The Cambridge Introduction to
English Theatre, 1660–1900

PETER THOMSON

CAMBRIDGE
UNIVERSITY PRESS

CAMBRIDGE UNIVERSITY PRESS
Cambridge, New York, Melbourne, Madrid, Cape Town, Singapore, São Paulo

Cambridge University Press
The Edinburgh Building, Cambridge CB2 2RU, UK

Published in the United States of America by Cambridge University Press, New York

www.cambridge.org
Information on this title: www.cambridge.org/9780521547901

First published 2006

Printed in the United Kingdom at the University Press, Cambridge

A catalogue record for this publication is available from the British Library

ISBN-13 978-0-521-83925-9 hardback
ISBN-10 0-521-83925-4 hardback

ISBN-13 978-0-521-54790-1 paperback
ISBN-10 0-521-54790-3 paperback

This one had better be for my grandchildren: Fraser, Joe, Abi, Eliza and Greta. If there are more to come, I'll write another book.

Contents

Illustrations

Preface

In offering an introduction to nearly 250 years of theatrical activity in Britain, I have tried to maintain a balance between the contribution of individuals and the historical and material conditions in which those contributions were made. The book is divided into five historically determined parts, but history is, of course, a continuum, and discreteness illusory. There are overlaps and, no doubt; many more inconsistencies than I am aware of. Part One is disproportionately long, because it was after the Restoration that the lines of development were laid down, and it seemed important to establish the origins before encountering the variations. Quotations, where they enrich the text rather than sustaining it, are separated out by shading. Illustrations have generally been chosen to serve the same purpose of enrichment. Although the pattern of chapters is common to all five Parts, I have allowed my different responses to each of the periods covered to dictate the choice of material represented by the subheadings of each chapter. It would be a foolhardy historian who claimed to be definitive. The proper function of an introducer is to bring two parties together in a friendly atmosphere. That is what I have endeavoured to do.

There is no bibliography, though some of the writing that has informed my thinking is mentioned in the text and its footnotes. Much more is not. Even a selective bibliography of books and essays on theatre and drama during the years between the restoration of Charles II and the death of Queen Victoria would need to be longer than this book. As far as possible, I have concentrated on plays available in modern editions, though some of the best of these are out of print. Years of cultural snobbery have discouraged familiarity with the popular drama of the past (as if Shakespeare were not a popular dramatist!), despite the obvious fact that popular plays provide unique access to vanished tastes, to what William Hazlitt called the 'spirit of the age' in attempting to unify his 1825 collection of essays on twenty-five prominent contemporaries. The spirit changes under pressure from external forces, and in less than twenty years Richard Hengist Horne was calling his parallel collection *A New Spirit of the Age* (1844). The cultural shift from the age of George IV to that of Victoria is nowhere more openly displayed than in the theatre. It is such shifts that this book aims to identify.

If there is anything unusual about my approach, it may be the outcome of my divided interest in history, playwrights and actors. That divided interest is reflected in the chapter divisions of each Part of the book.

Acknowledgements

The writing of this book has been a solitary experience, but I am in debt to all the authors who have enlivened it. My ideas and impressions have been formed over years – by teachers and scholars, some of whom have also been colleagues. No one can pretend to *know* 240 years of theatre history, but anyone who cares to can accumulate ideas and impressions. It was only on typing the final full stop that I remembered the opening sentence of Tom Henn's first lecture in an undergraduate series on 'English drama'. It went something like this: 'For the purposes of this lecture-course, I will assume that you are familiar with the work of Aeschylus, Sophocles, Euripides, Aristophanes, Terence, Plautus, the Wakefield Master, Marlowe, Shakespeare, Webster, Middleton . . .' and on and on he went. I am in Tom Henn's debt for the generosity of his assumption, but I am not sure that I went to his second lecture. I know enough now to know how little I know, and I am grateful to the hundreds of people who have alerted me to the delights of ignorance. Ignorance is, after all, one of the comparatively few things that we can *do* something about. Janette Dillon spurred me on by sharing with me, chapter by chapter, her own groundbreaking *Introduction* to pre-Restoration drama and theatre. Her example has encouraged me to look afresh at my old prejudices. But my principal debt is to Sarah Stanton, who invited me to write the book in the first place, and who has been my adviser and critic throughout the process.

Part One

The theatre restored: 1660–1700

The material circumstance

What can reasonably be called the 'modern' theatre began in England in 1660, and since the habits formed in the first decades of its existence had a lasting effect, and since this period produced a body of plays more remarkable than those of any other under review here, the first part of this book will pay particularly close attention to the rapid evolution of an institution. Who 'made' it and what materials went into its making (Chapter 1)? Who provided it with plays (Chapter 2)? How were they acted, and who acted them (Chapter 3)?

People who assume control of institutions – and a theatre, like a national government, is normally one of those – tend to delude themselves into thinking that they can accomplish something entirely new. At its most grandiose, this delusion involves an utter disregard of the vested interests of those already occupying subordinate positions in the institution and a bold belief that the network of dependencies that has so far, however flimsily, sustained that institution can be replaced at the drop of a new broom. Most of the deluded end up deep in the footnotes of history, where they might at best be used to point a moral or adorn the tale of today's stubborn dependence on yesterday. But in London, at the troubled dawning of the year 1660, there was no established theatre: had been none for eighteen years. Before the year was out, there were two. What the managers of these new theatres might have done is a subject for speculation. What they did is the starting point of this book.

Table of events referred to in Part One	
1642	Theatres closed by parliament
1658	Death of Oliver Cromwell
1660	General Monck's march to London. Restoration of Charles II
1662	Royal Society founded
1665	Great Plague of London
1665–7	Second Dutch War
1666	Great Fire of London
1667	Dutch fleet on the Medway. Fall of Earl of Clarendon
1672–4	Third Dutch War
1678	Titus Oates 'discovers' the Popish Plot

1679	Exclusion Bill to bar accession of James, Duke of York
1681	Charles II dissolves parliament to prevent passage of Exclusion Bill
1685	Death of Charles II. Accession of James II. Duke of Monmouth's rebellion quelled
1688	James II escapes to France. Accession of William and Mary
1689–97	War of the League of Augsburg
1694	Death of Queen Mary. Foundation of Bank of England
1701–13	War of the Spanish Succession
1702	Death of William III. Accession of Anne

The first theatre managers

The nationwide celebration of the restoration of the Stuart monarchy can easily mislead us into supposing that Charles II was inevitable. On the contrary, his crowning was the outcome of political improvisation in a country that was losing control of itself. By the end of 1659, the standing army was so profoundly at odds with parliament that a renewal of civil war seemed imminent. What proved to be the decisive action was taken by General George Monck, then occupied in the suppression of rebellion in Scotland. Monck is one of the abiding enigmas of history. What had he in mind when he marched his disciplined army southward across the Tweed on 2 January 1660? What were his intentions as he systematically disempowered the officers of the army in England? And what political resolution was he seeking when he led his troops into Westminster on 2 February 1660? It seems unlikely that so staunch a Cromwellian was already bent on preparing the way for a king. For more than two months he bided his time, evidently determined to support constitutional procedure. As a member of the parliament newly elected in April, he was among those who voted for the Stuart restoration on 1 May, and he was the first person to embrace Charles II when the gratified, and slightly flummoxed, uncrowned king landed at Dover on 25 May.

About noon (though the brigantine that Beale made was there ready to carry him) yet [the King] would go in my Lord's barge with the two Dukes. Our Captain steered, and my Lord went along bare with him. I went, and Mr. Mansell, and one of the King's footmen, with a dog that the King loved, and so got on shore when the King did, who was received by General Monk [*sic*] with all imaginable love and respect at his entrance upon the land of Dover. Infinite the crowd of people and the horsemen, citizens, and noblemen of all sorts. The Mayor of the town came and gave him his white staff, the badge of his place, which the King did give him again. The Mayor also presented him from the town a very rich Bible, which he took and said it was the thing that he loved above all things in the world. A canopy was provided for him to stand under, which he did, and talked awhile with General Monk and others, and so into a stately coach there set for him, and so away through the town towards Canterbury, without making any stay at Dover.

Samuel Pepys, *Diary*, 25 May 1660

Monck would be rewarded with the title of Duke of Albemarle, but it is difficult to believe that he could ever have explained just how things had turned out this way. In that respect, he would have been a true representative of the nation at large.

Charles II's instant performance of magnanimity at the beginning of his reign was politically brilliant. It was still being alluded to in the plays of the 1670s.

That I survive the dangers of the day,
Next to the gods, brave friends, be yours the honour;
And let heaven witness for me that my joy
Is not more great for this my right restored,
Than, 'tis that I have power to recompence
Your loyalty and valour. Let mean princes,
Of abject souls, fear to reward great actions;
I mean to show
That whatsoe'er subjects like you dare merit,
A king like me, dares give.

This is the first speech of the restored rightful king, Leonidas, in Act 5 of John Dryden's *Marriage à la Mode* (1671). There are many comparable passages in plays written between 1660 and 1678.

He relished the power to enhance the prospects of those who had smoothed his path to the throne, but not as much as he relished the power to reward the small group of royalists who had remained loyal to him during his penurious exile. The latter group included Thomas Killigrew, whom, in July 1660, Charles appointed as overseer of his own nominal company of players, the King's Men. The appointment, that is to say, was not based on proven managerial merit of the kind that might have been claimed for Sir William Davenant, given ten days later the oversight of a second company, nominally servants of the king's brother, and known from the outset as the Duke's Men. The political significance of these July appointments needs to be understood:

1)   Less than two months into his reign, Charles II was asserting his right to be royally entertained without reference to parliament or Privy Council,

and effectively bypassing Sir Henry Herbert, the long-serving Master of the Revels, who had been reappointed to that post in June.

2) At the same time, by sanctioning what amounted to a theatrical duopoly in London, he was signalling his determination to contain any threats to the state from a politically independent theatre. The warrants issued exclusively to Killigrew and Davenant, while encouraging them to take a fresh initiative, rendered illegal the theatrical enterprises already underway in the city.

3) Even so, Charles II was publicly setting the tone for a new style of government hospitable to stage-plays, those 'Spectacles of Pleasure' that had been banned by parliamentary directive in 1642.

Whereas the distressed Estate of Ireland, steeped in her own Blood, and the distracted Estate of England, threatened with a Cloud of Blood by a Civil War, call for all possible Means to appease and avert the Wrath of God, appearing in these Judgements; amongst which, Fasting and Prayer, having been often tried to be very effectual, have been lately and are still enjoined; and whereas Public Sports do not well agree with public Calamities, nor Public Stage-plays with the Seasons of Humiliation, this being an Exercise of sad and pious Solemnity, and the other being Spectacles of Pleasure, too commonly expressing lascivious Mirth and Levity: It is therefore thought fit, and Ordained, by the Lords and Commons in this Parliament assembled, That while these sad causes and set Times of Humiliation do continue, Public Stage Plays shall cease, and be forborne, instead of which are recommended to the People of this Land the profitable and seasonable considerations of Repentance, Reconciliation, and Peace with God, which probably may produce outward Peace and Prosperity, and bring again Times of Joy and Gladness to these Nations.

> Parliamentary directive against public stage-plays,
> issued 2 September 1642

But it was for Killigrew and Davenant to determine the direction of a reborn professional theatre. Who were they? And what had they to offer?

Thomas Killigrew (1612–83) belonged to the London gentry. It was almost certainly his father, vice-chamberlain to Queen Henrietta Maria, who introduced him to the royal court, where, by 1632, he was a page of honour to Charles I. He wrote his first play, *The Prisoners*, in 1635, and had earned himself a modest reputation as a playwright (and a decidedly immodest reputation as a wit) before the closure of the theatres in 1642. His most successful play, *The Parson's Wedding*, was written in 1640/1 and would be famously revived with an all-female cast in 1664. From 1635 until the outbreak of the first Civil War, Killigrew spent much of his time travelling in Europe (according to the 1664 edition of his *Comedies and Tragedies*, he wrote *The Parson's Wedding* in Basel), employed, if at all, on trivial missions; but he was carrying messages for Charles I and Henrietta Maria as political tension heightened in 1641–2, and was under house arrest in Covent Garden for several months in 1642–3.

After his release, like many displaced royalists, he took refuge on the Continent, and by 1647 was established in the circle of friends of the prince-in-exile. He served at various times as Charles's special envoy, his liaison officer and a groom of his bedchamber, but most significantly as a specialist in the morale-boosting job of remaining cheerful in adversity. Sometimes, and not always kindly, he was referred to as Charles's licensed jester, but there is something to be admired in a man whose good spirits survived the aimless time-passing of a wandering cavalier during the English Interregnum. It may have been in Madrid in 1654 that Killigrew completed the two-part comedy, *Thomaso*, in which he gave dramatic expression to the adventures (and mishaps) of the stateless royalists who travelled opportunistically from city to city in Europe. Too long and creakily put together, *Thomaso* survives best in Aphra Behn's brilliant compression, *The Rover* (1677); and the Killigrew of history can probably be glimpsed in the Willmore of Behn's recreation. He was certainly as much in need of a wealthy wife as any of Behn's roving cavaliers, and was lucky enough to find one in Holland, the territory in which he came closest to establishing himself. Charlotte van Hesse would later figure as 'north Holland's fine flower' in the Earl of Rochester's obscene poem 'Signior Dildo' (*c*.1673). (The marriage would eventually founder after Killigrew had exhausted Charlotte's fortune, and a few days after his death she was reduced to petitioning the king for relief: she was granted an annual pension of £200.) Samuel Pepys (1633–1703) met Killigrew, his spirits still high, on 24 May 1660, the eve of the restored king's embarkation for England, and marked him 'a merry droll . . . who told us many merry stories'. So far so good, but the biographical searcher for evidence that Killigrew had the makings of a theatre manager will find nothing.

Sir William Davenant (1606–68) – the knighthood was conferred by the beleaguered Charles I in 1643 – was much better equipped by experience, but never as close to Charles II. Davenant, the son of a prosperous vintner, spent his formative years in Oxford, of which city his father was elected mayor in 1621. The near-contemporary claim, given that father's known enjoyment of plays, that Shakespeare stood as young William's godfather is not implausible. Throughout his theatrical career Davenant said nothing to discredit it. Having left Oxford for London in 1622, he found employment first in the household of the Duchess of Richmond and then of the admired 'renaissance man' Fulke Greville, Lord Brooke. Before Greville's violent death at the hands of his man-servant in 1628, Davenant had married the first of three wives and had his first play, *The Cruel Brother* (1627), staged by the King's Men at the Blackfriars indoor playhouse, but the career of a young man on the make was interrupted in 1630 when Davenant contracted a venereal disease, probably syphilis, sufficiently virulent to entail the loss of most of his nose. The mercury cure was painful, but his gratitude to Queen Henrietta Maria's doctor Thomas Cademan, who tended him, found singular expression twenty years later when he married Cademan's widow. It was probably through Cademan that Davenant gained access to the queen, whose neoplatonic circle he joined and with whose support he wrote his courtly plays, *Love and Honour* (1634) and *The Platonic Lovers* (1635). From then until the outbreak of civil war, Davenant's theatrical work was centred on the royal court, above all in the staging of the elaborate masques through which the king and queen sought to celebrate their concept of benign rule. It was through writing these masques, from *The Temple of Love* (1635) to *Salmacida Spolia* (1640), that Davenant encountered the scenic innovations of Inigo Jones, and it is for his importation of scenic spectacle into the public playhouses of the post-Restoration period that he is best remembered. The idea was already in him when, in March 1639, he secured a warrant from Charles I to build a playhouse on the north side of Fleet Street. It was a dream that he would come close to realizing in 1661.

In the early years of the Civil War, Davenant was an active go-between for Charles I in England and his queen in France, but royalist defeats left him marooned in Paris. Without any of Killigrew's backseat skills, he embarked on the wasted labour of a vast 'heroic poem', modelled on the five-act structure of tragedy. Mercifully, only three books of *Gondibert* were ever completed. As unofficial poet laureate since 1638, Davenant was paying homage to the king by writing it. After Charles I's execution in January 1649, though, he returned to the service of the widowed queen, and it was on a mission instigated by her that he was captured and imprisoned by parliamentary forces, initially in Cowes Castle on the Isle of Wight and then, more ominously, in the Tower of London. Extremists argued for a treason trial, but the view that the impoverished Davenant constituted a threat to the state strained credibility, and he was released in the autumn of 1652. His immediate marriage to Anne Cademan brought short-term relief from accumulated debts, but his quick remarriage after her death in 1655 suggests that his financial problems remained. It was his French third wife, Henrietta du Tremblay, who supported and eventually inherited his management of the Duke's Men. Through Davenant's fifties and sixties, she provided him with nine sons and a home base secure enough to release him to the theatre.

Historians of the drama have given due credit to Davenant's groundbreaking initiatives. Confident of Oliver Cromwell's appreciation of music, he began as early as May 1656 with an 'entertainment' in his temporary home, Rutland House in Aldersgate Street. This was not a play – the ban on plays was still operative – nor was it merely a concert. Davenant had composed two debates, one on the value of 'moral representations' and one on the relative merits of Paris and London, interspersing them with songs and instrumental music. The audience was invited to consider the event as a first step on the road to 'our Elyzian field, the *Opera*'. A second, and much larger, step on that road was taken later in the same year, when Davenant staged his own *The Siege of Rhodes* at Rutland House. Within the constraints of a narrow room, perspective scenery provided a backdrop to a plain story, told in recitative. At this moment, the scenery mattered more to Davenant than the story. Even when transferred to the Cockpit in Drury Lane, this was a private performance, so that the evident presence among the singers of a Mrs Coleman cannot qualify her as the first woman to appear in a public theatre in England. But Davenant was sufficiently emboldened by the acquiescence of Cromwell and the parliamentary author-ities over the presentation of *The Siege of Rhodes* to follow it with two more 'operas', also staged at the Cockpit in 1658 and 1659. Only after Cromwell's death in September 1658 was he formally warned off; and by then London was caught up in pre-Restoration turmoil.

I have outlined the background of Killigrew and Davenant because, in their different ways, these first managers of the revived theatre set the pattern for the subsequent history of theatre management in England. Notably, and against Elizabethan, Jacobean and Caroline precedent, they owed their appointment to the court. The earliest managers of professional theatre companies in London worked within the companies they managed, and their authority was granted (or challenged) by their fellow-workers. But the limited egalitarianism of the Commonwealth ended abruptly with the restoration of the monarchy. The authority of Killigrew and Davenant shadowed the nation's return to gov-ernment by privileged aristocrats. Almost the only other things they had in common were their fluctuating aspirations as playwrights, continental wives and a constant shortage of funds to support their willingness to live beyond their means. In relation to the theatre, Killigrew was an amateur and Davenant a professional. The contrast is one that can be observed at almost any time over the next three centuries.

Managing the new theatres

Charles II's July decision to allow Killigrew and Davenant to share the future spoils of London's theatrical market was formally ratified by the issuing of a joint warrant the next month. The warrant sought to appease Puritan opponents of the stage by reminding its beneficiaries of their moral responsibilities.

We, taking the premises into our princely consideration, yet not holding it necessary totally to suppress the use of theatres, because we are assured that if the evils and scandals in the plays that now are or have been acted were taken away, the same might serve as innocent and harmless divertissements for many of our subjects; and having experience of the art and skill of our trusty and well-beloved Thomas Killigrew, Esq., one of the Grooms of our Bedchamber, and of Sir William Davenant, Knight, for the purposes hereafter mentioned, do hereby give and grant unto the said Thomas Killigrew and Sir William Davenant full power and authority to erect two companies of players, consisting respectively of such persons as they shall choose and appoint, and to purchase, build, and erect or hire at their charge, as they shall think fit, two houses or theatres with all convenient rooms and other necessaries thereunto appertaining, for the representation of tragedies, comedies, plays, operas, and all other entertainments of that nature in convenient places: and likewise to settle and establish such payments to be paid by those that shall resort to see the said representations performed as either have been accustomely given and taken in the like kind, or as shall be reasonable in regard of the great expenses of scenes, music, and such new decorations as have not been formerly used: with further power to make such allowances out of that which they shall so receive to the actors and other persons employed in the said representations in both houses respectively as they shall think fit; the said companies to be under the government and authority of them, the said Thomas Killigrew and Sir William Davenant. And in regard to the extraordinary licentiousness that has lately used in things of this nature, our pleasure is, that there shall be no more places of representation nor companies of actors of plays, or operas, and recitations, music or representations by dancing and scenes and any other entertainments on the stage, in our Cities of London and Westminster, or in the liberties of them than the two to be now erected by virtue of this authority. Nevertheless, we do hereby by our authority royal strictly enjoin the said Thomas Killigrew and Sir William Davenant that they do not at any time hereafter cause to be acted or represented any play, interlude, or opera, containing any matter of profanation, scurrility, or obscenity; and we do further hereby authorise and command the said Thomas Killigrew and Sir William Davenant to peruse all plays that have been formerly written, and to expunge all profanities and scurrility from the same before they be represented or acted.

Extract from the Warrant granted by Charles II on 21 August 1660

Its terms would be reaffirmed in 1662, with additions in the light of experience, by the delivery into the managers' hands of separate 'Letters Patent', thus initiating nearly two centuries of legal bickering about the duopoly rights of the current holders of the royal patent. While the authority of Killigrew and Davenant as patent-holders was made abundantly clear, the right to succession of their 'heirs and assigns' made the London theatre a hostage to familial and financial fortune. The disposal and vexed authority of the patents would be responsible for much that was inglorious in the subsequent history of the stage.

Both managers started purposefully. Under the King's Men's banner, Killigrew recruited most of the experienced actors and was granted the rights to the majority of the 'old' repertoire, in which plays by Ben Jonson featured prominently alongside those conventionally ascribed to Beaumont and Fletcher. (The 1647 publication in folio of the *Comedies and Tragedies* under the supposed joint authorship of Beaumont and Fletcher had been one of the Interregnum's sparse contributions to dramatic literature.) Davenant's actors were generally younger and unproven, and his company had a greater dependence on new plays. It was a division temperamentally suited to both men: Killigrew could sit back and leave the theatrical leadership to Charles Hart (1625–83) and Michael Mohun (c.1616–84), who had both been actors during the reign of Charles I and had served in royalist armies during the Civil Wars, while Davenant, a 'hands-on' professional, could lead his inexperienced troupe from the front.

Documentation of the early years of the post-Restoration theatre is scanty, and there is nothing to tell us about the backstage life of the actors. That there was an element of competition between the two companies from the outset is suggested by the evidence that they both gave their opening performances on 5 November (as the anniversary of James I's survival of the Gunpowder Plot, this was a significant date in the Stuart calendar) 1660, though there is a possibility that this was a joint production. Either way, the rapidity of the operation is notable. Within a few months, Killigrew and Davenant had assembled their troupes, determined an initial repertoire and furnished a playhouse. They were in close collusion with the royal court, and it may have been Charles II's mischievous prompting that emboldened Killigrew to employ a woman (exactly who she was has not been established) to play Desdemona when the King's Men (transformed by the presence of a pioneering woman into the King's Company) staged *Othello* in December 1660. The risk would not have been taken without at least a nod from the pleasure-loving monarch, whose experience of plays was largely confined to European theatres in which women customarily took the female roles. Political astuteness may have been in operation, too. It would be some time before Puritan forces could regroup without risk to their property or lives. In the event, those who took moral exception to the presence of actresses remained silent or were overruled, and the ethos of the English theatre was permanently transformed.

If the new generation of actors had little experience, the actresses had none, and Davenant's decision to board four of them in his own house typifies his engagement with the Duke's Company. We can assume that he provided personal coaching. The novelty of actresses was the second publicity coup for the new theatres. The first was changeable scenery.

When designing their playhouses, Killigrew and Davenant could have followed the architectural model of the great Elizabethan and Jacobean open-air amphitheatres. The Red Bull was still standing, and the fact that it could accommodate more than 2,000 spectators must have tempted any manager with his eye on the box office. Instead, they both chose to work in small indoor playhouses. Killigrew, cherishing the idea of a return to the old ways, refurbished a 'real' tennis court, Gibbons's, in the style of the Caroline 'private' theatres, an intimate space without significant scenic provision. Davenant, temporarily housed in just such a private theatre, in Salisbury Court, had still in mind the spectacular staging of Charles I's court masques. If a room in Rutland House could accommodate scenically elaborate operas, so, surely, could Salisbury Court, and so, certainly, would Lisle's converted tennis court near Lincoln's Inn Fields, into which he moved his company in the summer of 1661.

The attention paid to 'Restoration drama' by literary scholars has tended to obscure the significant contribution of scenery to the newfangled pleasures of late seventeenth-century theatre. In defining his share in the play that he co-wrote with Nathaniel Lee, John Dryden, the age's supreme wordsmith, explained in 1683 that 'I writ the first and third Acts of *Oedipus*, and drew the *Scenary* [*sic*] of the *whole Play*'.[1] Just how literally he was employing the verb 'drew' is uncertain, but the implication is as unmistakable as the fact that Davenant was the pioneer and mastermind of the transfer of perspective scenery from the privacy of courts to the public stage. Expenditure on the decoration and animation of the stage was bound to raise the price of admission, but Killigrew could not afford to ignore such a popular innovation.

> Sir *William Davenant* was the first who brought Scenes upon the Stage, towards the Middle of the last Century; and to defray the Expence of them, from time to time, rais'd the Theatrical Receipt about a third Part higher than it was before. The Pit, which was before but eighteen Pence, was rais'd to Half a Crown; the Boxes, which were Half a Crown before, were advanc'd to four Shillings; the first Gallery from a Shilling to eighteen Pence; and the upper Gallery, from Sixpence to a Shilling.
>
> John Dennis, 'Remarks on *The Conscious Lovers*' (1723)

While the Duke's Company retained its base in Lincoln's Inn Fields until 1671 (three years after Davenant's death), the King's abandoned the old Gibbons's tennis court in 1663, when the building of a new theatre, with provision for scenes and machines, was complete. When John Evelyn attended *The Indian Queen* there on 5 February 1664, he thought the text (by Dryden and Sir Robert Howard) well written, 'but so beautified with rich scenes as the like had never been seen . . . on a mercenary theatre'. Howard, Dryden's brother-in-law, was the scene-painter, and this mercenary theatre was the first of four to have been built on or near the site of the present Theatre Royal, Drury Lane.

Catering for a large, mixed audience was outside the vision of Killigrew and Davenant. They had informally contracted with Charles II to provide entertainment for a courtly coterie, and the capacity of their first playhouses cannot have exceeded 400. Even so, the selling of tickets was a matter of great moment and potential mistrust, as is clear from the articles of agreement between Davenant and the company he selected to share the risks and profits of performance. Of the fifteen shares, Davenant kept ten for himself (or his executives, administrators, assignees), with the remaining five to be divided among the actors. Financial responsibility was clearly demarcated, and an exaggerated attempt was made to dispel misgivings over the handling of receipts. So much so that the ticket office was as busy as the stage.

> That Sir William Davenant, his executors, administrators or assignees shall at the general charge of the whole receipts provide three persons to receive money for the said tickets in a room adjoining to the said theatre, and that the actors in the said theatre, now parties to these presents, who are concerned in the said five shares or proportions, shall daily or weekly appoint two or three of themselves, or the men hirelings deputed by them, to sit with the aforesaid three persons appointed by the said Sir William, that they may survey or give an account of the money received for the said tickets.
>
> From the articles of agreement between Sir William Davenant and his players, 5 November 1660

The mixed repertoire of predominantly old and occasionally new plays, with actresses freshly on display against cleverly painted backgrounds, proved sufficiently attractive in the early years to keep the ticket-sellers busy, particularly on days when the king or his brother were in attendance. The playhouses were fashionable meeting places, sites of opportunity for those given to self-display or for men and women alike at the sexual ready. If she chose, a woman could conceal her scrutiny of the male talent on the stage and off it behind a vizard-mask, and the men, when the action or dialogue on stage became sexually explicit, could switch their lascivious gaze between the actresses and their female audience (the women who smiled or those who pretended not to understand – where did opportunity lie?). Playgoers, then, enjoyed each other's company, sometimes more than the play. When Pepys adopted the new fashion for periwigs in 1663, he sported his purchase first in a coffee-house, then in Hyde Park and then in the theatre. The fact that a prominent and hardworking civil servant like Pepys went so regularly to the playhouses is a reminder that audiences were not confined to the nobility. To be sure, many adherents of the court went out of their way to be noticed, and it was the opinion of courtiers that Killigrew and Davenant were guided by, but as early as 19 January 1661, at the performance of a forgotten Fletcherian drama called *The Lost Lady*,[2] Pepys was 'troubled to be seen by four of our office clerks, which sat in the half-crown box and I in the 1s. 6d.', and he didn't much enjoy the play either.

There was nothing that Killigrew and Davenant could have done to stave off the double blow to their prosperity of the plague epidemic in 1665 and the Great Fire of 1666. An enforced closure for eighteen months, and, in the aftermath, a strengthening belief that London was being punished by God for its sinfulness, led to a decline in attendance which hit the King's Company particularly hard. Charles II's honeymoon period, too, was brought to an end by these disasters. Criticism of his open promiscuity was voiced more publicly, and the playhouse behaviour of his libertine associates caused such morally upright gentlemen as Evelyn to abandon the public theatres.

This night was acted my Lord Broghill's tragedy called *Mustapha* before their majesties at court, at which I was present, very seldom at any time going to the public theatres for many reasons now as they were abused to an atheistical liberty; foul and indecent women now (and never till now) permitted to appear and act which, inflaming several young noblemen and gallants, became their whores and to some their wives: witness, the Earl of Oxford, Sir Robert Howard, Prince Rupert, the Earl of Dorset and another greater person than any of those, who fell into their snares to the reproach of their noble families and ruin of both body and soul.
John Evelyn, *Diary*, 18 October 1666

Surveying his Theatre Royal auditorium, and comparing it with the playhouses he had known during the reign of Charles I, Killigrew betrayed to Pepys the kind of bewilderment that resourceful theatre managers keep to themselves. The occasion was a concert of Italian music at the home of the polymath Lord Brouncker, at that time still serving as the first president of the Royal Society and keeping as his mistress a minor actress called Abigail Williams (the willing ensnaring of noblemen by actresses was the kind of thing Evelyn deplored). The date was 12 February 1667, and Killigrew and Pepys had just listened to the composer Giovanni Baptista Draghi singing to his own harpsichord accompaniment an act of the opera which Killigrew planned to stage at Drury Lane:

> This done, T. Killigrew and I to talk: and he tells me how the audience at his house is not above half so much as it used to be before the late fire . . . That the stage is now by his pains a thousand times better and more glorious than ever heretofore. Now wax-candles, and many of them; then not above 3 lbs. of tallow: now all things civil, no rudeness

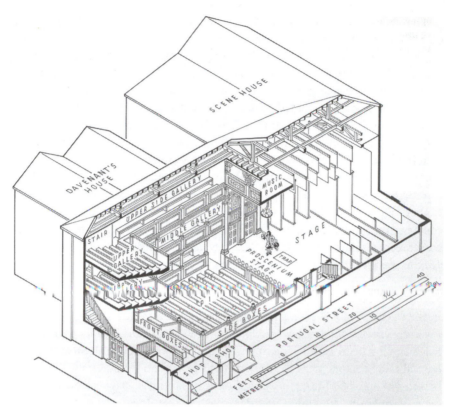

Figure 1. Lincoln's Inn Fields Playhouse in *c.*1661. Richard Leacroft's isometric cross-section shows clearly the stage doors and the ease of contact between the actor and the nine rows of pit benches.

anywhere; then as in a bear-garden: then two or three fiddlers; now nine or ten of the best: then nothing but rushes upon the ground, and every thing else mean; and now all otherwise: then the Queen seldom and the King never would come; now not the King only for state, but all civil people do think they may come as well as any. He tells me that he hath gone several times, eight or ten times, he tells me, hence to Rome to hear good music; so much he loves it, though he never did sing or play a note. That he hath ever endeavoured in the late King's time and in this to introduce good music . . .

Pepys captures the elegiac tone of a management in decline, though Killigrew soldiered on, in increasingly rancorous dispute with his actors, through the burning (in January 1672) and rebuilding of his Theatre Royal (opened March 1674), this time fronting on Drury Lane rather than Bridges Street, until, in 1677, his son and heir, Charles, took legal action to force him out.

The Duke's Company, under Davenant, recovered from the long closure of 1665–6 much more quickly than the King's. Its plays may have been no better, but they were better presented, and the intimacy of the auditorium at the Lincoln's Inn Fields playhouse was preferred by many to the comparative austerity of the Theatre Royal's. Davenant seems to have gained his actors' respect, and was thus enabled to demand the disciplined preparation of each new production. In a full season the Duke's Company might stage as many as fifty plays, of which ten might be 'new'. The 'new' is highlighted to draw attention to the fact that many supposedly new plays were reworkings of Jacobean and Caroline originals or adaptations from the French (Molière was regularly plundered). Davenant had a special interest in lavish, semi-operatic exploitations of plots from Shakespeare, for which he misleadingly retained Shakespearean titles. In the original division of the repertoire, Killigrew seems to have accepted Davenant's claims to a special relationship with Shakespeare.[3] *Hamlet* was among the first plays staged by the Duke's Men, and it was Thomas Betterton's playing of the title role that established him as a major actor. A grandiose production of *Henry VIII* was calculated to counter public interest in the wizardry of Killigrew's new stage at the Theatre Royal in 1663. But it is for his operatic interventions in *Macbeth* (?1664) and *The Tempest* (1667) that Davenant has been most frequently castigated by Shakespearean purists. There have always been people who consider the theatre bad for plays: they have not had to reckon with shifting tastes or box-office returns. Davenant would have been gratified by the king's attendance at his own 'new' (from the French) play, *The Man's the Master*, on 26 March 1668, but there was much unfinished business when he died suddenly on 7 April.

Management in disarray: Betterton to the rescue

The patents bestowed on Killigrew and Davenant in April 1662 made them *and their heirs and assigns* the exclusive purveyors of 'comedies, tragedies, plays or entertainment[s] of the stage' in the twin cities of London and Westminster. This meant, in effect, that anyone who inherited or purchased the patents had a legal right to manage the business of the two companies. In the case of the Duke's Company, this created few problems in the immediate aftermath of Davenant's death. His eldest son, Charles, was not yet of age to inherit, his widow was level-headed, and there was agreement among the actors that the management should be entrusted to their most eminent colleagues, Betterton (1635–1710) and Henry Harris (c.1634–1704). It was the actor-managers, not the patentee(s), who oversaw the design and construction of the grand new playhouse in Dorset Garden, which the Duke's Company opened in November

1671. This was the best-equipped of the post-Restoration theatres, but contemporaries considered it to be acoustically better-suited to opera than to plays. Actors have to grow into such demanding spaces, and it says much for Betterton's powers of persuasion that the necessarily egotistical members of the company learnt to concede to the demands of scenes and machines. There was no such harmony among the King's Company. Charles Killigrew's successful chancery suit against his father gave him the authority he craved, but, at the age of twenty-two in 1677, he was ill-equipped to lord it over such veterans as Hart, Mohun and the dance and dialect specialist, John Lacy (*c.*1615–81). Before the end of July 1677, the actors of the King's Company had withdrawn their labour, and the Lord Chamberlain had to intervene on behalf of the king.

> His Majesty being dissatisfied with the government of the players, His Servants at the Royal Theatre, upon their humble petition which I here send you, is pleased to gratify them in their proposition of governing themselves but withall, that Mr Killigrew's right to his shares and profits may be preserved and that he may have also security given him to indemnify him from those articles and debts which he alleges he is liable unto, as you will see in his answers to their petition which I here also send you. His Majesty desires it may be despatched by you with all conveniency that the Company may begin to play to support themselves because they suffer every day they lie still.
>
> The Lord Chamberlain to the Attorney General, 30 July 1677

There was no one of Betterton's steadiness among the angry players, and problems remained despite Charles II's uncharacteristically democratic intervention.

The political hurricane, latent from the time in 1673 when the Duke of York's Catholicism was made open (with the royal marriage childless, he was the lineal heir to the throne), and released on the country after Titus Oates's mischievous 'revelation' of a 'Popish Plot' in November 1678, need not necessarily have had an adverse effect on the theatres. Drama can thrive on turmoil, and the Catholic Duke's own company of players rode out the storm with only the occasional casualty.[4] Charles Killigrew, though, may have revealed his anti-Catholic bias too openly for the good of his actors. Dryden, who had been a shareholder and contracted playwright since 1669, and who would announce his conversion to Roman Catholicism in 1685, defected to the Duke's Company in 1678, and the next year a handful of Killigrew's disgruntled actors upped sticks and went to ply their trade in Scotland.[5] Having limped into 1682, the King's Company merged with, was in large measure absorbed by, the Duke's to form the United Company, and for the next thirteen years Betterton was effectively the inhouse manager of two playhouses (Dorset Garden and Drury Lane) and of the only theatrical enterprise in London.

The two patents remained, of course: Charles Davenant held one and Charles Killigrew the other. In signing an act of union, though, the two Charleses also amalgamated their patents. If law were foolproof, a single patent would then have held theatrical development to ransom, the shortcomings of such a monopoly would have been exposed, and 160 years of generally undignified litigation avoided. But once a family gets its teeth into a source of income, there is generally some sibling (or, failing that, an aunt, an uncle, a cousin) eager to pick up the pieces. When Charles Davenant wished to opt out, his brother Alexander bought his share of the patent. Since he could not afford it, he borrowed from a legal partnership fronted by Sir Thomas Skipwith, but powered by the financially astute Christopher Rich (*c.*1647–1714). So it was that, when Alexander Davenant, still in debt, fled to the Canary Islands in 1693, Charles Killigrew found himself with new co-patentees, Skipwith and Rich.

Almost immediately, the management policy changed. Whereas Killigrew had accepted an inherited agreement to reinvest a proportion of the profits in the two theatres' fabric and stocks, Rich was for radical reorganization and the cutting of costs. No one working in the public sector in twenty-first-century Britain need be surprised that the 'heavy' proponent of restructuring won the day, nor that the morale of the actors dipped. Driven to penning a petition to the Lord Chamberlain in December 1694, they complained that they were being treated 'not as . . . the Kings & Queenes servants but the Claimers slaves'. The petition was signed by all fourteen of the leading members of the United Company, and they were lucky in the Lord Chamberlain. Charles Sackville, Earl of Dorset, was a friend of the players and had been Nell Gwyn's lover before the king claimed her. He (after formal recourse to higher authority) allowed the petitioners to abscond from the United Company and to perform independently. Without a patent, and therefore in contradiction of the patents' terms, they refurbished once again the old theatre in Lincoln's Inn Fields, carrying with them the sympathy of most knowledgeable theatregoers.

The first play performed by the new Actors' Company was William Congreve's *Love for Love*, and its opening in April 1695 was one of those glittering occasions that are sprinkled across the history of the London stage. Congreve's prologue, spoken by Betterton, referred to the actors as husbandmen, 'transplanted to more kindly earth' from a place where their labours were 'lost upon ungrateful ground'. According to the prompter, John Downes, *Love for Love* was, very unusually for the time, presented thirteen times in uninterrupted succession. There is no doubt of the good intentions of the breakaway actors. There were to be ten equal sharers, and no nominated manager: they had seen enough of management. By 1700, though, the law of 'too many cooks' was in operation, and the Lord Chamberlain intervened again to put Betterton in charge.

The resumption of rivalry between two companies was generally welcomed, though not by Rich, who was left with a rump of lesser actors, among whom George Powell (1668–1714) and Colley Cibber (1671–1757) were the most visible, though not necessarily the most popular. Almost the only thing in Rich's favour was the Theatre Royal. Betterton's company was all too aware of the comparative inflexibility of its playhouse, and prompt to respond to Sir John Vanbrugh's proposal to design and build a new theatre in the Haymarket. Had Betterton known more of Vanbrugh's work-in-progress on Castle Howard, he might have been more cautious. Although Vanbrugh's architectural impulse to baroque ostentation was reined in when the new theatre was designed, it could not be totally suppressed, and the actors who transferred from the dilapidated playhouse in Lincoln's Inn Fields to the grandiose Queen's Theatre in 1705, under the management of the finest gentleman playwrights of their generation, Vanbrugh and William Congreve, would soon find themselves displaced by opera. At the time of the move, they were at the mid-point of what Curtis A. Price has identified as 'the critical decade for English music drama'.[6]

Music and theatre

The dominance of literary approaches to drama, which has obscured the significance of scenic innovation and actors in the late seventeenth century, has led also to a neglect of the lively contribution of music. As we know from his conversation with Pepys in February 1667, it was a source of pride to Killigrew that he employed as many as ten of the best fiddlers in England, and a theatrical orchestra was incomplete without woodwind and percussion instruments, too.

All the morning at the office, and at noon home to dinner, and thence with my wife and Deb to the King's House to see 'The Virgin Martyr' [adapted from a play ascribed to Dekker and, less certainly, Massinger], the first time it hath been acted a great while, and it is mighty pleasant; not that the play is worth much, but it is finely acted by Becke Marshal. But that which did please me beyond any thing in the whole world was the wind-musique when the angel comes down, which is so sweet that it ravished me, and indeed, in a word, did wrap up my soul so that it made me really sick, just as I have formerly been when in love with my wife; that neither then, nor all the evening going home, and at home, I was able to think of any thing, but remained all night transported, so as I could not believe that ever any musick hath that real command over the soul of a man as this did upon me: and makes me resolve to practice wind-musique, and to make my wife do the like.

Samuel Pepys, *Diary*, 27 February 1668

What makes the significance of music in the theatre difficult to measure is the fact that not until the twentieth century was it routinely segregated from the spoken drama. The audience for a seventeenth-century 'play' might also hear an overture, entr'acte or 'effects' music and plenty of songs, any or all of which they might prefer to the dialogue. Box-office receipts can never tell us why anyone in particular chose to buy a ticket, and account needs always to be taken of the impact of contemporary musical taste on the reception of plays: a historical poser which applies as much to the first performances of Shakespeare's plays in the Globe as to their revival in Henry Irving's Lyceum at the end of the nineteenth century. But it is the unsteady evolution towards a form of stage entertainment that can be distinctly labelled 'opera' that challenges definition over the final decades of the seventeenth century. A brief review of the theatrical records of two of the century's finest composers may demarcate the maze, even if the way out of it remains uncertain.

Matthew Locke (*c.*1622–77) made his first foray into theatre in 1656 when he responded to Davenant's invitation to contribute to the 1656 performance at Rutland House of *The Siege of Rhodes*. Not only did he compose some of the music, he also sang the part of the Admiral. A few years later, for what may have been a concert revival, he composed and arranged the music of James Shirley's masque *Cupid and Death* (1653). As a (perhaps secret) Catholic, Locke was as ill at ease during the Commonwealth as the arch-royalist Shirley, and it is a pity that we have no record of their collaboration in this curious one-off event. Early in the new year of 1660, with Monck's army bedded down in and around Whitehall, and Londoners in the mood to celebrate, Locke anticipated Charles II's return by composing 'Domine salvum fac Regem'. Pepys's record of a chance meeting with him and the father (or uncle) of Henry Purcell offers a memorable insight into the lost world of coffee-house society.

> After dinner I back to Westminster Hall . . . Here I met with Mr. Lock and Pursell, Masters of Music, and with them to the Coffee House, into a room next the water. Here we had variety of brave Italian and Spanish songs, and a canon for eight voices which Mr. Lock had lately made on these words: 'Domine salvum fac Regem', an admirable thing. Here out of the window it was a most pleasant sight to see the City from one end to the other with a glory about it, so high was the light of the bonfires, and so thick round the City, and the bells rang everywhere.
>
> Samuel Pepys, *Diary*, 21 February 1660

After the Restoration, high in the favour of the musically discriminating king, Locke continued to provide theatre music for both companies throughout his service (1662–71) as organist in the Catholic chapel of Queen Catherine, but his most significant work belongs to the last years of his life. He wrote some, though probably not all, of the music for the spectacular revival of Davenant's version of *Macbeth* and for the famously contentious[7] production of Elkanah Settle's *The Empress of Morocco* at Dorset Garden, both in 1673.

> *The Tragedy of Macbeth*, alter'd by Sir *William Davenant*; being drest in all its Finery, as new Clothes, new Scenes, Machines, as flyings for the Witches; with all the Singing and Dancing in it: The first Compos'd by Mr. *Lock*, the other by Mr. *Channell* and Mr. [Josias] *Preist*; it being all Excellently perform'd, being in the nature of an Opera, it Recompenc'd double the Expence.
>
> John Downes, *Roscius Anglicanus* (1708)

The inset masque which Locke composed on the Orpheus and Eurydice theme has a life independent of Settle's play, but his crowning theatrical achievement for the Duke's Company was the music he provided for Thomas Shadwell's operatic revamping of the already operatic adaptation by Dryden and Davenant of *The Tempest* in 1674.

> *The Tempest, or the Inchanted Island*, made into an opera by Mr. *Shadwell*, having all New in it; as Scenes, Machines; particularly, one Scene Painted with *Myriads* of *Ariel* Spirits; and another flying away, with a Table Furnisht out with Fruits, Sweet meats, and all sorts of Viands; just when Duke *Trinculo* [*sic*] and his Companions, were going to Dinner; all things perform'd in it so Admirably well, that not any succeeding Opera got more Money.
>
> John Downes, *Roscius Anglicanus* (1708)

These multi-media spectaculars carried theatre along the road from the operatic to opera itself, but there was still a way to go.

When Locke died in 1677, the youthful Henry Purcell (1659–95) mourned him in the elegy, 'What hope for us remains now he is gone', and Robert Thompson has noted Purcell's debt to Locke's famous curtain tune for *The Tempest* in the hurrying scale passages of his 'Stairre [*sic*] Case Overture',[8] but it is Purcell's own visual imagination that finds expression in that early work, and that underpinned his theatrical output. The 'several Entertainments of Singing' that he provided for the production of Nathaniel Lee's *Theodosius* at Dorset Garden in 1680 were, in the view of the prosaic Downes, high in the list of attractions that brought the court, 'especially the Ladies', to the theatre. For most of his reign, Charles II sponsored music drama in the palace of Whitehall, where Purcell was fully employed from 1680 until the king's death in 1685. He would have heard and watched the Earl of Rochester's *Valentinian* there in 1684, and *Dido and Aeneas* probably owed something to John Blow's *Venus and Adonis*, performed at court in the early 1680s. Often cited as the first English opera, *Dido and Aeneas* may have been seen at court before or after its known presentation at a boarding school for girls in Chelsea in 1689. The proprietor of this school, Josias Priest, was also the dancing-master of the United Company. He was well placed to ease Purcell's return to the theatre when the new regime of William and Mary led to the decline of music at court.[9] What followed was an annual succession of music dramas with Purcell's music and Betterton's scenic ambition giving colour to generally undistinguished texts: *The Prophetess* (1690), *King Arthur* (1691), *The Fairy Queen* (1692), and then, after a break, *Bonduca* and *The Indian Queen* in 1695. Of these, *The Fairy Queen* is the one that most demands attention.

Just who prepared the text has not been finally established, though the best-favoured candidate is Settle (1648–1724). The whole is a wild composite of startling songs, bursts of dialogue from *A Midsummer Night's Dream*, characters who have crept in, plotless, from pastoral whimsy trailing a drunken poet in their wake, and musical invitations to scenic spectacle. It is unlikely that the imperfect copy that has survived represents accurately a historical performance. When David Pountney produced *The Fairy Queen* for the English National Opera in 1995, he dispensed with the dialogue and divided it into three parts with nine masques/antimasques. More than two hours of Purcell's music served as a stimulus to riotous pictorial invention, and Settle had virtually disappeared. A full three centuries divided Pountney's production from the original, but the hallucinatory quality was surely present in 1692, despite Downes's sober commentary. *The Fairy Queen* stands towards *A Midsummer Night's Dream* like a drunken memory. Dryden, who had labelled Settle 'heroically mad' in 1681,[10] might have had a point. And yet, for sheer aesthetic nerve, this misshapen spectacular carries the hallmarks of the theatrical avant-garde. Its popularity with the most fashionable and sophisticated section of the audience should raise our awareness that dramatic coherence was not required where music and spectacle supervened.

> *The Fairy Queen*, made into an Opera, from a Comedy of Mr. *Shakespears*: This in Ornaments was Superior to [*The Prophetess* and *King Arthur*]; especially in Cloaths, for all the Singers and Dancers, Scenes, Machines and Decorations, all most profusely set off; and excellently perform'd, chiefly the Instrumental and Vocal part Compos'd by the said Mr. *Purcel*, and Dances by Mr. *Priest*. The Court and Town were wonderfully satisfy'd with it; but the Expences in setting it out being so great, the Company got very little by it.
>
>   John Downes, *Roscius Anglicanus* (1708)

Purcell's semi-operas are not the only part of the story. Between 1690 and his death in November 1695, he supplied music which was often more than incidental for more than forty plays. '[W]hat has been wanting on my part', wrote Dryden in the dedicatory letter to his admired comedy *Amphitryon* (1690), 'has been abundantly supplied by the excellent composition of Mr Purcell, in whose person we have at length found an Englishman equal with the best abroad.' He was referring to the impact in performance of three songs that can easily be skipped over by readers of this fast-moving piece. The way in which Purcell's music could counterpoint the dramatic action is well exemplified by his setting of 'Ingrateful Love' in Act 1, Scene 2 of Thomas Southerne's *The Wives' Excuse* (1691/2). The seriousness of this complex comedy, not yet evident in the plot, is here anticipated in the severity of the musical score. The point being made by way of Purcell is that music was integral to the theatrical experience of plays. But Purcell's example also advanced the development of a taste for opera. Unknowingly, in the bitter rivalry that followed the break-up of the United Company, Rich and Betterton were preparing the way for Handel's arrival in London in 1711.

The ten years that separated the actors' rebellion of 1695 from the opening of the Queen's Theatre may, in retrospect, be seen to have culminated in Rich's staging at Drury Lane of *Arsinoe* (1705), 'An opera, after the *Italian* manner: All sung'. Before that, Betterton had turned to John Eccles and Rich to Daniel Purcell as the leading competitors in a semi-operatic battle. After it, and certainly in the Handel years between 1711 and 1728, aficionados of opera and drama could take their separate ways. There was no absolute divorce between music and plays, rather a patriarchal marriage in which music was assumed to be an obedient wife unless called on as the active hostess for a special occasion. Only in opera could music play the husband.

Politics and patronage

Charles II's patronage of the theatre was inherently political. It advertised a joyful return to the ways of a legendary 'Merry England' that had been artlessly obliterated during two decades of puritanical parliamentary government. Over the years, though, the special interest of the most openly priapic monarch in British history proved to be a mixed blessing. A shameful episode in December 1670 illustrates the grumbling moral debate. Hearing of Sir John Coventry's intention to introduce in parliament a bill that would impose a tax on the playhouses, Charles II let it be known that 'the players were the king's servants, and a part of his pleasure'. Coventry, an independently minded Catholic, asked the House of Commons 'whether did the king's pleasure lie among the men or the women that acted'. That night, evidently on Charles's orders, Coventry was ambushed by twenty-five of the Duke of Monmouth's guard and had his nose slit to the bone. If this was an attempt to silence gossip about the royal sex life, it came far too late. The existence of ten illegitimate children (by five different mothers), of whom Monmouth was the eldest and the first by Nell Gwyn (*c.*1642–87) the most recent, had already been publicly acknowledged by 1670. Nor was Gwyn the first actress to share the king's bed. Moll Davis (*c.*1651–1708) beat her to it, and remained on the fringes of the king's favour long enough to provide him with his last bastard in 1673.

The Rivals, A Play, Wrote by Sir *William Davenant*; having a very Fine Interlude in it, of Vocal and Instrumental Musick, mixt with very Diverting Dances; Mr. *Price* introducing the Dancing, by a short Comical Prologue, gain'd him an Universal Applause of the Town . . . All the Womens Parts admirably Acted; chiefly *Celia*, a Shepherdess being Mad for Love; especially in Singing several Wild and Mad Songs. *My Lodging it is on the Cold Ground*, &c. She perform'd that so Charmingly, that not long after, it Rais'd her from her Bed on the Cold Ground, to a Bed Royal.

John Downes, *Roscius Anglicanus* (1708)

It would be too easy to claim that the notorious licentiousness of the plays staged between 1665 and 1685 was predicated on the equally notorious licentiousness of Charles II, but it is certain that the flamboyant adulterers and serial seducers who invite our sympathy in 'Restoration' comedies expressed the sheer carnality of the royal court. The king, it would seem, had an unusually ample penis and a (masculine?) urge to share it with his subjects.

Peace is his aim, his gentleness is such,
And love he loves, for he loves fucking much.
Nor are his high desires above his strength:
His scepter and his prick are of a length;
And she may sway the one who plays with th' other,
And make him little wiser than his brother.
Poor prince! Thy prick, like thy buffoons at Court,
Will govern thee because it makes thee sport.
'Tis sure the sauciest prick that e'er did swive,
The proudest, peremptoriest prick alive.
Though safety, law, religion, life lay on 't,
'Twould break through all to make its way to cunt.
Restless he rolls about from whore to whore,
A merry monarch, scandalous and poor.

John Wilmot, Earl of Rochester, 'A Satyr on Charles II' (1674)

PALAMEDE: My good genius would prompt me to find out a handsome woman: There's something that would attract me to her without my knowledge.

Figure 2. Charles II commissioned this painting of Nell Gwyn from Sir Peter Lely as an erotic pin-up. After his death, it found its way into the collection of James II.

DORALICE: Then you make a load-stone of your mistress?
PALAMEDE: Yes, and I carry steel about me, which has been so often touched that it never fails to point to the north pole.
John Dryden, *Marriage à la Mode* (1671), Act 4, Scene 4

His brother and heir, the Duke of York, was, or would have liked to be, equally promiscuous. These were the nominal patrons of the two licensed theatre companies, and they were encouraged and flattered by courtiers whose sexual appetite matched theirs. A glance at some of the dedicatees of the plays published between 1661 and 1688 is instructive.

William Wycherley (1641–1716) dedicated his first play, *Love in a Wood* (1671), to Barbara Villiers, Duchess of Cleveland, and his last, *The Plain Dealer* (1676), to Mother Bennet, famous only as a bawd. The implication that there is no essential difference between court and brothel can be biographically reinforced. Villiers (*c.*1640–1708) was recognized by audiences as the model for many of the sexually voracious and compulsively scheming ladies who propel the plots of contemporary plays. She had openly continued her liaison with the Earl of Chesterfield after her 1659 marriage to Roger Palmer, and had the first of her five children by Charles II less than ten months after his return to London. Throughout the 1660s she remained the *acknowledged* royal mistress and was influential – sometimes decisive – in political appointments or falls from grace, most crucially in the dismissal in 1667 of the king's political mentor, the Earl of Clarendon. While still in the royal favour, and with her husband fobbed off with the Irish earldom of Castlemaine, she took the courtier Henry Jermyn as a lover, and when Charles II's commitment to her was waning she turned successively to Jacob Hall, a rope-dancer, the actor Charles Hart and Wycherley. Knowing readers of the dedicatory letter to *Love in a Wood* were expected to snigger over the author's 'humble acknowledgements for the favours I have received from you', just as they may have doubted the veracity of his claim never to have received a favour from Mother Bennet, 'the great and noble patroness of rejected and bashful men'. As an address to those playgoers of the 1670s who, unlike the Duchess of Cleveland, pretend to ignorance of the way of the sexual world, the dedication of *The Plain Dealer* is an ironic *tour de force*.

Villiers (Mrs Palmer/Lady Castlemaine/Duchess of Cleveland) would not have figured in this book if her gift for self-promotion had not reached the theatre during a period when politics and drama were intricately intertwined. Readers of Pepys will have encountered his erotic obsession with her, and know through him how consciously she displayed herself in the playhouse, on one occasion (6 February 1664) ostentatiously leaving her box to join the king and his brother in theirs.

> Went to the theatre, and saw 'Brenoralt' [by Sir John Suckling], I never saw before. It seemed a good play, but ill acted; only I sat before Mrs. Palmer and filled my eyes with her, which much pleased me.
>   Samuel Pepys, *Diary*, 23 July 1661

It added piquancy to the theatrical experience of men like Pepys to watch women like Villiers watching actresses perform the roles of women like Villiers, but he was not present in February 1668 when she made a bejewelled appearance ('far outshining the queen', according to John Evelyn) in a court production of Corneille's *Horace*. Not that she needed to go on stage in order to act. The politics of theatricality are finely encapsulated in a trick that Villiers played on an adversary, Elizabeth, Lady Harvey, in January 1669. Temporarily in dispute over a court appointment with her cousin, the Duke of Buckingham, she was finding herself outfaced by the witty Lady Harvey, Buckingham's ally; so she paid an actress in the King's Company to imitate Lady Harvey in a performance of Ben Jonson's *Catiline*. The actress was imprisoned (though Villiers soon procured her release), but the resultant ridicule drove Lady Harvey from court.

It was more often male courtiers to whom playwrights dedicated their plays, because it was more often with male courtiers that the power to influence the theatre managers lay. Aristocratic poets and poetasters flourished at Charles II's court, and some of the best known were liable, through peer-group pressure, to bouts of hedonistic exhibitionism and random violence.

> [The] division between the 'old guard' and the 'new men' was reflected in Charles [II]'s social life, which revolved round a set of young, hard-drinking gad-abouts like Buckingham, Charles Sedley, Sir George Etherege, Charles Sackville, Lord Buckhurst (later Earl of Dorset), and John Wilmot, Earl of Rochester, whose verses, witty, unpolished, haunting and disgusted, express the angry futility and emptiness of an age poised between Faith and Reason. They were patrons of, many of them contributors to, a dramatic literature noted for its bawdry and false glamour, but possessing a vitality and drive equalled only by the Elizabethans. Amongst these 'angry young men' Charles polished his wit, and acquired a bawdiness of conversation that became habitual with him, even in the presence of women, and ran counter to his usual good breeding.
>   J. P. Kenyon, *The Stuarts* (1958)

Although most of them lived to regret their debauched youth, and were in positions of greater responsibility by the time they accepted dedications, their flagrant promiscuity bestowed a disturbing realism on that of the gallants in the plays whose publication acknowledged their patronage. Sir Charles Sedley (*c.*1639–1701), Lord Buckhurst, later the Earl of Dorset (1643–1706) and the Earl of Rochester (1648–80), with some encouragement from the older Duke of Buckingham (1628–87), were shameless roisterers, but all four were among the gifted writers of the age, and all wrote plays as well as patronizing playwrights and playhouses.

> [T]o the King's House, to 'The Maid's Tragedy'; but vexed all the while with two talking ladies and Sir Charles Sedley; yet pleased to hear their discourse, he being a stranger. And one of the ladies would and did sit with her mask on all the play, and, being exceedingly witty as ever I heard woman, did talk most pleasantly with him; but was, I believe, a woman of quality. He would fain know who she was, but she would not tell; yet did give him many pleasant hints of her knowledge of him, by that means setting his brains at work to find out who she was, and did give him leave to use all means to find out who she was but pulling off her mask. He was mighty witty, and she also making sport with him very inoffensively, that a more pleasant rencontre I never heard. But by that means lost the pleasure of the

play wholly, to which now and then Sir Charles Sedley's exceptions against both words and pronouncings were very pretty.

Samuel Pepys, *Diary*, 18 February 1667

Rochester's enemy, the Earl of Mulgrave, later first Duke of Buckingham and Normanby (1647–1721), was Dryden's most loyal patron through all the political and religious vicissitudes of the final decades of the seventeenth century, something which Dryden handsomely acknowledges in the address prefatory to *Aureng-Zebe* (1675): 'Your kindness, where you have once placed it, is inviolable; and it is to that only I attribute my happiness in your love.' But even the comparatively sedate and politically ambitious Mulgrave was banned from court in 1682 for an alleged attempt to seduce the future Queen Anne, who was seventeen at the time. (He was 'only ogling' her, Mulgrave protested.) Almost every dedication provides a link between theatre and politics. Perhaps the strangest, though, is that of Thomas Otway's *Venice Preserved* (1682).

Otway's tragedy, written while the debate over the succession of the Catholic Duke of York was still dividing the country, offers a deeply ambiguous argument in favour of the future James II. It was a debate fuelled by the childlessness of Charles II's marriage and the possibility that James might yet have a son by his second wife to add to the two daughters by his first. The Duchess of Portsmouth, the French Louise de Kéroualle (1649–1734), who had taken Villiers's place as Charles II's chief mistress in 1671, was intimately involved in the political machinations over the succession. Initially a supporter of those who wished to exclude James on religious grounds, she had recently been reconciled with the Duke and Duchess of York, and was active on their behalf. One of the greatest threats to the embattled Duke was the popularity of the Protestant Duke of Monmouth, Charles II's eldest acknowledged bastard, thirty-two years old when *Venice Preserved* was premiered by the Duke's Company at Dorset Garden. But the Duchess of Portsmouth had also borne a son to the king and overseen his early elevation to the dukedom of Richmond. Young Richmond was nine, already a Knight of the Garter (1681) and created Master of the Horse a month before Otway's play opened. It is not the dedication to the Duchess of Portsmouth that is strange, but Otway's conclusion in praise of bastards. Like the play, the 'Epistle Dedicatory' seems to point in the direction of the future James II while looking at the Dukes of Monmouth and Richmond.

The young prince you have given him, by his blooming virtues, early declares the mighty stock he came from; and as you have taken all the pious care of a dear mother and a prudent guardian to give him a noble and generous education, may it succeed according to his merits and your wishes. May he grow up to be a bulwark to his illustrious father, and a patron to his loyal subjects, with wisdom and learning to assist him, whenever called to his councils, to defend his right against the encroachments of republicans in his senates, to cherish such men as shall be able to vindicate the royal cause, that good and fit servants to the Crown may never be lost for want of a protector.

Thomas Otway, from the 'Epistle Dedicatory' to *Venice Preserved* (1682)

Unsurprisingly in view of its adherents, the theatre felt the force of, and responded to, the political upheavals of the age. The first new comedy to be staged in 1660, John Tatham's *The Rump*, pilloried the Puritans who had enriched themselves during the Interregnum by seizing land and property from Catholics and royalists, and found its happy ending in Monck's setting of the world to rights. Behn reworked Tatham's play as *The Roundheads* (1681) during the Exclusion Crisis, warning of a return to kingless chaos. In Sir Robert Howard's *The Great Favourite* (1668), an attack on the recently disgraced Earl of Clarendon, 'the voice of factionalism is heard for the first time on the Carolean stage'.[11] The wars against the Dutch during the 1660s and 1670s provided dramatic material as controversially as William III's war against Louis XIV's France, with the low point of the Dutch fleet's penetration of the Medway in 1667 matched by the high point of the victory over the French at Blenheim in 1704. The dizzying fact is that, torn between religious conviction and political expediency, playwrights changed sides as frequently as politicians. It was the heyday of the time-serving Vicar of Bray, and Dryden was not his only acolyte. The frenetic pace of so many late seventeenth-century plays echoes the frenetic activity of a nation constantly striving to reconstitute itself, and generally making a hash of it.

Summary of theatres in use, 1660–1705

1660	Duke's Company using Salisbury Court and, occasionally, the Cockpit in Drury Lane. King's Company settling into the former Gibbons's tennis court.
1661	Duke's Company to Lisle's tennis court, Lincoln's Inn Fields.
1663	King's Company to the Theatre Royal, Bridges Street.
1671	Duke's Company to Dorset Garden.
1672	Theatre Royal burned. King's Company to the empty Lincoln's Inn Fields theatre.
1674	King's Company to Theatre Royal, Drury Lane.
1682	United Company using both Drury Lane and Dorset Garden.
1695	Breakaway Actors' Company back to Lincoln's Inn Fields. (Dis)United Company continue at Drury Lane.
1705	Actors' Company to the Queen's Theatre, Haymarket.

Chapter 2

The drama

It is difficult to approach the plays written during this period without some kind of prejudice, since the way into them has been complicated by more than three centuries of bitter contention. The generally neglected fact is that about 500 of the pieces performed during these forty years have survived in print, while critical attention has been confined to about fifty. The canonical work is that of Etherege, Wycherley and Congreve, with Farquhar, Vanbrugh and, more recently, Aphra Behn as add-ons. There has been an observable tendency for literary critics to regret that the poet John Dryden wasted so much of his time on plays, and to argue that Thomas Otway might have been a greater writer if only he had lived in other times. Worst of all, the title of 'Restoration drama', subdivided into 'Restoration comedy' and 'Restoration tragedy', has been pasted over at least half a century of plays, as if to imply that Charles II was somehow responsible for them all, despite the fact that he was a decade dead by the time Congreve, Farquhar and Vanbrugh produced their first dramas.

Alternative titles could readily be found – 'Exclusion drama' for the plays written between 1680 and 1688, 'Revolution (or Usurpation) drama' for plays written during the reign of William III – but the damage is already done. Ever since 1698, when Jeremy Collier fired a famous salvo in his *Short View of the Immorality and Profaneness of the English Stage*, it has been accepted practice to lump together, often in order to condemn, two generations of playwrights and dramatic works of variety and distinction.[1] Even admirers of these plays have sometimes felt the need to adopt a defensive posture in order to parry blows from two directions: one kind of adversary attacking their dirty minds, the other accusing them of being too easily pleased.

> The cause of Congreve was not tenable: whatever glosses he might use for the defence or palliation of single passages, the general tenor and tendency of his plays must always be condemned. It is acknowledged, with universal conviction, that the perusal of his works will make no man better; and that their ultimate effect is to represent pleasure in alliance with vice, and to relax those obligations by which life ought to be regulated.
>
> Samuel Johnson, *Lives of the English Poets* (1779–81)

> The trouble is not that the Restoration comic writers deal with a limited number of themes, but that they bring to bear a miserably limited set of attitudes . . . The criticism that defenders of Restoration comedy need to answer is not that the comedies are 'immoral', but that they are trivial, gross and dull.
>
> L. C. Knights, 'Restoration Comedy: The Reality and the Myth' (1937)

The focus has generally been on comedy, because it is in that genre that the peculiar ethos of the age is most enticingly displayed.

Constituting 'Restoration' comedy

Plots and prologues

The typical plot of so-called 'Restoration comedy' brings together sexually predatory well-born men, adulterously inclined well-born women, well-born husbands who generally deserve to be cuckolded and well-born ingénues who are not as ingenuous as all that. It ends when the liveliest of the men and the sprightliest of the ingénues agree to get married, in apparent denial of everything the play has previously done to discredit marriage.

LADY GIMCRACK:	A husband's an insect, a drone, a dormouse –
HAZARD:	A foolish matrimonial lump –
LADY GIMCRACK:	A cuckoo in winter –
HAZARD:	An opiate for love –
LADY GIMCRACK:	A body without a soul –
HAZARD:	A chip in porridge –
LADY GIMCRACK:	A white of an egg –
HAZARD:	All phlegm and no choler –
LADY GIMCRACK:	A drudge –
HAZARD:	An excuse –
LADY GIMCRACK:	A necessary thing –
HAZARD:	A cloak at a pinch –
LADY GIMCRACK:	A pitiful utensil –
HAZARD:	Good for nothing but to cover shame, pay debts, and own children for his wife.
LADY GIMCRACK:	In short, a husband is a husband, and there's an end of him. But a lover is –
HAZARD:	Not to be express'd but in action. I'll show you what a lover is with a vengeance, madam. Come on.

Thomas Shadwell, *The Virtuoso* (1676), Act 4, Scene 2

Such plots are embryonically present in comedy from Aristophanes to Alan Ayckbourn, but never so ruthlessly explicit. The comedies that express the mood of high life in post-Restoration England have generally more truck with the genitals than with the heart, and there is no reason to doubt their accuracy as a commentary on the mores of a section of society. However discomforting their evident moral neutrality may be, these 'Restoration comedies' are not unrealistic. Jocelyn Powell, in an acute essay on Etherege's plays, calls them 'comedies of experience':

> The essential difference between the comedy of criticism and the comedy of experience is that in the former, though a good character may be given faults and a bad character virtues, there is never any serious doubt as to the category to which the character belongs; whereas in the latter there are no categories. Criticism sees characters from one angle, but experience is constantly modifying the angle from which a character is seen, so that, like a shot silk, his colour changes with the light.[2]

Etherege (1636–92) was one of the group of womanizing gamblers whose antics antagonized the London citizenry. As courtiers, they felt licensed to shock, and occasionally assault, their social inferiors.[3] Among more sober-minded contemporaries, there was a fear that such behaviour would contaminate the nation, and that plays like Etherege's might serve as an incentive to promiscuity that a malleable populace would be too feeble to resist. Interestingly, though, historical evidence offers little to support a claim that the flagrant promiscuity of the court (and of the characters in the courtly comedy that seemed to endorse it) was emulated in society at large. Parish registers of illegitimate births suggest, rather, a reduced incidence of extramarital sex after the Restoration. That need not surprise us: the popularity of Jane Austen's novels is unlikely to cause an exodus to country parishes any more than the bestselling books of Nancy and Jessica Mitford created a mass yearning for the life of the twentieth-century upper crust. 'Restoration comedy' – like the 'silver fork' novels of the early nineteenth century – capitalized on the interest of the 'middling sort' in the manners of their social superiors, so that, while a visit to the playhouse might provide a tradesman and his family with a fascinating glimpse of life among the 'quality', it did not make deviation from the habits of a lifetime imperative.

Intricacy, sometimes descending into fussiness, is habitual in the plotting of comedies that advance, and sometimes retreat, by way of sociosexual intrigues. John Crowne was reported to have found a play by his fellow-dramatist Nathaniel Lee too 'continually on the fret', and even so talented a writer as Aphra Behn (*c*.1640–89) can surrender control in search of a meretricious effect, as she does when exploiting beyond its theatrical limits the conventional impenetrability of disguise in *The Feigned Courtesans* (1679). Sexual brinkmanship ('not now, but maybe later') is too much the routine of this play's duplicitous heroines to carry the fictional weight placed on it. But to get the most out of *The Feigned Courtesans*, as is generally the case with 'Restoration comedy' and vehemently so with Behn's work, we need to review it in the context of social and political circumstance. As a woman venturing into the male world of authorship, Behn was often singled out for moral censure. Provoked to reply, in the preface to *The Lucky Chance* (1686) she would reasonably complain that the speeches in her plays that had been considered indecent 'right or wrong . . . must be criminal because a woman's'.

> Most in this depraved later Age think a Woman Learned and Wife enough if she can distinguish her Husband's bed from another's.
> Hannah Woolley, *The Gentlewoman's Companion* (1675)

But the provoked Behn was always provocative. *The Feigned Courtesans*, both in print and on stage, was given a feminine front cover. The printed version opened with an 'Epistle Dedicatory' to Nell Gwyn, who had been the king's part-time mistress for ten years, an actress in retirement for eight, and the mother of, in Behn's words, 'two noble branches, who have all the greatness and sweetness of their beautiful royal stock'. Behn knew that Gwyn was much more popular, and much less manipulative, than Charles II's official mistresses: she 'almost' says as much in the epistle, whatever the risk of antagonizing the Duchesses of Cleveland and Portsmouth.

> You never appear but you glad the hearts of all that have the happy fortune to see you, as if you were made on purpose to put the whole world into good humour whenever you look abroad; and when you speak, men crowd to listen with that awful reverence as to holy oracles or divine prophecies, and bear away the precious words, to tell at home to all the attentive family the graceful things you uttered, and cry 'but oh she spoke with such an air, so gay, that half the beauty's lost in the repetition'. 'Tis this that ought to make your sex vain enough to despise the malicious world that will allow a woman no wit, and bless ourselves for living in an age that can produce so wondrous an argument as your undeniable self, to shame those boasting talkers who are judges of nothing but faults.
> Aphra Behn, from the 'Epistle Dedicatory to Mrs Ellen Gwyn' (1679)

Gwyn's 'undeniable self' represents in print a woman's right to choose. On stage Behn's prologue invites the Irish actress Elizabeth Currer to do something similar. Currer specialized in whorish roles, probably in real life as well as on stage. But, in the intimacy of the prologue's interaction with the audience, Behn invites her to share a financial secret:

> Who says this age a reformation wants,
> When Betty Currer's lovers all turn saints?
> In vain, alas, I flatter, swear, and vow,
> You'll scarce do anything for charity now.

Something has happened in the outside world to interfere with Currer's sexual trade. Her former lovers (and what is to stop Currer fixing her eyes on one or two of them in the audience?) are pretending not to know her, and she refuses to let them get away with it. Here is a woman who, in this place and at this moment, cannot be ignored.

The social placing of women is at issue in *The Feigned Courtesans*, but the moment to which Currer's prologue refers is a politically fraught one. Her suddenly shy lovers are suffering from the Protestant paranoia consequent on revelations, emerging from late in 1678, of a Catholic conspiracy to kill the king. The 'Popish Plot' was the fantasy of Titus Oates, an inventive liar and one of the most unambiguously odious men to have affected the course of British history. His perjury led, over the period from October 1678 to early 1681, to the deaths (by execution or through harsh imprisonment) of about thirty-five men, and to the bitter debates about the right to accession of the Catholic Duke of York that have come to be known as the Exclusion Crisis. In April 1679 Oates would publish, by order of the House of Lords, his 68-page account of the Popish Plot, and *The Feigned Courtesans* was staged by the Duke's Company a month or so earlier. In its opening lines Behn's prologue alludes to the feverish speculation that Oates's accusations had aroused.

> The devil take this cursèd plotting age,
> 'T has ruined all our plots upon the stage;
> Suspicions, new elections, jealousies,
> Fresh informations, new discoveries,
> Do so employ the busy fearful town,
> Our honest calling here is useless grown.
> Prologue to *The Feigned Courtesans* (1679)

But the play goes much further than that. In the character of Sir Signal Buffoon's canting tutor, Tickletext, she provides a vicious commentary on Titus Oates. Tickletext is a Dissenter whose overt piety fails to disguise his lechery. (Oates was originally a Baptist, and possibly a sodomite.) In the light of the current witch-hunt, Behn's display of sympathy with Catholics is brave, even foolhardy, but the Popish Plot and the resultant Exclusion Crisis engaged many other playwrights at this time of national tension. As Derek Hughes has persuasively argued, a sophisticated reading of the drama produced during the reigns of Charles II, James II and William and Mary opens access to the politics of that fractious era.[4]

Conversation

Not until a few years into his reign did Charles II begin to disappoint those who had greeted his restoration with rapture. Unlike his father, he was gregarious and accessible. Strolling in St James's Park in the company of his spaniels, he would engage in witty conversation with all and sundry, and his court was open to the gentry as well as the nobility. Although lacking intellectual stamina, he had a genuine interest in experimental science, which found significant expression in the formation of the Royal Society in 1662. Membership of the Society was not confined to scientists. As a body, it represented a readiness to enquire into almost any area of human or nonhuman activity (Thomas Shadwell's play *The Virtuoso* (1676) wittily mocks some of its members' eccentricities), and the use and abuse of language was certainly one of those. A 1664 committee of the Royal Society, whose membership included Dryden and John Evelyn, advised writers to aim at 'a close, naked, natural way of speaking; positive expression; clear senses; a native easinesse, bringing all things as near the Mathematical plainnesse, as they can'. Dryden himself ascribed the new age's literary advantage to the availability of good conversation of the kind in which the king excelled, and the plays that best characterize the Restoration promote conversation as the apogee of human interaction. That 'advanced' conversation, to which Dryden aspires, may lead to 'criminal' conversation, for centuries the legal euphemism for adultery, is one of the ironies of 'Restoration comedy'.

The fourteen-word 'aside' with which Horner opens Wycherley's *The Country Wife* (1675) meets, almost parodies, the Royal Society demand for 'a close, naked, natural way of speaking': 'A quack is as fit for a pimp as a midwife for a bawd.' There is no artificial colouring here, the thirteen monosyllables varied only by the blunt 'midwife', which is effectively two further monosyllables conjoined. The actor who has this speech to set the play rolling (Charles Hart in 1675) faces a new kind of tonal challenge. He is *beginning* in the *middle* of a conversation with the audience. However extravagant his plots, Wycherley conducts them like everyday stories; but the general view is that it was Etherege whose verbal fluency brought the new style of conversational exchange to the stage. His first play, *The Comical Revenge; or Love in a Tub* (1664), predates the kind of comedy which it helped to create. Its serious 'love' plot, which is serious only if you shut your eyes to its absurdity, is framed in rhyming couplets, but the life is in the prose of the secondary action, where the tone is set by the faithless charmer, Sir Frederick Frollick. Sir Frederick's conversational skills flourish in taverns and pleasure gardens, central sites in the fashionable pursuit of – what?

Under the often glittering surface of Etherege's two mature comedies, *She Would If She Could* (1668) and *The Man of Mode* (1676), there is an unexplored hollow. No holds were barred to advanced conversation in the restive years that followed the Restoration. Revealed religion (that is, those elements of Christian faith dependent on the revelation of Christ's divinity in the Gospels), essential human nature and the business of good government were subjected to sceptical enquiry along with the principles of navigation, the source of light and the constitution of matter. There is very little certainty for Etherege's dissolute heroes to fall back on, and their preparedness to disregard the plight of the other owes more to a partial reading of Thomas Hobbes (1588–1679) than to Christianity. The view of humanity presented in Hobbes's *Leviathan* (1651) had a powerful influence on post-Restoration writing. For Hobbes, the manmade construction of society curbs, but cannot eradicate, the predatory self-interest and primitive fear of humanity in its natural, presocial state.

> [T]here is no place for Industry; because the fruit thereof is uncertain: and consequently no Culture of the Earth; no Navigation, nor use of the commodities that may be imported by Sea; no commodious Building; no Instruments of moving, and removing, such things as require much force; no Knowledge of the face of the Earth; no account of the Time; no Arts; no Letters; no Society; and which is worst of all, continuall feare, and danger of violent death; and the life of man, solitary, poore, nasty, brutish, and short.
>
> Thomas Hobbes on the 'state of nature' in *Leviathan* (1651)

> To the Exchequer and several places, calling on several businesses, and particularly my bookseller's, among others for 'Hobbs's Leviathan', which is now mightily called for; and what was heretofore sold for 8s. I now give 24s. for at the second hand, and is sold for 30s., it being a book the Bishops will not let be printed again.
>
> Samuel Pepys, *Diary*, 3 September 1668

Almost all the speeches of Etherege's best-known hero, the Dorimant of *The Man of Mode*, contribute to a cynical anatomy of love. In that they echo much of the verse of the man on whom Dorimant was popularly supposed to be modelled, the Earl of Rochester. A legend in his own lifetime, Rochester was a self-excoriating voluptuary with a gift of tongues and two distinct poetic voices. One voice is Dorimant's ('With wine I wash away my cares, / And then to cunt again'), but the other, silenced by Etherege, may be Dorimant's, too. This is the voice that can be heard in Rochester's bitter poem 'Upon Nothing' and in the savage 'Satyr against Reason and Mankind'.

> Were I (who to my cost already am
> One of those strange, prodigious creatures, man)
> A spirit free to choose, for my own share,
> What case of flesh and blood I pleased to wear,
> I'd be a dog, a monkey, or a bear,
> Or anything but that vain animal
> Who is so proud of being rational.
>
> Opening lines of Rochester's 'Satyr against Reason and Mankind' (c.1675)

Rochester represents supremely both the poise and the pose of Restoration conversation. Never at a loss for words, he told a dog that had just bitten him, 'I wish you were married and living in the country'; but it was a suppressed sense of sheer futility that found expression in his deathbed repentance. Rochester's most sympathetic biographer has called his life 'a brilliant experiment in the art of living',[5] but it was an experiment that failed. The same could be predicted for the afterlife of Etherege's eloquent heroes. Did Etherege himself see through the pose to the 'nothing' of Rochester's imagination? If we were to view the events of *The Man of Mode* through the eyes of the scorned Mrs Loveit, we would probably say 'yes': if we suppose that Etherege endorsed Dorimant's triumphant progress, we would probably say 'no'. It is the kind of question which has divided critics of 'Restoration' comedy. Conversation, however advanced, boils down to 'words, words, words', and it is not words, but people that *mean* things.

The country

Advanced conversation was an urban phenomenon, and life in the country was its butt. The social clumsiness of rural immigrants to London is a regular comic theme, and the prospect of prolonged rural residence is unspeakably grim. 'What a dreadful thing 'twould be to be hurried back to Hampshire!', says Young Bellair in *The Man of Mode* (Act 3, Scene 1), after sealing his nonmarriage pact with Harriet, and Dorimant's preparedness to visit Harriet there is the best available proof of his love.

LADY WOODVILL:	I have now so good an opinion of him, he shall be welcome.
HARRIET:	To a great rambling lone house, that looks as if it were not inhabited, the family's so small; there you'll find my mother, an old lame aunt, and myself sir, perched up on chairs at a distance in a large parlour; sitting moping like three or four melancholy birds in a spacious volary – does not this stagger your resolution?
DORIMANT:	Not at all, madam! The first time I saw you, you left me with the pangs of love upon me, and this day my soul has quite given up her liberty.
HARRIET:	This is more dismal than the country! Emilia! Pity me, who am going to that sad place. Methinks I hear the hateful noise of rooks already – kaw, kaw, kaw – there's music in the worst cry in London! 'My dill and cowcumbers to pickle.'

Sir George Etherege, *The Man of Mode* (1676), Act 5, Scene 2

The threat of exile in the country was not confined to the Earl of Rochester's dog or the world of fiction. When, in late 1662, the Duke of York was pressing his attentions on the Earl of Chesterfield's wife, the notoriously promiscuous earl (who had been one of the future Duchess of Cleveland's early lovers) punished her by banishing her to his Derbyshire estate. 'To send a man's wife to the Peak' was adopted as a catchphrase for this kind of discipline.

The supreme expression of the opposition between London and the country is Wycherley's *The Country Wife* (1675), which comes as close as any play need to fashioning art out of obscenity. Whereas for Horner, masquerading as a eunuch in order to gain open access to society ladies who would otherwise involve him in the tedium of intrigues, sex is a mechanical necessity, for Margery Pinchwife, the 'cuntry' wife of the title, it is a source of naïve fascination. Since her tormented husband is unable to satisfy her curiosity about sex, who better than Horner? The trouble is that Margery is unacquainted with the London rule: that you don't let the top half of the town know what your bottom half has been doing. At the play's sizzling climax, with all the characters assembled in Horner's lodging, she stands, an innocent among sophisticates, on the fringe of an incomprehensible conversation. There she is, fresh from the discovery her husband had never provided her with that sex is fantastic (still dancing in her head to the tune of Horner's whore-pipe), and here they all are, saying that Horner is impotent. Why are they all telling lies? This is ridiculous. Even Dorilant, who surely knows better, is calling Horner 'an arrant French capon' (and a countrywoman knows about capons): "Tis false sir,' unable to contain herself, 'you shall not disparage poor Mr. Horner, for to my certain knowledge. . .' 'Oh, hold,' shouts Lucy. 'Stop her mouth,' whispers Mrs Squeamish. It is a grotesque tableau of deceit. Had she been allowed to complete her sentence, Margery would have 'created' two cuckolds, two fornicators, two adulteresses and a proven lecher. When in London, do as London does: live a lie.

The satirical impulse was particularly powerful in Wycherley, but his plays never test his exposure of urban morality against a rural model. With rare precedents, such as Shadwell's *Bury Fair* (1689), George Farquhar (*c*.1677–1707) was the first significant writer of country plays, but Farquhar is only by artificial extension a 'Restoration' dramatist. *The Recruiting Officer* (1706) is dedicated to 'All Friends round the Wrekin', and the play is set in Shrewsbury, where Farquhar had only just completed a recruiting mission as a lieutenant of Grenadiers when the play opened at Drury Lane.

> Some little turns of humour that I met with almost within the shade of [the Wrekin] gave rise to this comedy, and people were apprehensive that, by the example of some others, I would make the town merry at the expense of the country gentlemen. But they forgot that I was to write a comedy, not a libel; and that whilst I held to nature, no person of any character in your country could suffer by being exposed. I have drawn the justice and the clown in their *puris*

naturalibus: the one an apprehensive, sturdy brave blockhead; and the other a worthy, honest, generous gentleman, hearty in his country's cause, and of as good an understanding as I could give him, which I must confess is far short of his own.
George Farquhar, 'Epistle Dedicatory' to *The Recruiting Officer* (1706)

Even Farquhar, it might be argued, was surprised to find intelligent human life in the English provinces, but the amiability of this and his last play, *The Beaux' Stratagem* (1707), sets him outside the 'Restoration' tradition, in a dramatic world altogether more inclined to benevolence.

Wit and marriage

Wit, the distinguishing characteristic of advanced conversation, was assumed to be outside the range of the countryman. The literary quarrels over its possession remained virulent through most of the eighteenth century, entering the realm of moral, as well as intellectual, discourse. Hobbes had divided man's rational faculty into two – judgement (the ability to *separate*, analyse, discriminate) and fancy (the ability to *combine*, compare, surprise) – and 'both Fancie and Judgement are commonly comprehended under the name of Wit'. For Dryden, strong in defence of 'modern' plays, repartee was the new addition to fancy and judgement in the domain of dramatic wit, and it was above all through Dryden's work that the King's Company popularized the joyful verbal sparring of a witty, predatory gentleman and his equally witty female prey. This heterosexual pairing ('gay couple' as critics used to be able to term it) drew most of the plaudits when, as in Dryden's *Secret Love* (1667), the combatants were Hart and Gwyn, but they operated within a predominantly masculine triangle of the genuinely clever (Truewits), those who wished to be thought clever (Witwoulds) and those who hadn't a chance (Witlesses). It was a format derived from the merciless comedies of Ben Jonson, but given a new twist in plays that accepted the rationale of sexual consummation outside marriage.

Why should a foolish marriage vow,
  Which long ago was made,
Oblige us to each other now,
  When passion is decayed?
We loved, and we loved, as long as we could,
  'Till our love was loved out in us both;
But our marriage is dead, when the pleasure is fled:
'Twas pleasure first made it an oath.
        Song from John Dryden's *Marriage à la Mode* (1671), Act 1, Scene 1

For most of the dramatic wits, neither revealed (by Christ) nor 'natural' (evident through observation of the natural world) religion had much of authority to say about sex. Under scrutiny in their judgement, fantasy and repartee, the hallowed institution of 'holy matrimony' was vulnerable. Almost the best that the playwrights of the period could say for it was that it offered to gratify temptation by providing easy opportunity. Partly because witty jibes at marriage were so habitual in the drama, wit itself became an object of abuse. Dryden was not alone in being troubled by the imputation that it was either the Devil's instrument or the fancy dress of folly.

> There are a middling sort of courtiers, who become happy by their want of wit; but they supply that want by an excess of malice to those who have it. And there is no such persecution as that of fools: They can never be considerable enough to be talked of themselves; so that they are safe only in their obscurity, and grow mischievous to witty men, by the great diligence of their envy, and by being always present to represent and aggravate their faults . . . These are the men who make it their business to chase wit from the knowledge of princes, lest it should disgrace their ignorance.
>
> John Dryden, 'Epistle Dedicatory' to *Marriage à la Mode* (1671)

Playwrights might fairly have argued (some did) that, because marriage was a desperately serious business, and divorce a virtual impossibility, comedy had a duty to scour it. Although civil marriages had been legalized in 1653, the restoration of the monarchy had seen the Church reclaim its established rights under canon law. Matrimony was once again officially holy, but this was an adjective that could scarcely be applied to the bonding of John Manners, Lord Roos and Anne Pierrepont, daughter of the Marquis of Dorchester. Married in 1658, they had separated before the end of the year, and their highly public wrangling (who was the father of the child born to Anne in 1663?) continued throughout the 1660s, culminating in 1670 when the House of Lords passed an act enabling Lord Roos to remarry. The account of Lady Anne's sexual exploits caused some hilarity in the House, and Charles II, who attended the debates perhaps in the hope of applying the precedent to his own childless marriage, commented that it was 'better than a play' before giving the bill his royal approval. The Roos Act was a small breach in a big dam, but it was long into the nineteenth century before divorce would provide a realistic escape from even a brutal marriage.

The comedy of this period is vulnerable to the accusation that it endorses adultery and rewards concupiscence, but there is something serious at stake. Particularly after the revolutionary settlement of 1688, the nature of the contract between man and wife was under scrutiny. England had 'divorced' its Catholic king for misconduct and 'remarried' the Protestant William and Mary under terms to be negotiated. If the relationship of monarch and people was negotiable, what about that of a man and his wife? The analogy is active in the most famous of the many 'proviso' scenes – passages of dialogue in which the 'gay couple' establish the conditions on which they will marry – in comedy, that between Mirabell and Millamant in Congreve's *The Way of the World* (1700).

Congreve (1670–1729) has the most secure reputation of post-Restoration dramatists, and the strongest claim to 'wit', in its modern sense. Unmarried himself, though long in love with the actress Anne Bracegirdle, around whose personal style he fashioned Millamant, he wryly observed the effect of marriage on others. The happiness of Mirabell and Millamant is confined to the afterlife of *The Way of the World*, and the play's only married couple, the Fainalls, promise nothing to each other but perpetual torment. It is above all through the plight of wives like Mrs Fainall that 'Restoration' comedy reveals the underside of laughter. The emotional void of Lady Brute's future at the end of Vanbrugh's *The Provoked Wife* (1697) has tragic undertones. Vanbrugh (1664–1726), a brilliant dabbler, was probably provoked into playwriting by irritation at the disingenuously happy ending of Colley Cibber's *Love's Last Shift* (1696). Cibber had contrived for the rakish husband, Loveless, a fifth-act reformation that brought joy to the heart of the virtuous wife, Amanda. Vanbrugh's *The Relapse* (1696) showed what happened next. This is not so much cynicism as reproof: the contract of marriage is open to breakage, not codicils. Cibber himself was surprisingly complacent about Vanbrugh's implicit rebuke. In the new play his role as Sir Novelty Fashion had him promoted to the peerage as the exemplary fop, Lord Foppington, and he shared with his fellows a delight in the ease with which Vanbrugh's words could be committed to memory.

> There is something so catching to the ear, so easy to the memory, in all he writ, that it has been observ'd by all the actors of my time, that the style of no author whatsoever gave their memory less trouble than that of Sir John Vanbrugh . . . And indeed his wit and humour was so little laboured, that his most entertaining scenes seem'd to be no more than his common conversation committed to paper.
> Colley Cibber, *An Apology for His Life* (1740), Chapter 6

Perhaps the most complex of the 1690s marriage plays, though, is Thomas Southerne's *The Wives' Excuse* (1691/2). Southerne (1660–1746) has, until recently, been largely neglected, and there is room for a wholesale reappraisal. *The Wives' Excuse* has Mrs Friendall at its centre. Her husband is a 'Witwould' addicted to adulterous rambling, and she has every excuse to surrender to the 'Truewit' Lovemore.

WELLVILE:	I am scandalised extremely to see the women upon the stage make cuckolds at that insatiable rate they do in all our modern comedies, without any other reason from the poets, but because a man is married he must be a cuckold. Now, sir, I think the women are most unconscionably injured by this general scandal upon their sex. Therefore, to do 'em what service I can in their vindication, I design to write a play and call it –
FRIENDALL:	Ay, what, I beseech you? I love to know the name of a new play.
WELLVILE:	*The Wives' Excuse; or, Cuckolds Make Themselves.*
FRIENDALL:	A very pretty name, faith and troth; and very like to be popular among the women.
WILDING:	And true among the men.
FRIENDALL:	But what characters have you?
WELLVILE:	What characters? Why, I design to show a fine young woman married to an impertinent, nonsensical, silly, intriguing, cowardly, good-for-nothing coxcomb.
WILDING (*aside*):	This blockhead does not know his own picture.
FRIENDALL:	Well, and how? She must make him a cuckold, I suppose.
WELLVILE:	'Twas that I was thinking on when you came to me.
FRIENDALL:	O, yes, you must make him a cuckold.
WILDING:	By all means a cuckold.
FRIENDALL:	For such a character, gentlemen, will vindicate a wife in anything she can do to him. He must be a cuckold.

Thomas Southerne, *The Wives' Excuse* (1691/2), Act 3, Scene 2

Indeed, it is expected of her, and she has to apologize for the stubborn fidelity which she maintains even after Friendall has been discovered *in flagrante*. The private action of the play is subtly enclosed in public occasions – concerts, card parties, masked balls – which highlight Mrs Friendall's solitariness. There is more emotional intensity, and less decorum, in the images of 'woman alone' than there ever is in the portrayal of love. As in all the finest comedies of the period, the playwright's achievement is to deny the plot, even within the fiction, a total resolution. It takes more than a play to correct the ways of the world.

The pursuit of tragedy

While English comedy attained one of its peaks in the four decades following the restoration of the monarchy, tragedy began its long decline. The reasons for this decline are complex, but the argument that tragedy can be effective only when writer and audience share a unified, religious view of the human condition cannot be ignored. Aristotle's identification of a capacity to arouse pity and terror as the essential mark of tragedy was known to post-Restoration theorists, but it is not easy to terrify a sceptical audience. Most of the writers who attempted tragedy settled for pity. It is difficult to admire even Dryden's two-part *Conquest of Granada* (1670 and 1671), commonly cited as the best example of the heroic tragedies staged in the 1660s and 1670s. The style's brief time has long passed.

It was characteristic of the Restoration, with its love of paradox, of contradictions and false faces, that it should have created a tragedy that was less serious than its comedy . . . Faced with the real issues of the age, with the new science and the doctrines of Hobbes, with the split between faith and reason, appearance and reality, [tragedy] retreated in confusion to a land of rhetorical make-believe.
        Anne Righter on 'Heroic Tragedy' (1965)

Dryden must carry most of the blame not for originating, but for prolonging, the ill-judged experiment with serious drama in rhyming couplets. Familiar with the work in French of Corneille and Racine, he convinced himself that the English could do better. He was wrong. The French alexandrine allows its speaker leisure to reflect: the English heroic couplet is always in a hurry to reach its clinching rhyme-word. No one, not even Alexander Pope, is better than Dryden at driving narrative through rhyme, but the aural effect is like that of being pelted with a succession of pellets. When, as in *The Conquest of Granada*, the pelting continues for ten acts, the impact is deafening. But this is not to deny Dryden an awesome talent for arguing in rhyme. *Aureng-Zebe* (1675), his last play in this style, is more accomplished than could reasonably be expected. The rhetorical treatment of the conflict between natural love and patriotic honour/duty – a more or less compulsory theme – is here comparatively restrained.

The excesses of heroic drama did not go unnoticed at the time. They are targeted in *The Rehearsal*, a burlesque accumulated by various hands, under the guidance of the Duke of Buckingham, first written in 1664, and frequently revised and updated thereafter. When John Lacy played the part of the foolish playwright Bayes in 1671, he imitated Dryden's well-known mannerisms, but as played by David Garrick from 1742 almost until his retirement in 1776, Bayes was no longer Dryden. The plasticine text had been moulded by Garrick to feature a burlesque of contemporary actors, not writers. But in 1671 *The Conquest of Granada* was the target: 'Now, here, she must make a *simile*. . . Because she's surpris'd. That's a general rule, you must ever make a *simile*, when you are surpris'd; 'tis the new way of writing' (*The Rehearsal*, Act 2, Scene 3). Mockery, ranging from the benign to the vicious, was in the spirit of the age, and theatre thrived on it. The second part of *The Conquest of Granada* had opened to acclaim in January 1671, and was still in the repertoire of the King's

Company in December when *The Rehearsal* was staged *by the same company*. Nor should we forget that Dryden was a shareholder and attached playwright. We do not know whether he took the jest in good part or bit his tongue in order to avoid the double jeopardy of showing that he was hurt. Perhaps it was bravado that motivated the couplets of *Amboyna* (1673) and *Aureng-Zebe*, with its prologue announcing the *voluntary* abandonment of rhyme.

> Our author by experience finds it true,
> 'Tis much more hard to please himself than you;
> And out of no feigned modesty, this day,
> Damns his laborious trifle of a play.
> Not that it's worse than what before he writ,
> But he has now another taste of wit;
> And, to confess a truth (though out of time),
> Grows weary of his long-loved mistress, rhyme.
>
> John Dryden, prologue to *Aureng-Zebe* (1675)

The heroic drama had tended to pluck its plots from remote history: Indians and Moors abounded. When Dryden switched to blank verse, he sought his inspiration in Shakespeare. *All for Love* (1677) is *Antony and Cleopatra* regulated for the post-Restoration stage. The tendency to read, or present, the two plays in parallel does no favours to Dryden, who can be seen to tame whatever he borrows. But *All for Love*, like Nahum Tate's unjustly reviled *History of King Lear* (1680/1), is a professional dramatist's commonsense appropriation of an old-fashioned text.

Tate's play was one of a clutch of tragedies written (but not all staged – censorship, though lax, was not sleeping) during the Oates hearings. The Popish Plot might have spawned a civil war; instead, it created party politics. The group of 'Whigs' that adhered to the Earl of Shaftesbury used the Plot to further the Protestant cause, proclaiming the rights of freeborn Englishmen. The 'Tories' stood firmly for the royal family's rights of succession.

Whig and Tory

Party (as opposed to partisan) politics was unknown when government was controlled by the reigning monarch. Charles II had necessarily yielded some ground to parliament, but formal power remained in his hands. It was when the nation divided over the question of his Catholic brother's succession to the throne that two definably different 'parties' came into being. Those who supported the Duke of York's right to the throne, regardless of his religious affiliation, came to be known as 'Tories', those who opposed it in the national interest as 'Whigs'. For 150 years or so, it remained possible, though not always meaningfully, to describe British politicians as either Whig or Tory, and it was these two parties that evolved, in the nineteenth century, into Liberals and Conservatives. At least until the quelling of Charles Stuart's 1745 uprising, it was a routine response to national crisis for Whigs to accuse Tories of Jacobitism. Thereafter, opposition of one party to another was more often the outcome of circumstance and opportunism, and division *within* parties was as rife in the eighteenth century as division *between* parties.

Each party could claim to be more patriotic than the other, but neither could claim to be united on any issue other than that of Exclusion. The Duke's Company hedged its bets. *The History of King Lear*, anti-Whig and fervently royalist, was in the Dorset Garden repertoire at much the same time as Lee's Whiggish *Lucius Junius Brutus* (1680), whose brief run was interrupted by order of the Lord Chamberlain on 11 December. Out of historical context, Lee's play is nothing more than the violently extravagant story of a patriotic father who orchestrates the death of his sons in the defence of a Rome threatened by tyranny. In 1680 its poetic fervour breathed the politics of a nation in disarray. The same is true of the most remarkable of late seventeenth-century tragedies, Thomas Otway's *Venice Preserved* (1682).

Otway (1652–85) was troubled and is troubling. In an epigram dating from late in 1679, the Earl of Rochester attacked him for preferring rapture to nature, and it is not easy to distinguish those passages, or whole plays, in which he is following fashion from those in which he is purging himself. Rape or attempted rape, a common feature of comedies as well as tragedies in the new age of actresses, is both a political and a personal metaphor for Otway, who dramatized himself as both rapist and victim of a transgressive society. In *Venice Preserved* the crucial turn of Jaffier from conspirator against the state to betrayer of the conspiracy is brought about by Belvidera's exploitation of the assault on her.

He drew the hideous dagger forth thou gav'st him,
And with upbraiding smiles he said, 'Behold it;
This is the pledge of a false husband's love!'
And in my arms then pressed, and would have clasped me;
But with my cries I scared his coward heart
Till he withdrew, and muttered vows to Hell.
These are thy friends! With these thy life, thy honor,
Thy love, all's staked, and all will go to ruin.
Thomas Otway, *Venice Preserved* (1682), Act 3, Scene 2

To be sure, the conspirators have rogues like the would-be rapist Renault among them, but Jaffier's friend, Pierre, is an honest revolutionary, and it is Jaffier's tragedy to be torn between the two people he loves, his (Whig) friend and his

(Tory) wife. If Otway is advancing the Tory line in *Venice Preserved*, he makes curiously crabwise progress. What are we to make of the scenes – as strange as any in tragedy – in which the masochistic senator, Antonio, plays out his sexual fantasies? He is a rancid Venetian representative of the hardline royalists of Otway's England.

> AQUILINA: Now your Honor has been a bull, pray what beast will your Worship please to be next?
>
> ANTONIO: Now I'll be a Senator again, and thy lover, little Nicky Nacky! (*He sits by her*) Ah toad, toad, toad, toad! Spit in my face a little, Nacky – spit in my face, prithee, spit in my face never so little; spit but a little bit – spit, spit, spit, spit when you are bid I say! Do, prithee spit – now, now, now, spit. What, you won't spit, will you? Then I'll be a dog.
>
> AQUILINA: A dog, my lord?
>
> ANTONIO: Ay, a dog – and I'll give thee this t'other purse to let me be a dog – and to use me like a dog a little. Hurry durry – I will – here 'tis. (*Gives the purse*)
>
> Thomas Otway, *Venice Preserved* (1682), Act 3, Scene 1

In 1682 these scenes were played out fully by Anthony Leigh and Elizabeth Currer. They were cut from eighteenth-century performances. Times had changed.

Half-and-half drama

Dryden, Southerne, Otway and even Behn and Congreve tried their hands at both comedy and tragedy, though the effort necessitated the adoption of dual personalities. The very passions that are inflated in their tragedies are systematically deflated in their comedies. But the post-Restoration era also accommodated hybrid dramas that straddled both worlds. The tone of these plays, though unique to this period, owes something to the action-packed tragicomedies of John Fletcher (1579–1625), which figured prominently in the repertoire of the King's Company. The post-Restoration hybrids do not fit easily into any category, but they merit brief consideration in their own right, particularly insofar as their popularity bespeaks the eclecticism of a relaxed audience. Two examples will serve.

Etherege's *The Comical Revenge; or Love in a Tub* 'got the [Duke's] Company more Reputation and Profit than any preceding Comedy', claims Downes, adding that ticket sales over its first month brought in an astonishing £1,000. It is, though, a broken-backed piece, in which a contrived love plot, conducted in rhyming couplets, is overwhelmed by a seemingly random sequence of comic episodes, conducted in prose. Both title and subtitle belong to one of these episodes, the 'tubbing' of an overreaching French servant, which *must* have been funny on stage to compensate for its lack of dramaturgical weight. In the love plot two 'truewit' friends are rivals for the hand of Graciana, who, once promised to Colonel Bruce (believed dead in the royalist cause during the Civil Wars), has fallen for Lord Beaufort: 'My heart does double duty; it does mourn / For you brave Bruce; for you brave Beaufort burn' (Act 3, Scene 7). Resolution is achieved when the heartbroken Bruce, after challenging his friend to a duel and then attempting to commit suicide by falling on his sword, accepts his fate and agrees to marry Graciana's sister instead. It is probably a good thing that the prose scenes, centred on the opportunistic gallant Sir Frederick Frollick, dominate the action, but it is impossible to reconcile these comic episodes with the sententiousness of the love plot. 'Honour with justice always does agree,' says Colonel Bruce (Act 5, Scene 1). Try telling that to Lucy, Sir Frederick's mistress, when he casually offloads her on to the witless Sir Nicholas Cully once a rich widow makes herself available.

Dryden's *Marriage à la Mode* (1671) similarly mixes the rhyming couplets of a 'serious' plot, involving the rightful succession to a throne and a tragic conflict between love and duty, with the lively prose of a (more serious, in fact) comic subplot, in which a sexy foursome finally untangle the knots they have tied for themselves. The perfunctorily plotted and rather silly 'serious' plot is utterly undermined by its comic playmate. 'Let me die,' says Leonidas in the serious plot – and means it: 'Let me die,' reiterates the delightful Melantha, a constant flurry of exits and entrances, in the comic plot – because it is a fashionable catchphrase: and, in one of his bawdiest songs, Dryden reverts to the time-honoured *double entendre* that links death and sexual intercourse.

> Thus entranced they did lie,
> Till Alexis did try
> To recover new breath, that again he might die:
> Then often they died; but the more they did so,
> The nymph died more quick, and the shepherd more slow.
> John Dryden, *Marriage à la Mode* (1671), Act 4, Scene 3

Under such circumstances, Leonidas (the rightful king) has little chance of maintaining his dignity. At one point (Act 3, Scene 1) he even threatens, like Harlequin in a commedia *lazzo*, to hold his breath until he dies. If Dryden is taking his serious plot as unseriously as this, what is expected of the audience? *Marriage à la Mode* effortlessly exemplifies the superiority of comedy in an age that continued, officially, to rank tragedy at the top of the dramatic hierarchy.

Changes in the audience

Social classes were clearly defined in the immediate aftermath of the Restoration. Theatre companies aimed first to please the court, then the gentry of the 'town', then the merchants of the 'city', and only then the visitors from the country.

> [Y]our little courtier's wife, who speaks to the king but once a month, need but go to a town lady, and there she may vapour and cry, 'The king and I', at every word. Your town lady, who is laughed at in the circle, takes her coach into the city, and there she's called Your honour, and has a banquet from the merchant's wife, whom she laughs at for her kindness. And as for my finical cit, she removes but to her country house, and there insults over the country gentlewoman.
>
> John Dryden, *Marriage à la Mode* (1671), Act 3, Scene 1

But over the closing years of the century, the landed aristocracy (and even more the landed gentry) had to accommodate itself to the advance of money. By 1696 the early statistician Gregory King was confident that prosperous merchants had substantially higher incomes than the majority of the gentry. Financial institutions developed to meet the demands of capital (and war): Lloyds of London was founded in 1688, the Bank of England in 1694. The patronage of the court could no longer be depended on after the 1688 Revolution. Queen Mary had little interest in the theatre, King William none. The shifts in the audience are clearly signalled by changes in the timing of performances. In the 1660s the play began at half past three; by the early 1690s the start had been pushed back to four o'clock; and as the century turned, five o'clock was early, half past five preferred and six o'clock acceptable. Merchants and civil servants had work to do. They were ready for a different kind of drama, and most of them were content, after the play, to go home to bed.

Chapter 3

Actors and acting

Acceptable styles of acting are determined by the nature of the spaces in which performance occurs. In the common experience of today's theatregoers, a play takes place in a vividly lit area and is watched in darkness. Light separates the actors from the audience and allows them authority over us. To challenge that authority requires bravado and will probably result in expulsion. We go to a theatre in the expectation of remaining silent except when licensed to laugh or called on, by convention, to clap. When Tom Courtenay, performing Shakespeare in Manchester's University Theatre in the late 1960s, halted mid-speech to ask a school party to be quiet, the audience applauded him. A Restoration audience would have been more likely to lynch him. Although certain actors achieved something like star status, they were all regarded as subservient to audiences, who shared the light with them. The playhouses of the late seventeenth century were small: stage, auditorium and lobby at the first Theatre Royal in Bridges Street (1663) were contained within a building 30.5 metres long by 18 metres wide, and even Sir John Vanbrugh's grandiose Queen's Theatre (1705) was only 39.6 metres long by 18 metres wide. And since the space in front of the proscenium arch was permanently lit by chandeliers, the actors could see the audience as clearly as the audience could see them. They were in a room together, and social convention, while sometimes tolerant of indecorous behaviour among the spectators, demanded decorum from the actors. The fact that actors, by virtue of their status as servants of the monarch, could be legally prosecuted only on the Lord Chamberlain's say-so, did not diminish, but if anything strengthened this demand.

Stage and auditorium: 1660–1705

In one significant respect, the measurements cited above are misleading. Almost two-thirds of the interior length of the rebuilt Theatre Royal (1674) was occupied by the stage, and the stage itself was divided into two parts by a proscenium arch. The area in front of the arch, about 6.4 metres in depth and about

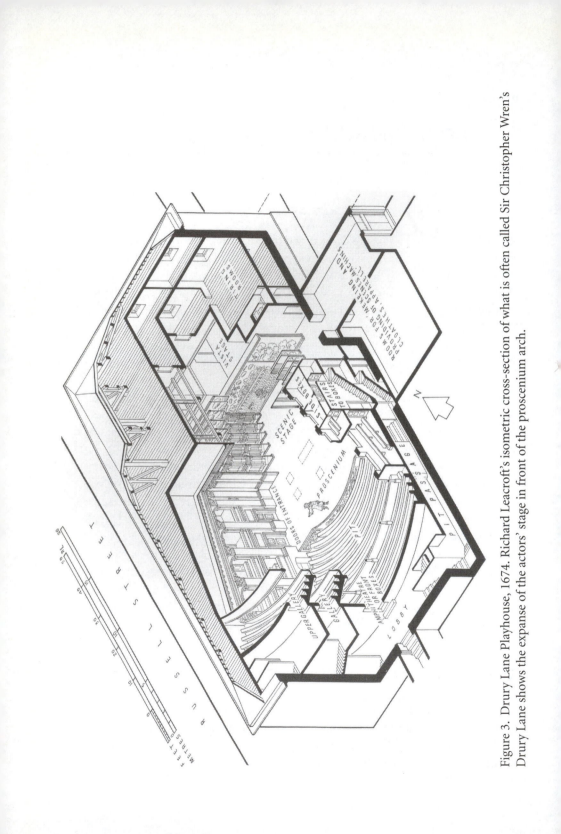

Figure 3. Drury Lane Playhouse, 1674. Richard Leacroft's isometric cross-section of what is often called Sir Christopher Wren's Drury Lane shows the expanse of the actors' stage in front of the proscenium arch.

12 metres wide, belonged to the actors, though they might have to share it with pushy members of the audience. The area behind the arch, upwards of 10 metres in depth, housed the scenery and was rarely entered by the actors. This 'scenic' stage provided the visual background for the aural forestage, and was an active contributor to each performance. Imminent scene changes – carried out by stagehands – were announced to the expectant spectators by the blowing of a whistle. They might involve the blocking-off of the previous 'scene' by the sliding of screens from either side of the stage (to meet in the middle) along grooves, or the sliding back of screens to reveal a new scene further upstage, and the turning of revolving wings to provide an appropriate frame for the different backgound. On occasions, for grand processions primarily, the upstage screens could be pulled open to reveal a recess, or 'vista stage'. The whistle was an open invitation to the audience to enjoy the visible transformation. The back wall of the auditorium, itself divided into pit, boxes and galleries, was about 10 metres from the front of the stage (the remaining length being occupied by the lobby). Estimates of the capacity of this Theatre Royal vary from 800 to 1,200, but a full house, mostly sitting on backless benches, would have been cooped up cheek by jowl, and this must have affected behaviour. (Do I easily ignore the person whose right thigh is pressing my left thigh?)

The performance of the audience began before the performance of the play, and when the piece was a new one, it was the performance of the audience that was decisive. Let us take, as an example, the afternoon of 11 December 1676 at the Theatre Royal in Drury Lane. *The Plain Dealer*, a new play by William Wycherley, has been announced. By now in his mid-thirties, Wycherley is known to belong to the still-charmed circle of the Duke of Buckingham,[1] but the slurs on female virtue in *The Country Wife* (1676) have given rise to scandalous gossip and vocal abuse from a section of society ladies – something to which Wycherley cannot resist alluding in *The Plain Dealer*.

> OLIVIA: Cousin . . . You are one of those who have the confidence to pardon [*The Country Wife*].
> ELIZA: Why, what is there of ill in't, say you?
> OLIVIA: O fie, fie, fie, would you put me to the blush anew? Call all the blood into my face again? But to satisfy you then, first, the clandestine obscenity in the very name of Horner.
> ELIZA: Truly, 'tis so hidden I cannot find it out, I confess.
> OLIVIA: O horrid! Does it not give you the rank conception or image of a goat, a town-bull or a satyr? Nay, what is yet a filthier image than all the rest, that of an eunuch?
> ELIZA: What then? I can think of a goat, a bull or satyr without any hurt.
> OLIVIA: Ay, but cousin, one cannot stop there.

ELIZA: I can, cousin.

OLIVIA: O no, for when you have those filthy creatures in your head once, the next thing you think is what they do, as their defiling of honest men's beds and couches, rapes upon sleeping and waking country virgins under hedges and on haycocks. Nay, farther –

ELIZA: Nay, no farther, cousin. We have enough of your comment on the play, which will make me more ashamed than the play itself.

OLIVIA: O, believe me, 'tis a filthy play, and you may take my word for a filthy play as soon as another's, but the filthiest thing in that play, or any other play, is –

ELIZA: Pray keep it to yourself, if it be so.

OLIVIA: No, faith, you shall know it. I'm resolved to make you out of love with the play. I say, the lewdest, filthiest thing is his china; nay, I will never forgive the beastly author his china. He has quite taken away the reputation of poor china itself and sullied the most innocent and pretty furniture of a lady's chamber, insomuch that I was fain to break all my defiled vessels. You see I have none left; nor you, I hope.

ELIZA: You'll pardon me, I cannot think the worse of my china for that of the playhouse.

OLIVIA: Why, you will not keep any now sure! 'Tis now as unfit an ornament for a lady's chamber as the pictures that come from Italy and other hot countries, as appears by their nudities, which I always cover or scratch out, wheresoe'er I find 'em. But china! Out upon't, filthy china, nasty, debauched china.

ELIZA: All this will not put me out of conceit with china nor the play, which is acted today or another of the same beastly author's, as you call him, which I'll go see.

William Wycherley, *The Plain Dealer* (1676), Act 2

Prominent among the audience on 11 December are the Duke of Buckingham, the Earl of Rochester, the future Earl of Dorset, the Earl of Mulgrave (John Dryden's patron) and the fashionable poets Sir John Denham and Edmund Waller. The atmosphere in the small auditorium is not unlike that at a party when the arrival of a provocative guest is imminent. Conversation overrides the opening music, and the actor Charles Hart, who is to deliver the prologue in the role of the 'plain dealer', Manly, has to time his arrival. He is to enter through one of the four doors (two each side) on the forestage, and must be feeling some of the trepidation of the provocative guest. But he has Wycherley's prologue immediately ahead of him as he bows and bobs his way through the onstage gallants, with, of course, the necessary acknowledgement to those in the side-boxes overlooking the forestage:

> I the Plain-Dealer am to act today
> And my rough part begins before the play.

What he proceeds to do – and this prologue is by no means unique in requiring this – is to address the nearest sections of the audience in turn. First the wits (some of them on stage, some in the stage-boxes), who 'with faint praises one another damn'; then 'the fine, loud gentlemen o' th' pit', who 'damn all plays'; and then the 'shrewd judges who the boxes sway' and like to protect their female companions from too much truth. The abuse of audiences in prologues of the period is, I suppose, a defensive routine. By predicting their hostile reaction, the playwright hopes to reverse it. What is said matters less than the fact that the audience's presence is openly acknowledged. The actors know we are here, and admit that they are afraid of us: now we can get on with the play. But *The Plain Dealer* is a disconcerting amalgam of Molière's *Le Misanthrope* and Shakespeare's *Twelfth Night*, a dense play with a sting in most of its tails. The audience reacts uncertainly, until Wycherley's aristocratic cheerleaders guide it to applaud, thereby establishing for the play a place in the national repertoire. It might easily have come out differently: the interrelationship of playwrights, players and audiences was a volatile one. Assembled together in a small space, around the common territory of a play, they take the measure of each other before casting their votes. In the case of *The Plain Dealer*, the outcome, narrowly, is favourable, but there are reservations, and the alert actors have noted them. The spoken text is not sacred, and there will be revisions before the second performance. It became the custom, in the late seventeenth century, to stage premieres on Saturday – to allow a responsive author time to accommodate the audience by rewriting on Sunday. That author's first aim, after all, was to nurse the play through to a third performance, for which he would receive his first additional financial reward. Nor was there any guarantee that the actors would respect the writer's wishes. From his study of promptbooks, Edward Langhans has concluded that 'meeting a reasonable running time' mattered more to the actors than the ambitions of playwrights.[2]

The impact of actresses

Knowing well the moral opposition to the introduction of actresses, Charles II disingenuously turned Puritanism back on itself in his instructions to Thomas Killigrew and Sir William Davenant.

[F]or as much as many plays formerly acted do contain several profane, obscene and scurrilous passages, and the women's parts therein have been acted by men in the habit of women, at which some have taken offence, for the preventing of these abuses for the future, we do hereby strictly command and enjoin that from henceforth no new play shall be acted by either of the said companies containing any passages offensive to piety and good manners . . . And we do likewise permit and give leave that all the women's parts to be acted in either of the said two companies for the time to come may be performed by women so long as their recreations, which by reason of the abuses aforesaid were scandalous and offensive, may by such reformation be esteemed not only harmless delight, but useful and instructive representations of human life, to such of our good subjects as shall resort to the same.

Charles II, Letter Patent to Thomas Killigrew, 25 April 1662

Cleansing the theatre of cross-dressing was presented as a moral project, though its authority was already being blandly undermined by the popularity of breeches roles. Close to a quarter of the plays staged between 1660 and 1700 called for an actress (or two) to expose normally concealed parts of the body in male costume, never more brazenly than in Thomas Southerne's *Sir Anthony Love* (1690), whose title role was expertly created by Susannah Mountfort. Perhaps uniquely, Mountfort was there invited to disguise her femininity, for a while at least, rather than, as was the norm, flaunting it from the start.

Opposition to actresses may not initially have been confined to the morally fastidious. Charles II was probably colluding with Killigrew in the overriding of objections from some of his actors. None of the plays in the available repertoire displayed a capacity that Aphra Behn would later cultivate – to redirect the gaze onto the bodies of the male actors. Edward Kynaston (*c.*1643–1712) was particularly at risk under the new dispensation, since he owed his early popularity to his playing of beautiful young women.

To the Cockpitt play, the first that I have had time to see since my coming from sea, 'The Loyal Subject', where one Kynaston, a boy, acted the Duke's sister, but made the loveliest lady that ever I saw in my life, only her voice not very good.

Samuel Pepys, *Diary*, 18 August 1660

Colley Cibber would 'remember' the 'Ladies of Quality' who enticed Kynaston into their coaches, after the play but still in his female costume, for drives through Hyde Park. But Kynaston was young enough to adapt, and he became a serviceable performer of male roles. It was probably harder for men of Michael Mohun's generation to stomach female competition, particularly when it was the actress's body rather than her talent that attracted admiration. Actors were essentially soloists, inclined to think of *parts* rather than *plays*, and it was a severe threat to a man's vanity to find he had lost control of the audience's gaze. Increasingly irascible, Mohun could *see* the eyes of his audience wandering from him towards Nell Gwyn, or any of the other inexperienced beauties whose bodies were on display. *The Plain Dealer* opened during one of his unexplained periodic absences from the King's Company. We may surmise that he found the new world harder to live in than Charles Hart, Kynaston, William Cartwright and Joseph Haines, senior actors who appeared in Wycherley's play.

It is, however, the actresses in *The Plain Dealer* who command attention here, not so much because they have a special claim on it as because they are straightforwardly representative. Elizabeth Knipp (*c.*1640–80), who played the tolerant Eliza, is best known to history through Samuel Pepys's *Diary*, where she is first referred to on 6 December 1665 as 'the most excellent mad-humoured thing, and sings the noblest that ever I heard in my life'. A martyr to the sexual excitability properly known as 'erethism', Pepys 'spent the night in extasy almost'. By 2 January 1666, and not for the first time in his life, Pepys was mingling his passion for singing and his impulse for sex by joining Knipp in a coach, where he 'got her upon my knee (the coach being full) and played with her breasts and sung'. It was generally assumed that actresses were sexually available, and Knipp, though married to a horse-trader whom Pepys considered 'an ill-natured fellow', was certainly open to flirtation, but there is no evidence of consummation before the spring of 1668. Pepys was always happy to confide his manual gropings to his *Diary*, but reticent when it came to copulation. The entry for 7 May 1668 speaks openly about his backstage ogling and the sexual traffic in the green room of the Theatre Royal, but offers nothing more than 'and so the rest' about what happened after he 'set Mrs. Knepp at her lodgings'.

[C]alled Knepp from the King's house, where going in for her, the play being done, I did see Beck Marshall come dressed off the stage, and looks mighty fine and pretty and noble: and also Nell [Gwyn] in her boy's clothes, mighty pretty. But, Lord! Their confidence! And how many men do hover about them as soon as they come off the stage, and how confident they are in their talk! Here I did kiss the pretty woman newly come, called Peg [Hughes], a mighty pretty woman. Here took up Knepp into our coach, and all of us with her to her lodgings, and thither comes [John] Bannister with a song of her's. Here was also [Joseph] Haynes, the incomparable dancer of the King's house, and a seeming civil man, and sings pretty well, and they gone, we abroad to Marrowbone [Marylebone], and there walked in the garden, the first time I ever was there; and a pretty place it is, and here we eat and drank and stayed till 9 at night, and so home by moonshine. And so set Mrs. Knepp at her lodgings, and so the rest.

Samuel Pepys, *Diary*, 7 May 1668

Only the censorious could use Pepys's records as evidence that Knipp was a peculiarly 'loose' woman. She lived modestly, and was understandably at a loss to resist *every* attempt (she did some) by her important admirer to get his hands on her. Never in the front rank of actors, she shone most brightly as an entr'acte singer and dancer, and little is known of her after Pepys abandoned his *Diary*. She was probably with Haines, the actor/dancer whom Pepys contrived to outstay on 7 May 1668, among the group of actors who ventured (desperately) to Scotland in 1679, and may have died giving birth to a daughter by Haines.

We know even less about Katherine Corey (born *c.*1635), who played the litigious Widow Blackacre in *The Plain Dealer*, and was entrusted with the epilogue. To have the last word with the audience was a cherished privilege, and we can assume that Wycherley admired her. A good epilogue was an opportunity for intimate conversation with the audience, and playwrights quickly learnt the wisdom of letting the audience's last encounter be with a seductive woman. The most famous example is that of Gwyn, dead on stage at the end of John Dryden's heroic tragedy *Tyrannick Love* (1669), but springing up to obstruct the stagehand deputed to remove her corpse, with:

> Hold! Are you mad, you damned, confounded dog?
> I am to rise, and speak the epilogue.

Having commanded the freedom of the stage, Gwyn focused on her male admirers, promising to haunt their bedrooms:

> And faith you'll be in a sweet kind of taking
> When I surprise you between sleep and waking.

Coincidentally (or perhaps not), it was not long after delivering this epilogue that Gwyn became Charles II's mistress. Corey was a different kind of actress, and her epilogue focused primarily on law students at the Inns of Court, future beneficiaries of the Widow Blackacre's thirst for litigation,

> For with young judges, such as most of you,
> The men by women best their business do.

Corey had been among the first actresses recruited by Killigrew in 1661, and it was she whom Lady Castlemaine suborned to imitate Lady Harvey on stage in 1669. From an examination of the roles she played, particularly in the later stages of her career, Elizabeth Howe deduced that she was 'large and plain', a specialist in 'ugly, comic parts'.[3] Twice married, she vanishes from the records after 1692, with no scandal attached to her name.

The creators of *The Plain Dealer*'s two leading female roles have been casually traduced in many accounts of the Restoration stage. Like their more famous successors, Elizabeth Barry and Anne Bracegirdle, Rebecca Marshall (creator of hair Manly's demanding mistress, Olivia) and Elizabeth Boutell (in male disguise as the faithful Fidelia, whose love for Manly finally triumphs) hunted best as a pair. During the 1670s, their partnership of contrasts flourished predominantly in tragedy: Marshall (born *c.*1640) played strong women, whose impetuosity might lead to villainy, Boutell (1648–1715) the timorous and generally innocent victim. Both have been assumed, on flimsy evidence, to have benefited from the sale of sexual favours. Both might equally well be portrayed as women who achieved, through their talents and self-belief, a right of command over their own lives that was more available to actresses (and Quakers) than to almost any other women.

The case for a reappraisal of Boutell has been powerfully argued by Kirsten Pullen.[4] There is no hard evidence to support the description of her in an anonymous verse lampoon, 'The Session of the Ladies' (1688), as 'chestnut-maned Boutell, whom all the Town fucks', but the legitimacy of this canard has been silently accepted as further confirmation of the concupiscence of Restoration actresses. The 'truth' may be that the marriage between Elizabeth Davenport and Barnaby Boutell was a good one, or, to approach 'truth' from a different angle, it may be that her contemporaries confused the roles that Boutell played on stage with her 'real' life. This, after all, was the original 'Country Wife', and this was the woman who commonly displayed herself in breeches. As the cross-dressed Fidelia in *The Plain Dealer*, she would have her peruke pulled off and her breasts felt by Olivia's husband; as Dryden's Cleopatra in *All for Love* (1677), those same breasts may have been fully exposed to asp and audience.[5] Given the roles she played over an uncommonly long stage career (*c.*1663–97), and given the eagerness of town and court to purchase them as lovers, the preservation of a reputation for virtue was a rare commodity for actresses. Whoever was playing Evadne in one of the periodic revivals of the Beaumont and Fletcher favourite, *The Maid's Tragedy* (*c.*1608), could be guaranteed a laugh on the line, 'A maidenhead, Amintor, at my years?' So, probably, could the boy who created the role for Shakespeare's company – but there are laughs and laughs.

Rehearsal and the actor's method

The critical concern with 'theory' as the necessary underpinning of all cultural activity has led scholars of acting to attempt to uncover the coherent basis, sometimes almost a philosophy, of acting on the late seventeenth-century stage. The stubborn fact is that such coherence is as much a chimera as any belief in a unifying theory. Actors, I have already suggested, came on to the proscenium through a side-door with the same kind of intention as they might have had when self-consciously 'making an entrance' to a social occasion already in progress. The space they then occupied was one in which they were allowed to

shine conversationally. In tragedy the conversation was formally more heightened, less open to the audience, than in comedy: poetically ambitious playwrights such as Dryden, Thomas Otway and Nathaniel Lee consistently broke
it up into a sequence of spoken arias, for the delivery of which the most available
models were manuals of rhetoric. The exemplar, for Cibber (writing thirty years
after the actor's death), was Thomas Betterton.

> In the just delivery of poetical numbers, particularly where the sentiments are
> pathetick, it is scarce credible upon how minute an article of sound depends their
> greatest beauty or inaffection. The voice of a singer is not more strictly ty'd to
> time and tune, than that of an actor in theatrical elocution: the least syllable too
> long, or too slightly dwelt upon in a period, depreciates it to nothing; which very
> syllable, if rightly touch'd, shall, like the heightening stroke of light from a
> master's pencil, give life and spirit to the whole. I never heard a line of tragedy
> come from Betterton, wherein my judgement, my ear, and my imagination, were
> not fully satisfy'd; which, since his time, I cannot equally say of any one actor
> whatsoever.
>
> Colley Cibber, *An Apology for His Life* (1740), Chapter 4

The apparent detail of Cibber's observations is deceptive: what he writes might
equally be applied to Sir Johnston Forbes-Robertson (1853–1937), Henry
Ainley (1879–1945), Sir John Gielgud (1904–2000), or any other honey-voiced
actor from James Quin in the eighteenth century to Michael Gambon in the
twenty-first. There is no reason to doubt that Betterton spoke finely. According
to contemporary accounts, he was neither handsome nor particularly graceful,
so that it was most likely his vocal dexterity that pleased audiences when, at
the age of sixty, he created the role of the young lover Valentine in William
Congreve's *Love for Love* (1695), and that was still sustaining him as Hamlet
fourteen years later. The craft was in what Colley Cibber called 'sensible pronun-
ciation', a way of speaking that captured both the sense and the sensuousness
of language. It is much harder to know what he did with his body. In trying
to describe Betterton's physical presence, Cibber is reduced to 'this inexpress-
ible somewhat'. The commonplace assumption was that, in order effectively
to convey a passion (we tend to prefer 'emotion'), the actor had to feel it, and
the measure was always 'nature'. But 'nature' is a slippery word, one which, on
stage, elides with 'convention'. Betterton's naturalness would look and sound
to us now comically artificial, 'over the top', but the same could be said of any
actor born before 1920. In his time he was admired for his control, something
which his ardent young challenger George Powell lacked.

Joseph Roach, in his attempt to reconstruct past performances, has argued
that Betterton 'had mastered the rhetorical mode',[6] by which he means a

mode of acting, derived from readings of Quintilian's *De Institutione Oratoria* (*c.* AD 90), that registered human passions with conviction. Closely linked to ancient medicine, rhetorical acting, Roach argues, embodied mental passions. His primary sources, apart from Quintilian, are Thomas Wright's *The Passions of the Minde* (1604) and John Bulwer's *Chirologia* and *Chironomia* (1644). Bulwer, in particular, ascribes precise meaning to gesture, outlawing the raising of the hand above the level of the eye or dropping it below that of the belly and privileging the right hand over the left. There are two obvious problems about all this: the first, that the passions are the domain of tragedy, which leaves most of the action of comedy unaccounted for, and the second that there is no secure evidence that any known actor read Wright and Bulwer, let alone Quintilian. In a more recent essay on Restoration performance,[7] Roach has scaled down his claims, referring convincingly to the 'public intimacy' of the Restoration stage and to the mutual reinforcement of 'passion' and 'manners' as a constituent of a distinctive style. Most tellingly, he presents the theatrical occasion in social terms:

> In performance the most important element of the unfolding action of the play was the grouping, which may be defined as the roll-call of actors assembled on the stage at a particular moment . . . The performance of a Restoration play consisted of a series of continuous groupings – solos, duets, trios, quartets etc. A reader of these plays today needs to be attentive to the by-play between characters in each grouping, including the presence of silent characters (who tend to be forgotten in reading, though not in performance). (26)

It is Roach's recognition of the sociosexual significance of performance that distinguishes his essay.

During the Restoration period successful performances made carefully planned use of the three hours or so that audiences could spend at the playhouse – from the 'first music', which summoned the spectators to their seats, to the announcement of the next day's offering, which ended the performance by inviting them back. In between there occurred a variety of exciting incidents calculated to stir involvement: in tragedy a rising pulse of lurid violence, frequently erotic; in comedy a concatenation of intrigues and cross-purposes, always erotic.

Joseph Roach, 'The Performance', *The Cambridge Companion to English Restoration Theatre* (2000)

From what we can learn about systems of rehearsal, it would be astonishing if there were any coherent application of theory to practice. As a general rule, four weeks elapsed between the distribution of 'parts', marked up, as they had been on the Elizabethan stage, with short cues and no indication of the speaker of those cues, and the first public performance, whether of a new play or the revival of an old one. During these four weeks, as well as acting in as many as seven repertoire pieces, the actors were expected to learn their words. They had probably attended a reading of the play – by the author, if available,[8] by a leading actor if not – but there was no complete text to which they could refer. Even those older plays that had appeared in print would have been adapted for performance; a text as originally written would already have been altered before rehearsals began and would undergo further revisions in the light of performance. A play published 'as it is acted' probably represented a final version as approved by actors and audiences. An unhappy author might pursue a publisher prepared to bring out the original, but it was the acting company that owned the performed text, and it was on actors rather than playwrights that audiences focused. Dryden pronounced it an innovation when Congreve's name appeared on the playbill for *The Double-Dealer* (1693), and Pepys, always likely to single out an actress or, less frequently, an actor, rarely recorded the author of the plays he attended. The text was dumb until spoken on stage.

Modern assumptions about the purpose of rehearsal are profoundly misleading. Restoration actors worked on and from their 'parts'. When Betterton complained of actors who no longer felt obliged to 'make our Study our Business', as he had been trained to do by Davenant, he was endorsing the 'best practice' of completing work on a part *before* rehearsals began. Such study might be carried out in private, or in the presence of trusted advisers. The young men who 'scarce ever mind a Word of their parts but only at *Rehearsals . . .* when the Mind is not very capable of considering so calmly and judiciously on what they have to study' were, for Betterton, delinquents.[9] But we miss his point if we think in terms of today's painstaking piecing together of a play through collaborative discovery. Secondary actors were required to attend the theatre at stated hours, not to rehearse scenes in orderly sequence, but to ensure that they knew their parts. Principal actors, shareholders in the business, were trusted to work alone. An outsider at a 'rehearsal' might have heard six or seven people simultaneously mouthing lines, with 'instructors' moving between them. Group, or 'partial', rehearsals were not the norm, and 'full company' rehearsals likely to be delayed until the day before opening. On occasions, influential 'friends' of the company were invited to attend previews, after (or even during) which their advice on improvements would be solicited. John Evelyn was one of a group who, in 1662, went to 'heare the Comedians con, & repeate' one of the first great successes of the Restoration stage, Sir Samuel Tuke's swashbuckling *The Adventures of Five Hours*. Tiffany Stern has described an occasion like this as 'a performative "rehearsal" for gentlemen'.[10] Fictionalized versions, featuring authorial misbehaviour, dictate the progress of *The Rehearsal* and the anonymous *The Female Wits* (1696), both of which present their plays-within-a-play as roughly ready dress rehearsals. For actors less conscientious than Betterton, the pursuit of perfection before the first public audience had passed judgement was unnecessarily strenuous.

Actors as celebrities

It is comparatively easy to name the 'stars' of the Restoration stage, not so easy to define their distinctness. Sagacious playwrights wrote parts that fed off the known strengths of a company, and the perceived quality of individual actors is best discerned in the roles they were asked to create. Some of the most telling examples are to be found in the disposition of double-acts, like the 'gay couple' of Hart and Gwyn or the villainess/victim of Marshall and Boutell. Betterton was given a new lease of life by the brilliance of Elizabeth Barry (*c.*1658–1713) in both tragedy and comedy. By virtue of the fact that they played opposite each other in an astonishingly high proportion of the best plays of the era – *The Man of Mode* (1676), *The Rover* (1677), Thomas Otway's *The Soldiers' Fortune* (1680), *The Lucky Chance* (1686), Dryden's *Amphitryon* (1690), *The Wives' Excuse* (1691/2), *Love for Love* (1695) and *The Way of the World* (1700) among comedies; Nathaniel Lee's *Lucius Junius Brutus* (1680), Otway's *The Orphan* (1680) and *Venice Preserved* (1682) among tragedies – it can reasonably be argued that, for well over twenty years, they raised the level of drama as well as performance. But Barry does not need Betterton as a prop. She was one of the most powerful women of her era, the first actor to be awarded a personal benefit, thus inaugurating a system of huge financial significance to her fellow-professionals, a voice to be reckoned with in theatrical management, and the chief stimulus for a subgenre crudely called 'she-tragedy'. From a sequence of plays by John Banks (*c.*1652–1706), Nicholas Rowe (1674–1718) and others, we can be certain that Barry had a command of pathos that would not be rivalled until the heyday of Sarah Siddons at the end of the eighteenth century. And all this without the obvious physical beauty that consistently distorts theatrical comment on actresses. Barry was plump and big-hipped, and her face (aquiline nose, pronounced cheeks and a lopsided mouth) would nowadays probably be called 'horsey'. She had lovers, Etherege and the Earl of Rochester among them, and was prepared to take advice from them, but was never subservient to the men in her life. She acted with Betterton as his equal.

Figure 4. Sir Godfrey Kneller's portrait of Elizabeth Barry, while conveying her strength, makes no attempt at flattery.

The same is true of her double-act with the younger and prettier Anne Bracegirdle (1671–1748).

[S]he had no greater claim to beauty than what the most desirable *brunette* might pretend to. But her youth, and lively aspect, threw out such a glow of

> health and chearfulness, that, on the stage, few spectators that were not past it,
> could behold her without desire. It was even a fashion among the gay, and
> young, to have a taste or *tendre* for Mrs. Bracegirdle.
>
> Colley Cibber, *An Apology for His Life* (1740), Chapter 5

Popular in breeches, a good singer, and chosen even more frequently than
Barry to deliver prologues (nine known) and epilogues (twenty-two known),
Bracegirdle was something of a specialist in being stage-raped, a specialism she
sustained alongside a cultivated reputation for chastity in private life. Her early
stage partnership with the dashing William Mountfort (*c.*1664–92) was brought
to a sudden end in a way that vividly illustrates the seriousness with which
the sexual game could be played in and around the London theatre. Captain
Richard Hill, obsessed with Bracegirdle and convinced that Mountfort was his
successful rival for her body, teamed up with the serial duellist Lord Mohun to
abduct the actress after a performance on 9 December 1692. They were foiled,
and Bracegirdle took refuge in her Howard Street home, but Mohun and Hill
lingered outside the house, drinking even more than they already had. Exactly
what happened when Mountfort appeared (on his way home, or . . .) is not
clear from the accounts of Mohun's subsequent (and sensational) trial before
the House of Lords, but it is certain that Hill stabbed Mountfort with his sword,
and that the actor died nine hours later. Bracegirdle cannot be held responsible
for the turbulence she unleashed, but her mode was to be provocative, and
playwrights exploited it. She and Congreve might have married if society had
been as expansive as it soon became. Thomas Shadwell, from a gentry family,
had married an actress, but the royalist Shadwells had forfeited their estates
during the Civil Wars; and Mary Lee continued to perform as Lady Slingsby
after her putative marriage to a baronet, but Sir Charles Slingsby had taken
continental refuge from his creditors before that marriage could be accredited.
Congreve had Lord Halifax as a powerful patron, and Halifax, much as he
admired the actress,[11] was more likely to suppose her a suitable mistress for his
protégé than a wife. The best Congreve could do was to marry her in fiction,
as Araminta in *The Old Bachelor*, as Angelica in *Love for Love* and above all as
Millamant in *The Way of the World*. The growth of a passionate relationship can
be traced from play to play. For the audiences of 1700, as well as for Congreve,
Millamant *was* Bracegirdle.

There was never any rivalry between Barry and Bracegirdle. Dramatically
paired as opposites (Barry was the dangerous Mrs Marwood in *The Way of the
World*), they teamed up in theatrical affairs. Having been Betterton's ward in her
early youth, Bracegirdle shared with him and Barry the effective leadership of
the breakaway Actors' Company from 1695, and Barry left her the considerable
sum of £220 in her will. Before that will was proved, Bracegirdle had retired

from the stage, sensing perhaps that her thunder was being stolen by Anne Oldfield. Five years earlier, the Earl of Scarsdale had left her an unexplained £1,000: something to help her on the way to forty years in retirement.

This was a period in which the possession of a part remained with its creator until retirement or death intervened. Whoever inherited it was expected to copy the original as closely as possible. Only around the turn of the century was the introduction of original touches by inheritors beginning to be admired. Cibber acknowledged that he played the title role in his own adaptation of *Richard III* (1699) in imitation of the outstandingly ugly Samuel Sandford, recently retired: 'I imagined I knew how Sandford would have spoken every line of it.'[12] Even more telling is Cibber's recollection of a revival of *The Old Bachelor* by the rump of actors under Christopher Rich, after the 1695 defection of the leading lights of the United Company. The decision to stage Congreve's play was, in itself, a defiance of actors' claims to the possession of the roles they had originated, and it is doubtful that anyone other than George Powell would have been brash enough to steal Betterton's role while Betterton was still active. It was surely Powell who demanded the footnote to the playbill, 'The part of the Old Batchelor [*sic*], to be perform'd in imitation of the original', but it must have been Cibber's choice to copy Thomas Doggett (*c.* 1670–1721) as Alderman Fondlewife: 'I had laid the tint of forty years, more than my real age, upon my features, and, to the most minute placing of an hair, was dressed exactly like him. When I spoke, the surprise was still greater, as if I had not only borrow'd his cloaths, but his voice too.'[13] This is less acting than mimicry, a craft dependent on the celebrity of the person being mimicked. Richard Estcourt (1668–1712) based his stage career on his skills as a mimic, as Samuel Foote and Tate Wilkinson would in the later eighteenth century. Cibber, still a tyro, had not yet developed his line in excessive foppery. He and Doggett would later work together in management, but they were not at all similar. It was Doggett's show-stealing performance as Ben Legend in *Love for Love* that had established his stardom, and it is worth wondering just what the Drury Lane audience was invited to relish when Powell played Betterton and Cibber Doggett. Whatever Powell's motives, the very idea involves a metatheatrical homage to the status of actors in *fin-de-siècle* London.

It has generally been the case in theatre history that 'low' or 'eccentric' comedians are harder to replace than 'straight' actors, and one pair merits particular attention here. James Nokes (*c.*1642–96) was one of the original members of the Duke's Company, and came to prominence as the witless Sir Nicholas Cully in Etherege's *The Comical Revenge* (1664). His knack of naturalizing the grotesque encouraged later playwrights to create for him foppish buffoons whose unlikely antics he could make plausible. Calling such people a 'nokes' meant something

Figure 5. Anthony Leigh as Father Dominic in *The Spanish Friar* (1680).
Sir Godfrey Kneller's 1689 painting is a rare early portrait of an actor in role.

to contemporaries (there is, for example, reference to 'a natural Nokes' in Rochester's satirical poem 'Tunbridge Wells' and the *OED* records a 'nokes' as a fool or dullard). Dryden created a 'nokes' for Nokes as the accident-prone title character of Pepys's favourite play, *Sir Martin Marall* (1667). Nokes, then, was an established favourite before Anthony Leigh (d.1692) joined the Duke's Company early in the 1670s to set up the most famous comic partnership of the era. They formed a classic double-act, with Nokes playing the foolishly imperturbable against Leigh's volatile nitwit. Shadwell placed them knowingly in *The Virtuoso* (1676), with Leigh creating the role of the unstoppable orator, Sir Formal Trifle, and Nokes that of the put-upon Sir Samuel Hearty. The opening scene of Act 4, with a cross-dressed Nokes desperately resisting Leigh's sexual advances ("Sdeath! The rogue begins to pry into the difference of sexes and will discover mine'), is designed for virtuoso slapstick artists.[14] Cibber would remember how, in play after play, 'they returned the ball so dextrously upon one another, that every scene between them seem'd but one continued rest of excellence';[15] without a knowledge of this dexterity, Dryden would never have written the second act of *Amphitryon* as he did. Aphra Behn's *The Lucky Chance* is comic only if the two old men who cling ineffectively to young wives are played with the kind of humour that belonged naturally to Nokes and Leigh. They could work independently – there was no part for Nokes in *Venice Preserved*, in which Leigh's Antonio was such a startling presence – but, like all the best double-acts, they complemented each other. You can tell how wholehearted an actor Leigh was by looking at Sir Godfrey Kneller's portrait of him in the National Portrait Gallery. Kneller presents him in the role of the pimping Father Dominic in Dryden's *The Spanish Friar* (1680), a play in which his energy was expended on cuckolding Nokes's Gomez. Nokes retired from the stage in 1692, and Leigh died after a short illness in December of the same year. Mountfort had been murdered less than two weeks earlier. For the United Company, the loss of three such actors meant also the, at least temporary, loss of all the plays with which they were particularly associated.

Part Two

The theatre reformed: 1700–1737

Chapter 4

The material circumstance

At the beginning of the new century, London's theatre companies had no cause for complacence. The playhouses, to be sure, were established on the social circuit, but their activities were subject to uncomfortably close moral scrutiny, and received no support from the joyless royal court.

Table of events referred to in Part Two	
1688	James II escapes to France. Accession of William and Mary
1691	Society for the Reformation of Manners founded
1694	Death of Queen Mary
1695	Stationers' Company's monopoly of printing lapses. Proliferation of newsprint
1701	Act of Settlement establishes the Hanoverian succession
1702	Britain joins War of the Spanish Succession as enemy of France. Death of William III. Accession of Anne
1704	Duke of Marlborough's victory at Battle of Blenheim
1707	Act of Union with Scotland
1709	Copyright Act
1713	Treaty of Utrecht ends War of the Spanish Succession
1714	Death of Anne. Accession of George I
1715	Jacobite rebellion
1720	South Sea Bubble bursts
1727	Death of George I. Accession of George II
1733	Defeat of Walpole's Excise Bill
1736	Marriage of Frederick, Prince of Wales to Augusta, Princess of Saxe-Gotha
1737	Stage Licensing Act

Encouraged by the Protestant devoutness of Queen Mary, the submerged forces of Puritanism had reasserted themselves in London, most overtly in the foundation, in 1691, of a Society for the Reformation of Manners. This was an aristocratically supported 'top down' faction committed to correcting the behaviour of the masses, one which would claim, in its 1727 'Account of The Progress', to have mounted 94,322 prosecutions over thirty-six years 'in or near London

69

only'. Actors – as utterers on stage of blasphemy or obscenity – were among those prosecuted, and attacks on plays proliferated through the 1690s. The 160th published sermon of John Tillotson (1630–94), whose influence on English religious thought (and on English prose) lasted deep into the eighteenth century, is an unforgiving diatribe from an Archbishop of Canterbury noted for his moderation.

[A]s the Stage now is, [plays] are intolerable, and not fit to be permitted in a *civilized*, much less in a *Christian* Nation . . . And therefore I do not see how any Person pretending to Sobriety and Virtue, and especially to the pure and holy Religion of our blessed Saviour, can without great guilt, and open contradiction to his holy Profession, be present at such lewd and immodest plays, much less frequent them, as too many do, who yet would take it very ill to be shut out of the Community of Christians, as they would most certainly have been in the first and purest Ages of Christianity.

    John Tillotson, extract from Sermon CLX in *Works* (1722), preached
    *c.*1693

It was, then, in fertile ground that Jeremy Collier planted his notorious *Short View of the Immorality and Profaneness of the English Stage* (1698). Passages from Tillotson's sermon on 'the evil of corrupt communication' were reprinted and circulated during the virulent controversy stirred up by Collier's (extremely long) *Short View*. For the next forty years, it became the significant project of some of those professionally engaged to demonstrate the theatre's ability to clean its own Augean stables.

The modern Poets seem to use smut as the old ones did Machines, to relieve a fainting situation.

    Jeremy Collier, *A Short View* (1698)

Steele and Addison

Richard Steele (1672–1729) had seen three of his plays performed in London before founding his periodical, the *Tatler*, in 1709. Published three times a week, and running to 271 issues before its discontinuance in January 1711, the *Tatler* virtually created theatrical criticism as a journalistic genre, as well as fostering the development of the periodical essay. In its maturity in the *Spectator* (1711–12), jointly produced by Steele and Joseph Addison (1672–1719), the periodical essay led the English pursuit of national virtue which was a concomitant to the eighteenth century's near-continuous wars with France.

It was a pursuit in which Steele and Addison did more than anyone to embroil the theatre. To ignore their efforts is to lose direction.

Steele was a serving soldier in 1701 when he published his first successful pamphlet, *The Christian Hero*, and sold his first play, *The Funeral*, to the young company at Drury Lane. They constitute a matching pair: the play's Lord Hardy, discarded heir to Lord Brumpton and altruistic in his impoverished courtship of his father's ward, is a Christian hero, a military man in the service of the soldier-king, William III. Steele's patriotic devotion to the unlovely Dutchman who occupied the English throne and led the opposition to Catholic France was, at this time, wholehearted, however tinged with sycophancy. For him, as for many indoctrinated soldiers, William, whom Lord Hardy is proud to serve, exemplified the Christian hero.

> LORD HARDY: How shall I keep myself even above worldly want? – Shall I live at home, a stiff, melancholy, poor man of quality; grow uneasy to my acquaintance as well as myself, by fancying I am slighted where I am not, with all the thousand particularities which attend those whom low fortune and high spirits make malcontents? No! we have a brave prince on the throne, whose commission I bear, and a glorious war in an honest cause approaching, (*clapping his hand on his sword*) in which this shall cut out bread for me, and may, perhaps, equal that estate to which my birth entitled me.
>
> Richard Steele, *The Funeral* (1701), Act 2, Scene 1

The purpose of Steele's pamphlet is to place the king on a pedestal, and to encourage emulation. The purpose of *The Funeral* is similar. By its popularity, far in excess of the company's expectations, it signalled the viability of the theatre's turning over a new leaf in public; which is not the same as saying that it is a particularly good play. The plot is an old one (by feigning death, husband discovers the true wickedness of the young wife who has besotted him), and the plotting conventional. The deceitful are found out and the virtuous rewarded, in line with Thomas Rymer's recently formulated principles of 'poetic justice'.[1] But Rymer's concern was with tragedy. The transfer of poetic justice from tragedy to comedy carries with it a risk of blurring sentiment with sentimentality, a risk fully embodied in Lord Brumpton's extravagantly benevolent steward, Trusty. By entrusting his mission to mealy-mouthed missionaries, Steele oversold it. The many who know him only through his most easily available and dreadfully mawkish last play, *The Conscious Lovers* (1722), are doomed to misjudgement.

The Funeral was carried by the energy and enthusiasm of three of London's new young stars, Colley Cibber, Anne Oldfield and Robert Wilks. 'Nothing can make the Town so fond of a Man as a successful Play,' Steele would remember after his expulsion from the House of Commons in 1714. The mere fact of that expulsion witnesses to the fervour of his political engagement. Throughout the fierce battles between Whigs and Tories that divided parliament and country after the unfought revolution of 1688 – the extraordinarily contained convulsion that had sent James II to exile in France and seen his daughter and her Dutch husband crowned Queen and King of England – Steele was the most eloquent, sometimes the most outspoken, of the Whig propagandists. His expulsion from parliament, on the ground of his authorship of a 'seditious' pamphlet on the 'crisis' of the royal succession, came in the closing months of Tory ascendancy, and was expedited by the greater eloquence of his arch-adversary, Jonathan Swift. It was a brief setback. Queen Anne's death in August 1714 threw the Tories into disarray. That October, with the enthusiastic endorsement of its actor-managers, Steele was appointed governor of the Theatre Royal, Drury Lane. It was an appointment that made him, formally, the top man in London's theatre world, and it would be rounded off by his knighthood and the reward of a safe parliamentary seat in 1715.

Affable and unfailingly well-intentioned, Steele was determined to do his best for Drury Lane. In the event, and given life's knack of undermining him, he did about as much good as harm. It was seven years before he produced a new play for the company, and when he did it sparked off a lingering controversy. *The Conscious Lovers*, not entirely accurately, is generally described as the originating 'sentimental comedy'. As a master of prepublicity, and of the whole culture of print, Steele carries some of the responsibility for this historical judgement. He ensured that rehearsals were attended by 'many excellent Judges' and himself puffed it as a new kind of comedy. Much of the plot was derived from Terence's first known play, *Andria* (166BC), and the choice of source is anything but casual. Terence was viewed as the moralist of the Roman theatre, a spokesman for *humanitas* and author of the often quoted Latin tag, *Homo sum: humani nil a me alienum puto*. Steele's overtranslation of the original in the *Spectator* 502 – 'I am a Man, and cannot help feeling any Sorrow that can arrive at Man' – significantly identifies the sharing of sorrow as the emblem of humanity. In his life, as well as his works, Steele strove to live up to Terence's precept, but he had always a fatal tendency to approximate. Terence, after all, says nothing to rule out the sharing of joy. To be fair to Steele, though, sorrow and joy are mingled in the excruciating, and surely risible to a modern audience, recognition scene in Act 5 of *The Conscious Lovers*. '*In her disorder [Indiana] throws away a bracelet, which Mr. Sealand takes up, and looks earnestly on it*': eighteenth-century onlookers wept as father and long-lost daughter, in the aftermath of this unlikely bracelet-tossing, came to terms with the glorious truth. We have lost their capacity to be moved by blatant contrivance.

The Conscious Lovers is Steele's attempt to consummate in the theatre a literary project initiated in *The Christian Hero*: to replace the fashionable prestige of the promiscuous rake with that of the socially responsible monogamist. The problem is that his vehicle, Bevil Junior, is a dreary prig who destroys the life of the play almost every time he opens his mouth. In his preface to the published text, Steele, perhaps honestly, claimed that '[t]he chief design of this was to be an innocent performance', adding that 'the audience have abundantly showed how ready they are to support what is visibly intended that way'. To understand the play's hold on the mid-eighteenth-century stage,[2] we would need to *feel* with the age.

Bevil Junior makes his first entrance 'reading' a philosophical tale of Addison's in the *Spectator* 159. Steele and Addison were schoolmates and lifelong friends. Sadly, although they were both Whigs, they quarrelled publicly in early 1719 over governmental policy in the House of Lords. Within a few months Addison was dead. We can assume that Bevil's reading matter is one of Steele's many gestures towards posthumous reconciliation. Although they shared many views, both political and social, the two men were temperamentally different. Steele was a natural participator, Addison an observer. Tattling was Steele's métier, spectating Addison's, and it is Addison's voice that speaks most insistently through the *Spectator*. We can hear it in the mission statement published in the tenth issue of this six-days-a-week mass-circulation (for the time) journal.

> I shall endeavour to enliven morality with wit, and to temper wit with morality, that my readers may, if possible, both ways find their account in the speculation of the day. And to the end that their virtue and discretion may not be short, transient, intermitting starts of thought, I have resolved to refresh their memories from day to day till I have recovered them out of that desperate state of vice and folly into which the age has fallen. The mind that lies fallow but a single day sprouts up in follies that are only to be killed by a constant and assiduous culture. It was said of Socrates that he brought philosophy down from heaven to inhabit among men; and I shall be ambitious to have it said of me that I have brought philosophy out of closets and libraries, schools and colleges, to dwell in clubs and assemblies, at tea-tables and in coffee-houses.
>
> Joseph Addison, extract from *Spectator* 10 (1711)

The cultivation of active spectatorship was, for Addison, a way of improving the day, every day. It offered, incidentally, to civilize the practice of theatregoing and to bring about the improvement of drama by the force of audience demand.[3] The Addisonian project of transforming thought into a social custom was, however unachievable, influential. More reliably than Steele, he could saturate bias with sweet reasonableness, and this made him an unrivalled architect of public opinion. It was in the *Spectator* that readers might find explanations of all that was explicable in Isaac Newton's *Opticks* (1704), a new theory of vision that Addison could link to the pleasures of the imagination (*Spectator* 412). The *Spectator* was the medium through which the ideas formulated in John Locke's *Essay Concerning Human Understanding* (1690) came to permeate eighteenth-century literature. In the *Spectator* 62, for example, he character-istically develops Locke's definition of wit into a literary recipe: 'Thus when a Poet tells us, the Bosom of his Mistress is as white as Snow, there is no Wit in the Comparison; but when he adds, with a Sigh, that it is as cold too, it then grows into Wit.' It is on this recipe, 'mix familiarity with surprise', that the century built its dramatic repertoire. In common with Steele, Addison took advantage of the age's continuing delight in public intimacy,[4] a delight which necessarily benefited theatre in general and actors in particular.

Although fascinated by the stage, Addison was nervous of it. After the failure of *Rosamond* (1707), an English opera whose text he had supplied in criticism of the fashion for incomprehensible Italian libretti, he shelved the manuscript of a tragedy before completing it, and it was probably at Steele's urging that he turned to it again. The outcome was sensational. Addison's *Cato* was staged, with a ragged fifth act hastily compiled, at Drury Lane in April 1713, two weeks after the Treaty of Utrecht had ended the War of the Spanish Succession. It was a Tory treaty, vehemently opposed by the Whigs, who wished to fight on. The furore over *Cato* is the eighteenth century's first significant example of the interconnection of political controversy and theatrical success. Steele had rallied an audience for the first night, and advance rumours of Whiggish triumphalism in a play by the people's spokesman made Tory attendance imperative. Leading figures of both parties showily applauded Addison's sententious blank verse. There was very little other than verse to applaud. Not until Act 4, and then for the only time, does any significant action occur on stage. Addison had turned his back on English renaissance tragedy in favour of the neoclassicism of seventeenth-century France. The contrast is extreme: 'Shakespeare's poetry surrounds events; Racine's poetry replaces events.'[5] Yet this turgid experiment in political tragedy ran uninterrupted for a month, and was regularly cited as a masterpiece for a century more.

It is the first production of *Cato* that concerns us here, because it represents a theatre embedded in politics. Alexander Pope's prologue – Pope was a Tory, but not yet Addison's enemy – promises the audience the spectacle of

> A brave man struggling in the storms of fate,
> And greatly falling with a falling state!

What we witness is the republican Cato's doomed defence of Roman values against the tyrannical threat of an (offstage) Julius Caesar. If Addison was mounting a political platform, it was a platform which faced both ways. For the Whigs, Cato was the Duke of Marlborough, a mighty general in the war against France and an opponent of the Treaty of Utrecht. For the Tories, Marlborough was the warmongering Julius Caesar. The same lines could be clapped by both parties, and the Tory spokesman Viscount Bolingbroke could trump the Whigs with his flamboyant gesture of calling to his box Barton Booth, who had just finished playing Cato, and rewarding him with fifty guineas. It was only the passages on liberty that the Whigs could claim as a slogan – *Cato* is an early monument to the Whiggish appropriation of liberty – but the treacherous Sempronius has the best speech on that theme.

> Lucius seems fond of life; but what is life?
> 'Tis not to stalk about, and draw fresh air
> From time to time, or gaze upon the sun;
> 'Tis to be free.
>
> Joseph Addison, *Cato* (1713), Act 2

The hinge of the play's success is Addison's fastidious dislike of factional politics,[6] voiced in a couplet from the final speech:

> From hence, let fierce contending nations know
> What dire effects from civil discord flow.

Politics aside, the status accorded to *Cato* led English tragedy up a dead end.

Theatre managers and audiences

Insensitive management, in which Christopher Rich was a specialist, damaged the London stage in the first decade of the eighteenth century. Although still in control of one of the patents, Rich was eventually banned from Drury Lane by the Lord Chamberlain in 1709. Not easily silenced, he set about rebuilding the old theatre in Lincoln's Inn Fields, but died in November 1714, a month before the playhouse was ready to open. The patent passed to his two sons, effectively to the elder. John Rich (1692–1761) is rarely recognized as the great theatre manager that he was. Routinely recorded as the originator of English pantomime (which he wasn't), he is almost as regularly dismissed as a man who degraded the drama in search of an audience. Since pantomimes became his moneyspinning fare, and he himself an expressive Harlequin, the verdict hangs on the jury's attitude to pantomime, which, under Rich, supported music and dance with humour and scenic spectacle. During his forty-seven years of management (at Lincoln's Inn Fields until the phenomenal success of John Gay's *The Beggar's Opera* (1728) enabled him to open a fine new playhouse in Covent Garden in 1732), his repertoire's proportion of new plays, revivals and pantomimes differed little from that of Drury Lane, and his actors, generally speaking, liked and trusted him.[7]

After a turbulent first decade of the new century, Drury Lane, too, achieved a kind of stability, if stability can accommodate storms, under the effective management of a triumvirate of actors from 1710 to 1732. The wily Colley Cibber, who knew when to temper provocation with diplomacy, was at the heart of it. Anne Oldfield (1683–1730) would have been, but for Thomas Doggett's resistance. Politics, as well as prejudice, may have been involved. A fervent Whig, Doggett had probably listened to gossip about Oldfield's disloyalty to her Whig lover, Arthur Mainwaring MP, and when, in 1714, Queen Anne commanded that the Tory Barton Booth (1683–1733) be added to the management team, Doggett resigned, leaving the field to Cibber, Booth and the avowedly apolitical Wilks (*c.*1665–1732).

With or without Booth's concurrence, and particularly after Steele's appointment as (absentee) governor, Drury Lane became clearly identified with the Whig cause, and, more by default than intention, Rich's company with that of the Tories. The Drury Lane staging of Cibber's *The Non-Juror* (1717) is a landmark. (Rich's production of Christopher Bullock's *The Perjuror* (1717) was a comparatively lame counter.) The play is a wickedly partisan version of Molière's *Tartuffe*, anti-Catholic, anti-Jacobite and, by association, anti-Tory. The very title was inflammatory; non-jurors were the tolerated minority who, having refused to sign the oath of loyalty to William and Mary after the 1688 Revolution, implicitly maintained the right to the throne of James II and his heirs. Less than two years before, James II's son, the self-styled James III, had sanctioned a Scottish rebellion against the Hanoverian George I. The Jacobite forces had penetrated no further south than Preston, but the memory lingered, and it was common practice for Whig polemicists to accuse Tories of Jacobitism. It tells us something about the hothouse atmosphere inside an eighteenth-century playhouse that, after *The Non-Juror*, no new play of Cibber's was allowed a hearing at its first performance in Drury Lane. Tory cabals saw to that.[8]

Drury Lane and Lincoln's Inn Fields had more to compete with than each other. The fashionable taste for Italian opera, endorsed by successive Hanoverian courts and curiously slanted by the cult of the castrati, was the greatest threat to the drama. Social cachet easily overrode the grumblings of such arbiters as

Addison and Steele, and a significant section of the coveted genteel audience deserted to the King's Theatre, home of the Italian opera in England under the management, from 1713 to 1732, of George Frederick Handel (1685–1759). Handel first came to London, direct from the court of the future George I, in 1710, and staged his first 'London' opera, *Rinaldo*, in 1711. Directing orchestra and singers from the harpsichord, he made himself known as composer, performer and executant in a single virtuosic display, and would remain the largely unchallenged maestro until the establishment in 1733 of the rival Opera of the Nobility at the playhouse in Lincoln's Inn Fields.[9] The slippery interconnection of drama and opera is neatly illustrated by the fact that, when the Opera of the Nobility unseated Handel from the King's Theatre in 1735, he arranged with John Rich to present his operas at Covent Garden.

The nation's growing prosperity was already affecting the constitution of playhouse audiences. Luxuries (looking-glasses, tobacco, coffee, tea, sugar, seats for plays or operas) were within reach of the 'middling sort'. By 1740 there were 550 coffee-houses in London, tobacco consumption peaked in the first quarter of the century, purchases of sugar increased twentyfold between 1663 and 1775, and the East India Company's importation of tea, worth some nine million pounds in the 1720s, was on the rise to eighty-seven million by the 1750s.[10] The moralist in Addison might see fit to reiterate the old association of luxury with vice, but he had the views of an equally witty apologist to contend with. Bernard Mandeville, offering an economic gloss on Hobbes's *Leviathan* in *The Fable of the Bees* (1714), would argue that the pursuit of luxuries is a natural consequence of human self-interest and vanity, and that this is a *good* thing because it leads to an expansion of the labour market.

> Wednesday: from eight to ten drank two dishes of chocolate in bed, and fell asleep after them, exhausted by the effort.
>
> Joseph Addison's 'diary of a lady', in *Spectator* 428 (1712)

The way was already being paved for Adam Smith's *The Wealth of Nations* (1776).

With so many merchants, tradesmen and their families visible in the audience, playwrights sensibly began to rephrase or obliterate the old opposition of land and money. Even to envisage a play like George Lillo's *The London Merchant* (1731) would have been inconceivable forty years earlier. But, with all its faults, that assertively middle-class tragedy was decades ahead of its time. The Drury Lane triumvirate would never have staged it. Barton Booth, in particular, was resistant to the staging of new plays anyway: they were costlier, and less reliable, than revivals. It was Cibber's tragicomic son Theophilus (1703–58), given the run of Drury Lane during the summer closure, who promoted Lillo. By then Cibber Senior's loyalty to the Whigs had been rewarded with the Poet Laureateship, a potato that was already too hot for him to hold before Pope scalded him with the crown of Dullness in the final version of *The Dunciad* (1743).

Other theatres in London and the provinces

The legal status of Charles II's letters patent was always flimsy once the original holders had died. In 1709, with Christopher Rich's patent in suspension and Betterton's breakaway Actors' Company sharing the Queen's Theatre with the opera, under licence but without patent, London was without an active patented playhouse, a situation that persisted until the lifting of Rich's suspension in 1714. Having transferred their licence from the Queen's Theatre to Drury Lane, Cibber and his colleagues were now at a disadvantage: the unpredictable Christopher Rich knew how to stretch the law, and John Rich was an unknown quantity. Steele's 1714 appointment to the governorship of Drury Lane was a lifeline, particularly when, in January 1715, he was granted a *personal* patent for Drury Lane, to last his lifetime plus three years. Steele died in 1729, and Poet Laureate Cibber was able to negotiate a handover of the patent when three years had elapsed. From 1732, then, London had once again two patent theatres, Covent Garden and Drury Lane. No one could have predicted that their legal monopoly would continue uninterrupted until 1843. But of what did they have a monopoly? And how far did it extend? They were in no position to obstruct all forms of theatrical entertainment elsewhere in London, let alone in the rest of England, all of Wales and (after the Act of Union in 1707) Scotland. What about fairs (of which, in 1756, 3,200 were recorded in England and Wales alone)? Over the years, the power of the patents had become attenuated, until it was securely applied only to the *spoken* ('legitimate') drama. How else could opera develop within the law? And where exactly was the dividing line between 'legitimate' and 'illegitimate' drama? Pantomime, vital to the financial health of both Drury Lane and Covent Garden, was surely on the illegitimate side of the line. And ballad opera, the new genre introduced by the runaway success of Gay's *The Beggar's Opera* in 1728?

There was enough promise in the hiving off of 'illegitimate' entertainment to encourage a speculative builder or entrepreneur. A little theatre in the Haymarket, opposite the prestigious home of Handelian opera, opened in December 1720 with a performance by 'French Comedians' under the powerful patronage of the Whig Duke of Montagu. This building's adventurous history would last for exactly 100 years. Shorter lived, but with a significant part to play over the next twelve years, was a theatre in Goodman's Fields, Whitechapel, opened in 1729. Whitechapel was a busy working district, and the distraction of a playhouse there was an invitation to the Whig bugbear, the 'idle apprentice'. When, in 1735, the building of yet another theatre, *in the heart of the City*, was rumoured, Sir John Barnard, wine importer and independent Whig, introduced a Playhouse Bill to the House of Commons. Barnard's bill proposed a restriction on the number of theatres in view of 'the Mischief done to the City of London by the Play-houses, in corrupting the youth, encouraging Vice and Debauchery, and being prejudicial to Trade and Industry'.

Mr. James Erskine in particular reckon'd up the number of Play-houses then in London, viz. The Opera House, the French Play-House in the Hay-Market, and the Theatres in Covent-Garden, Drury-Lane, Lincoln's-Inn-Fields, and Goodman's Fields; and added, 'That it was no less surprizing than shameful to see so great a Change for the worse in the Temper and Inclinations of the British Nation, who were now so extravagantly addicted to lewd and idle Diversions, that the Number of Play-Houses in London was double to that of Paris; That we now exceeded in Levity even the French themselves, from whom we learned these and many other ridiculous Customs, as much unsuitable to the Mien and Manners of an Englishman or a Scot, as they were agreeable to the Air and Levity of a Monsieur: That it was astonishing to all Europe, that Italian Eunuchs and Singers should have set Salaries, equal to those of the Lords of the Treasury and Judges of England.'

The History and Proceedings of the House of Commons,
Volume IX (March 1735)

The bill was withdrawn only because Robert Walpole considered impolitic an additional clause enlarging the power over theatres of the Lord Chamberlain. He would change his tune in 1737.

The first Theatre Royal outside London had opened in Smock Alley, Dublin, in 1662. Its reputation grew during the management (1684–1720) of Joseph Ashbury (1638–1720), but the Dublin repertoire and taste were largely dictated by the viceregal court, and therefore dependent on London. Throughout the eighteenth century, and well into the nineteenth, Ireland exported playwrights (from George Farquhar to Oscar Wilde and George Bernard Shaw) and actors (Robert Wilks, James Quin, Peg Woffington, etc.). Those it imported, London stars on their summer break, stayed for a season or two – to make money. Without its London accolade, a reputation made in Ireland stayed in Ireland.

The same can be said of the slowly emerging English provincial theatre. Norwich, the second largest city as the seventeenth century ended, was the first to develop an independent theatrical life. (Even London was nervous of East

Anglians.) Bristol rejected bids to build a playhouse until after 1730, despite the example of its much smaller neighbour, Bath. Not until the mid-1730s had Beau Nash established Bath as a fashionable resort, but a small theatre had been erected there as early as 1705. York had a resident company from 1734. In general, though, the provinces remained dependent on touring companies, roughing it on a road system that would not be greatly upgraded until the economic boom of the 1750s, for their theatrical entertainment. The transition from a wood-based to a coal-based economy was to change the face of Britain, but it got off to a fairly slow start. In 1720 England's population (exclusive of Wales and Scotland, that is) was about 5.5 million, of whom more than 520,000 lived in London. By 1800 the population had risen to about 8.6 million and London's to 900,000, but the distribution elsewhere was etched by an economic revolution.

Table of England's largest cities

In 1670	In 1800
1. London	1. London
2. Norwich	2. Manchester
3. Bristol	3. Liverpool
4. York	4. Birmingham
5. Newcastle	5. Bristol
	6. Leeds
	7. Sheffield
	8. Plymouth
	9. Newcastle
	10. Norwich

Walpole and the Robinocracy

Robert Walpole (1676–1745) rose to power after the users of money to make money had overreached themselves. The bursting of the South Sea Bubble in 1720, the eighteenth century's equivalent of the Wall Street Crash of 1929, was a direct result of governmental sharp practice. It seemed a clever idea to convert the national debt into shares in the stock of the South Sea Company, but there was never enough 'real' money to match the token banknotes issued by the Sword Blade Company on behalf of its South Sea sponsors. Those in the know, leading politicians among them, sold before the rumours reached the public ear, while stockbrokers (who matched buyers to sellers) and stockjobbers (who bought and sold for themselves) were gulling and being gulled.

> *Jonathan's Coffee House in Exchange Alley. Crowd of people with rolls of paper and parchment in their hands; a bar and Coffee Boys waiting. Enter Tradelove and Stockjobbers, with rolls of paper and parchment.*
>
> FIRST STOCKJOBBER: South Sea at seven-eighths! Who buys?
> SECOND STOCKJOBBER: South Sea bonds due at Michaelmas 1718! Class Lottery tickets!
> THIRD STOCKJOBBER: East India bonds?
> FOURTH STOCKJOBBER: What, all sellers and no buyers? Gentlemen, I'll buy a thousand pound for Tuesday next at three-fourths.
> COFFEE BOY: Fresh coffee, gentlemen, fresh coffee?
> TRADELOVE: Hark ye, Gabriel, you'll pay the difference of that stock we transacted for t'other day.
> GABRIEL: Ay, Mr. Tradelove, here's a note for the money, upon the Sword Blade Company.
> COFFEE BOY: Bohea tea, gentlemen?
>
> Susanna Centlivre, *A Bold Stroke for a Wife* (1718), Act 4 Scene 1

Cibber was one of the bubble's many victims. Typically resilient, he reworked another man's version of Molière's *Les femmes savantes* as a satire on the mercantile cheats who had inflated the bubble in the first place. (*The Refusal* (1721) was drowned out at its first performance, but Cibber was in a position to ensure that he collected a second 'author's benefit' for a sixth night before calling it off.) Catapulted by crisis into the chancellorship of the exchequer, Walpole was meanwhile patching up the nation's finances at the same time as disguising the involvement of courtiers, politicians and even some of the directors of the South Sea Company. This was something he had to do if he was to gain the necessary support of George I, but it earned for him the scabrous nickname of 'screen-master general'. Let a self-interested party hide behind a screen on any stage from then until as late as Sheridan's *The School for Scandal* (1777), and someone might shout Walpole's name, and the image of a screen appeared regularly in satirical prints attacking minister or ministry during Walpole's twenty-year supremacy. For his opponents, Whig as well as Tory since parties have always split apart under settled leadership, this was the 'Robinocracy', government by corruption. There was substance in the accusations. Walpole maintained his authority by the shrewd 'placing' of dependants in secure parliamentary seats and through the undeclared bribes of office, just as previous and future leaders had done and will continue to do. Success on such a scale multiplies enemies.

Literary opposition hardened significantly in 1726. In September Walpole was transparently disguised as Flimnap, the devious High Treasurer of Lilliput in Book One of Swift's *Gulliver's Travels*, and in December the first issue of the *Craftsman* was published. For a decade in its columns Bolingbroke (high Tory) and William Pulteney (disaffected Whig) would sustain a campaign that created the concept of political opposition as an *activity*. Among the brilliant circle that included Swift, Bolingbroke and Pulteney was John Gay (1685–1732). The idea for a 'Newgate pastoral', a folksy poem set among the inhabitants of London's grimmest prison, was Swift's – Gay needed encouragement, and such a poem was within his range – but it was Gay's decision to make a theatrical piece out of it. *The Beggar's Opera* was seen, and rejected, by the Drury Lane management before it reached John Rich at Lincoln's Inn Fields, and even Rich had no idea that he was handling a share of a goldmine when the 'opera' opened on 29 January 1728. For a play to run for twelve nights was remarkable: *The Beggar's Opera* ran uninterruptedly for thirty-two and had notched up sixty-two performances before the season's end.

Gay's intentions were not as clear-cut as historians of the drama have some-times maintained. His 'ballad opera', lightheartedly plundering tunes for its sixty-nine airs from sources as various as folksongs and *opera seria* (Handel was among the composers drawn unwittingly into service), was certainly dif-ferent from Italian opera, but difference is not necessarily a sign of hostility; and yes, Polly Peachum and Macheath *could* be seen as a Walpolean diptych, but equally as Jonathan Wild (*c.*1682–1725), duplicitous master-criminal, and Jack Sheppard (1702–24), highwayman and escape artist. It was Henry Fielding, in his mock-heroic *Jonathan Wild the Great* (1743), who nailed down the compar-ison between a 'great' man and a 'great' rogue, and it was Gay's interpreters, in and out of Lincoln's Inn Fields, who identified Walpole in *The Beggar's Opera*.

This Comedy contains likewise a Satyr, which without enquiring whether it affects the present Age, may possibly be useful in Times to come. I mean, where the Author takes the Occasion of comparing those common Robbers of the Publick, and their several Stratagems of betraying, undermining and hanging each other, to the several Arts of Politicians in Times of Corruption.
    Jonathan Swift, *Irish Tracts* (1728–33)

What is certain is that Gay's example released into the eighteenth century a new and distinctive form of entertainment, the ballad opera, and that Walpole, though stung, was unrepentant. As his mouthpiece, the *British Journal*, admit-ted on 31 May 1729, 'Men are always corrupt, and must often be manag'd. Corruption is good or bad in its Effect as good or bad Governors apply it.'

The Golden Rump and the Licensing Act of 1737

To hold on to power for as long as he did, Walpole needed the support of both George I and George II (the royal prerogative, though diminished since the 1688 Revolution, was still a force), and that required dexterity. To get on well with either of them was hard; to get on with both was distinctly clever, since they cordially loathed each other. Although affirmed by the Act of Settlement (1701), George I's succession had not been universally welcomed. That he spoke hardly any English did not endear him to 'patriots', and both his appearance and his behaviour were easily satirized.[11] He had left his wife in Hanover, where she was incarcerated for adultery from 1694 until her death in 1726, and imported to the English court two German mistresses, one uncommonly skinny and the other extraordinarily fat. Walpole had to deal with them, too, and they made an indelible impression on his fourth son.

> Lady Darlington [Charlotte Kielmansegge], whom I saw at my mother's in my infancy [he was born in 1717], and whom I remember by being terrified at her enormous figure, was as corpulent as the Duchess [Ehrengard von Schulenberg] was long and emaciated. Two fierce black eyes, large and rolling beneath two lofty arched eyebrows, two acres of cheek spread with crimson, an ocean of neck that overflowed and was not distinguished from the lower parts of her body, and no part restrained by stays – no wonder that a child dreaded such an ogress, and that the mob of London were highly diverted at the importation of so uncommon a seraglio.
>
> Horace Walpole, recollecting in maturity (c.1750)

Drama was of no interest to George I[12] – he couldn't follow the words – but as Handel's former patron in Hanover, he lent the cachet of his presence to the opera. This preference was shared by his son, and it was during the reign of George II that theatrical attacks on Walpole and the royal family took hold.

The Beggar's Opera was a portent of what was to come in the 1730s, and the political background to the Licensing Act of 1737 implicates George II much more than has been commonly recognized.[13] Walpole saw to it that Gay's sequel, *Polly*, was kept off the stage, but its publication by subscription kept it in the public eye, and there was little Walpole could do to screen the trouble in the palace, though he did his best by enduring long conversations with the indefatigably speculative Queen Caroline. The trouble was Frederick, Prince of Wales (1707–51), whom his father bullied and despised and whom his mother despised and stubbornly believed, on grounds lost to history, to be impotent. Frederick's adult response was to dedicate his life to complicating that of his parents and, by association, Walpole. Culturally alert, he liked the theatre. With his friend, the court gossip Lord Hervey, he even wrote a play, *The Modish Couple*, which was ascribed to 'Charles Bodens' when given a rumour-laden production at Drury Lane in January 1732. But Frederick wanted a wife. After his father (unlike a later royal father) prevented him from marrying Lady Diana Spencer, he took a mistress – Lord Hervey's mistress – and boasted, against his mother's scepticism and Hervey's denial, paternity of Lady Anne Vane's daughter. An anonymous satirist published *Vanelia; or, The amours of the great* (1732), calling it 'An opera. As it is acted by a private company near St. James's'. It is just possible that this was the work of the ambitious but impecunious Henry Fielding (1707–54).

Fielding was already a performed playwright, with five pieces at Drury Lane in 1732 alone, but his early work had been largely confined to the little theatre in the Haymarket. It is the sheer audacity of this early work, its energetic mockery of the managers of the patent playhouses (*The Author's Farce*, 1730) or of contemporary tragedy (*Tom Thumb*, 1730), that distinguishes Fielding from the mass of minor dramatists. But *The Welsh Opera* (1731) carried audacity into the realms of *lèse majesté*. In the newly fashionable ballad opera style, Fielding presented to Haymarket audiences a hen-pecked George II, a pretentious Queen Caroline and an amorous but impotent Frederick. They are given a Welsh domicile and a Welsh surname, Apshinken, which, for those who knew their Welsh prefixes and Hanoverian nouns, signified 'son of ham'. They are also given a set of household servants supervised by a light-fingered butler called Robin (Walpole's stage name) whose adversary is William (Pulteney), the coachman. The tone is mischievous rather than malicious, but Walpole cannot have relished either the ridiculing of the royal foibles or the implication that he was enriching himself on pickings from court. When Fielding's intention to expand *The Welsh Opera* into three acts, albeit disguised under the new title of *The Grub-Street Opera*, leaked out, Walpole ensured that performance was proscribed. It was published, of course, complete with its sixty-five jauntily satirical songs. There had been no control of printed material since 1695. But the Lord Chamberlain, by way of the Office of Revels and the holders of the theatrical patents, had retained a contested authority over the theatrical repertoire. Increasingly through the 1730s, Walpole employed his spies to sniff out trouble. Fielding bided his time, contenting himself with the proceeds of publication, the composition of an epilogue for *The Modish Couple* (1732) and the production at Drury Lane of a sequence of generally unexceptionable plays and afterpieces. It was probably financial exigency rather than political passion that motivated his next significant move in the theatrical war against Walpole. In the interim Walpole had enflamed public opinion by his attempt to carry a moneyspinning Excise Bill (1733) through parliament and Frederick, Prince of Wales had joined the opposition.

To launch his new campaign, Fielding returned to the 'illegitimate' Haymarket, which he leased in January 1736 in the name of 'The Great Mogul's Company of Comedians'. His first offering, *Pasquin*, opened in the spring, around the time that Frederick married (at last) a German princess, and held the stage through the summer. Less a play than an improvisatory satire, it deals with electoral corruption in its first half and with the defeat of Queen Common-Sense by Queen Ignorance in its second. What seems to have endowed the generalized satire of *Pasquin* with a special pungency was the well-advertised attendance of the Prince of Wales. In the new confidence of his married state, Frederick was assembling what amounted to a court-in-opposition, ready to cheer the lament of the defeated Queen:

> Could Common Sense bear universal sway,
> No fool could ever possibly be great.

Since *The Beggar's Opera*, the adjective 'great' carried, in theatrical parlance, a latent reference to Walpole, here portrayed, under the sway of Queen Ignorance, as a 'great' fool. Such ascriptions were routine in the opposition press, and it can only have been the audience, not the text, that made *Pasquin* a serious challenge to the government.

Fielding now found himself linked with Prince Frederick and the group of alienated aristocrats who formed the nucleus of the Rumpsteak Club – men who felt aggrieved that George II had turned his back on them; in the language of the day, 'rumped' them. The King's rump, a notoriously large one, was to play a leading part in the theatrical events of 1737. He was on one of his regular trips to Hanover when the new year dawned, and when storms delayed his return, there were rumours that he had been drowned. Briefly, Walpole had to confront the grim prospect of the accession of Frederick I. But George arrived safely on 15 January, in one of his foul tempers: to his recurrent affliction of piles was now added an adjacent fistula. When he heard of the opposition's intention to bring before parliament a bill calling for the doubling of Frederick's annual allowance, he was incandescent, and Walpole, as ever, turned to Queen Caroline as an emollient intermediary. But the situation was inflamed by the 19 March issue of the opposition periodical *Common Sense* and by the opening at the Haymarket, two days later, of Fielding's theatrical squib, *The Historical Register for the Year 1736*.

Common Sense offered its readers a two-part 'Vision of the Golden Rump', in which the visionary dreamer 'landed in a pleasant Meadow, in which were

Figure 6. 'The Vision of the Golden Rump'. The play, if there ever was one, was probably derived from this scurrilous cartoon.

several fine Walks, like Greenwich Park'. He encounters there 'the Noblesse of the Kingdom' on their way to celebrate the Festival of the Golden Rump. This Golden Rump is George II, easily identified by his bowel problems and his well-known habit of kicking his servants when angry, just as the Queen is identifiable by her attempts to placate him.

> She had in one Hand a Silver Bell, and a Golden Tube in the other, with a large Bladder at the End, resembling a common Clyster-Pipe. The Bladder was full of *Aurum potabile*, and other choice Ingredients, which at proper Seasons, was injected . . . into the fundament of the Pagod, to comfort his Bowels, and to appease the Idol, when he lifted up his cloven Foot to correct his Domesticks.
>
> Extract from *Common Sense*, 19 March 1737

In attendance, of course, to pocket the 'annual Offerings, to which the whole Body of the People were obliged', is Walpole in the penetrable disguise of Chief Magician. In London's print-shops that spring, the vision of the Golden Rump was purchasable in cartoon form. A naked George II (as a satyr) stands on a pedestal, farting one way while lifting his foot to kick out the other way. Queen Caroline hopes to calm him by administering an enema of liquid gold while a fat-bellied Walpole (he weighed more than 20 stone) makes a placatory gesture. The cartoon's caption is a rendering in dog-latin of *Common Sense*'s 'Whoever envies me, let him be RUMPED'.

Beside the scurrility of this assault, *The Historical Register* is quite tame. But Walpole was tired of being pilloried in the theatre, and the sheer plenitude of surrogate Walpoles in Fielding's satiric medley may have seemed one insult too far. That is speculative, but the fact is that, amid other urgent parliamentary business, on the brink of the summer recess, and with his government rockier than it had ever been, he piloted through both Houses a Licensing Act which required the kind of detailed preparation of which he was always capable, but sometimes disinclined to undertake. And the vehicle he used was the manuscript of a play called *The Golden Rump*, a text which, above any other he could have envisaged, was guaranteed to offend George II and thus to expedite the royal assent to a bill passed by parliament.

The manuscript has not survived, and there is a fair possibility that it never existed. Any government hack, using the text of *Common Sense* or the cartoon it spawned, could have supplied the passages that Walpole read to the House of Commons as 'excerpts' from a manifestly objectionable play. Purportedly, the 'set' was an immense pair of (George II's) buttocks, and characters were to make their entrance through its anus. The manuscript had reached Walpole by way of the manager of the unlicensed theatre in Goodman's Fields, Henry Giffard, to whom it had (allegedly) been submitted for performance. It was outrageous enough to silence most of the opposition: only Pulteney in the Commons and Lord Chesterfield in the Lords (in a famous speech in defence of liberty) are recorded as having spoken against the bill, which was rapidly passed and received the royal assent on 21 June 1737.

The two central provisions of the Licensing Act were first, that the performance of plays for money be limited to playhouses (not only in London but throughout England, Wales and Scotland) with a royal patent or a licence from the Lord Chamberlain, and second, that a 'true copy' of all words to be sung or spoken be submitted for the Lord Chamberlain's licence prior to performance. The intention was to limit the number of London's theatres to three – Drury Lane, Covent Garden and the King's (opera house) – to ensure control over theatre building nationwide and to prevent the performance anywhere (as at the Haymarket at the very time the bill was passing through parliament) of dramatic entertainments that had not been scrutinized by the Lord Chamberlain. It was, in effect, a reinforcing Bill, since the legislation had been in place from the first year of Charles II's reign, but a law in abeyance is as permissive as no law at all. It was only after 1737 that government, through the Lord Chamberlain, asserted its active control of both playhouses and their repertoire.

That there were loopholes and evasions is amply proved by subsequent history (was it for services rendered that a blind eye was turned to Giffard's continuing activity in Goodman's Fields?), but the impact of the Licensing Act should not be underrated. It is to be felt in plays that were never written, or plays that, having been written, were never performed. The act, emblematic of the Lord Chamberlain's deterrent effect, turned Fielding into a novelist. Self-censorship, combined with the pettiness of successive examiners of plays within the Chamberlain's office, deprived the theatre of an authorized voice on politics, religion and the great issues of contemporary debate. There is too much truth in what one of the most authoritative writers on the drama of the period has recently written: 'London was a rapidly growing city, and in the natural course of events more theatres should have sprung up to cater to different segments of the audience and offer different sorts of plays. The fundamental mediocrity of English drama after 1737 may be attributed directly to the suppression of competition and multiple venues imposed by the Licensing Act.'[14]

Chapter 5

The drama

In the *Spectator* 219 (1711), Joseph Addison addressed his 'Fraternity of Spectators', among whom he included 'every one that considers the World as a Theatre, and desires to form a right Judgment of those who are actors on it'. So far as it concerns would-be dramatists, the metaphor is double-edged: on one side, it adorns the practice of theatre with a representative solemnity, on the other, it reduces every play to the status of a little-play-within-a-greater-play. Either way, though, the playhouse is a site within which the actor as puppet-character behaves in such a way as to inform the spectator as actor. For playwrights engaged in the new century's moral crusade, its pursuit of national virtue, the stage had some of the properties of a pulpit. Shorn of their contemporary colouring, Addison's *Cato* (1713) is a sermon on patriotism, Richard Steele's *The Conscious Lovers* (1722) an invocation to benevolence and, most extraordinary of all, George Lillo's *The London Merchant* (1731) a parable on the Whig diptych of the industrious and the idle apprentice.

Tragedy and *The London Merchant*

No eighteenth-century tragedies are likely to feature in the repertoire of a modern theatre because no modern audience would believe a word that was said. Without some sort of narrative conviction, an acted tragedy exhibits a group of people pretending to get so absurdly overwrought, usually about matters of state, that a predictable handful of them will have to pretend to die in about eighty minutes from now. That the defects were recognized is apparent from burlesques of the style, most famously in the multiple deaths at the climax of Henry Fielding's *Tom Thumb* (1730).

GHOST:	Tom Thumb I am – but am not eke alive.
	My body's in the Cow, my Ghost is here.
GRIZZLE:	Thanks, O ye Stars, my Vengeance is restor'd,
	Nor shalt thou fly me – for I'll kill thy Ghost. *(Kills the Ghost)*

HUNCAMUNCA:	O barbarous Deed! – I will revenge him so.	(*Kills Grizzle*)
DOODLE:	Ha! Grizzle kill'd – then Murtheress beware.	(*Kills Huncamunca*)
QUEEN:	O wretch! – have at thee.	(*Kills Doodle*)
NOODLE:	And have at thee too.	(*Kills the Queen*)
CLEORA:	Thou'st kill'd the Queen.	(*Kills Noodle*)
MUSTACHA:	And thou hast kill'd my Lover.	(*Kills Cleora*)
KING:	Ha! Murtheress vile, take that.	(*Kills Mustacha*)
	And take thou this.	(*Kills himself*)

Henry Fielding, *Tom Thumb* (1730)

It can be argued that extremity, the condition of tragedy, was becoming increasingly alien to the complacent worldview of Augustan commentators, but tragedy retained its place as the major dramatic genre; aspirants to Parnassus had to write it and culturally assertive theatre companies had to stage it, even to audiences no longer sympathetic to the renaissance quest for glory.

I am Content, I do not care,
    Wag as it will the World for me;
When Fuss and Fret was all my Fare,
    It got no ground, as I could see:
So, when away my Caring went,
    I counted Cost, and was Content.

With more of Thanks, and less of Thought,
    I strive to make my Matters meet;
To seek, what ancient Sages sought,
    Physic and Food in sour and sweet;
To take what passes in good Part,
And keep the Hiccups from the Heart.

John Byrom, opening stanzas of 'Careless Content' (c.1728)

It is a disservice to the posthumous reputation of Nicholas Rowe to say that he was the best of a bad bunch. At least three of his tragedies remained in the repertoire throughout the eighteenth century, and the latest of them, *Lady Jane Grey* (1715), is a respectable contribution to the subgenre of the 'English History' play. Rowe was sufficiently wealthy to neglect the law in favour of literature,[1] and sufficiently shrewd to recognize and exploit the hold over audiences of Elizabeth Barry and Anne Oldfield. Barry created Calista in *The Fair Penitent* (1703), the first of Rowe's admired 'she-tragedies'.[2] Having allowed Lothario to seduce her before her marriage to Altamont, Calista is not only doomed to die by her own hand but condemned to rhetorical paroxysms, along with all the other leading characters bar Lothario (a Restoration rake), on the slow road to suicide. It is difficult to justify the voyeuristic relish of female anguish, which reached new heights when Oldfield played the title role in Rowe's *Jane Shore* (1714), and which would be indulged at inordinate length in Samuel Richardson's mid-century novels.[3] At best, it might be patriarchy's attempt to repay a debt to the sex it continues to wrong, but it is not at its best in Rowe's she-tragedies. A shadowy figure in Shakespeare's *Richard III*, mistress of the late King Edward IV and now of Lord Hastings, Jane Shore dominates Rowe's play, not the indulgent courtesan of history but the sorrowful widow reliving the virtue she abandoned when she chose the king's bed above her husband's. In the play's most sensational episode, she fights off Lord Hastings's attempt to rape her, but she later defies the demand of the future Richard III that she incriminate Hastings. She is a *good* woman, not the 'moppet made of prettiness and pride' that Richard expects, justly rewarded (poetic justice blunting the blade of tragedy) when she dies in the arms of her husband, whom Rowe has conveniently resurrected.

The Fair Penitent is a version of Philip Massinger's *The Fatal Dowry* (*c*.1617), with the unities improbably observed and the focus shifted from bridegroom to bride. Despite its setting in Genoa and its peopling by aristocratic Italians, its thoroughly English and fundamentally domestic concerns are exposed by its bathetic final couplet:

> If you would have the nuptial union last,
> Let virtue be the bond that ties it fast.

Jane Shore is domestic, too, despite its Shakespearean reference and pseudo-Shakespearean language. Even Lady Jane Grey, fatally embroiled in national history, becomes, in Rowe's hands, a modest English housewife in the making. This is not the failure of tact or taste that it may be made to appear. Rowe's instinct was sound. If tragedy were to have a future, that future could not be in the past world of remotely mighty monarchs and legendary heroes. The proliferation of newspapers and periodicals which followed the 1695 lapse of the Stationers' Company's monopoly had brought affairs of state into the street. More than 8,000 political pamphlets (not including books and broadsheets) were published in the first fifteen years of the eighteenth century. The age of the mighty monarch was over: Queen Anne was quite as 'middle class' as William and Mary had been. As for the legendary heroes of Elizabethan England, they had dwindled into the squabbling creatures of party politics. Rowe moved amicably among the leading Whigs without making enemies of Tories. He had served as under-secretary of state for Scotland, and his appointment as Poet Laureate in 1715 was broadly welcomed. His tragedies, less sensationally but no less shrewdly than Addison's *Cato*, took close account of national politics. There is no deviation into subplots, no significant variation of tone: all is measured. Rowe is an Addisonian spectator who 'considers the World as a Theatre, and desires to form a right Judgment of those who are actors on it'. In his safe hands tragedy preserved an antiquarian dignity, comparable with that of history painting, which stood supreme among the visual arts, like tragedy among dramatic genres.

Rowe's status among playwrights was like that of James Thornhill among painters. In 1707 Thornhill was chosen to paint the allegory of the Protestant succession in the Great Hall of the Royal Naval Hospital in Greenwich and, in 1715, to paint the cupola of St Paul's Cathedral. By 1720, when he was knighted, he was Serjeant Painter to the King.[4] Self-consciously grand, he had kicked over the traces of his first recorded commission, to design the scenery for the English opera *Arsinoe* at Christopher Rich's Drury Lane in 1705. Thornhill's lofty baroque has aspirations in common with those of writers of neoclassical tragedy. Rowe's *Ulysses* (1705), more than his she-tragedies, expresses this aspect of eighteenth-century taste. Such work is peopled by characters of more than life size, distanced from the spectator by the magnitude of their history and with nothing on the canvas to bring them closer. Something quite different, and infinitely more exciting, was opened up by Thornhill's son-in-law, William Hogarth.

Hogarth (1697–1764) was sometimes troubled, and always fascinated, by the theatricality of London life: for sheer artistry, the finest dramatic achievement of the period from 1700 to 1737 was the sequence of six pictures that defined 'A Harlot's Progress' (1730). This low-life tragedy of corrupted innocence owed its provenance as much to plays and printed sources as to Hogarth's own street prowlings. Daniel Defoe's *Moll Flanders* (1722) is in the background, along with Steele's typically compassionate description of a Covent Garden prostitute,

> She affected to allure me with a forced Wantonness in her Look and Air; but I saw it checked with Hunger and Cold: Her Eyes were wan and eager, her Dress thin and tawdry, her Mien genteel and childish. This strange Figure gave me much Anguish of Heart.
>
> Richard Steele, *Spectator* 266 (1712)

but the foreground belongs to John Gay. Hogarth's painting (1729) of a scene from *The Beggar's Opera* had brought theatre and the visual arts into a novel alignment, and it was in the career of Macheath's rejected mistress, Polly Peachum, that he found the initial inspiration for his 'harlot', Moll Hackabout. Here was an example of a *modern* moral subject – the reviled whore as victim of a society governed by 'great' men.

> [I] turn my thoughts to still a more new way of proceeding, viz painting and Engraving modern moral Subjects a Field unbroke up in any Country or any age.
>
> William Hogarth, *Autobiographical Notes* (1753)

Fielding's *Rape upon Rape* (1730) touched lightheartedly on the theme, but it was in the wake of an altogether more sombre play about corrupted innocence, *The London Merchant* (1731), that Hogarth launched the sale of his own copperplate engravings of 'A Harlot's Progress' in 1732. The impact of Lillo's tragedy, its absorption in a 'modern moral subject', contributed to the rush to buy Hogarth's prints. That, at least, is in its favour.

 The London Merchant is almost irredeemably flawed by its author's earnestness. Lillo (*c.*1693–1739) was probably brought up according to the Calvinist tenets of the Dutch Reformed Church, convinced of the palpable existence of heaven and hell and persuaded that the individual's post mortem residence was predestined. But Calvinism like his, or like that of the Methodist evangelist George Whitefield (1714–70), whose charismatic preachings were soon to be heard across England and in the new world of America, was distinct from *laissez-faire* fatalism. *The London Merchant* is possessed by a reforming zeal that amounts almost to a readiness to pinion the audience in order to impregnate it with virtue. The story is taken from the old ballad of 'George Barnwell' in which a virtuous apprentice, seduced by the 'gallant dainty dame', Sarah Millwood, is led by her first into robbery, then murder and finally to the gallows, and the play adds little narrative flesh to the ballad's skeleton. It does, however, provide a balance of 'good' characters to offset, though scarcely to threaten, Millwood's potent charms. There is Barnwell's employer, the benign merchant Thorowgood, to hymn the virtues of trade.

> Methinks I would not have you only learn the method of merchandise and practice it hereafter merely as a means of getting wealthy. 'Twill be well worth your pains to study it as a science, see how it is founded in reason and the nature of things, how it has promoted humanity as it has opened and yet keeps up an intercourse between nations far remote from one another in situation, customs, and religion; promoting arts, industry, peace, and plenty; by mutual benefits diffusing mutual love from pole to pole.
>
> George Lillo, *The London Merchant* (1731), Act 3, Scene 1

There is Thorowgood's daughter, Maria, whose selfless love for Barnwell has led her to spurn the advances of courtiers. And there is Trueman, fellow-apprentice, who stands by him to the bitter end. It has to be presumed that the play's original audience was not deterred by Trueman's tendency to spin his speeches out of pseudobiblical texts: 'he who trusts Heaven ought never to despair. But business requires our attendance – business, the youth's best preservative from ill, as idleness his worst of snares' (Act 2, Scene 2).[5] It would be easy to excuse the erring Barnwell for responding to that mouthful from his bosom-pal by punching him on the nose. But no. *The London Merchant* not only loads the dice in favour of virtue, it also employs a tedious tautology in doing so: the good characters do good things, express sentiments that show they are good and then, often in asides, explain to us how good they are. I began by saying that the play is *almost* irredeemable: the saving disgrace is the monstrous Millwood, with her pathological hatred of the male sex and her conscienceless habitation of the world according to Thomas Hobbes: 'I have done nothing that I am sorry for. I followed my inclinations, and that the best of you does every day. All actions are alike natural and indifferent to man and beast who devour or are devoured as they meet with others weaker or stronger than themselve' (Act 4, Scene 18). Even Lillo cannot keep the best tunes from the Devil.

What was utterly new about *The London Merchant*, what makes its fifth-rate author remarkable, was the decision to confine its characters to the 'middling sort' and to write it in prose throughout.[6] This lowering of tragedy, which had its greatest effect in eighteenth-century Germany (by way of Lessing's plays and theorizing) and has allowed Lillo a claim as the ancestor of Lenz, Büchner and even Ibsen, was startling enough to excite Hogarth and Fielding. Had it not been for the novel's almost immediate colonization of the new territory, it might have transformed English tragedy. As it was, *The London Merchant* proved sturdy enough to last into the nineteenth century, particularly in provincial theatres where it was routinely trotted out at Christmas for the edification of young apprentices like Pip in Charles Dickens's *Great Expectations* (1860–1). In his dedication to the published text, Lillo wrote of his tragedy, not in Aristotelian terms of catharsis – the purging of infection – but as a remedy against disease. When Mr Wopsle inflicts on Pip the cautionary tale of George Barnwell, he is reminding us of the play's long life. Reading Lillo, we can grimly foresee the Victorian family going hand-in-hand to church for purgation on Christmas Day, and hand-in-hand to *The London Merchant* for a preventative remedy the day after.

Mr. Wopsle had in his hand the affecting tragedy of George Barnwell, in which he had that moment invested sixpence, with the view of heaping every word of it on the head of Pumblechook, with whom he was going to drink tea. No sooner did he see me, than he appeared to consider that a special Providence had put a 'prentice in his way to be read at; and he laid hold of me, and insisted on my accompanying him to the Pumblechookian parlour . . . When Barnwell began to go wrong, I declare I felt positively apologetic, Pumblechook's indignant stare so taxed me with it. Wopsle, too, took pains to present me in the worst light. At once ferocious and maudlin, I was made to murder my uncle with no extenuating circumstances whatever; Millwood put me down in argument on every occasion; it became sheer monomania in my master's daughter to care a button for me; and all I can say for my grasping and procrastinating conduct on the fatal morning, is, that it was worthy of the general feebleness of my character. Even after I was happily hanged and Wopsle had closed the book, Pumblechook sat staring at me, and shaking his head, and saying, 'Take warning, boy, take warning!' as if it were a well-known fact that I contemplated murdering a near relation, provided I could only induce one to have the weakness to become my benefactor.

Charles Dickens, *Great Expectations* (1860–1), Chapter 15

Comedy part-laundered

For more than thirty years, the surest way to gauge London's theatrical temperature would have been to hang Colley Cibber like a thermometer in the lobby of Drury Lane and take a reading from him. As actor, playwright and eventually manager, he was the supreme opportunist. His first comedy, *Love's Last Shift* (1696), anticipated the corrective moralizing of Jeremy Collier's *Short View* by two years, and his last, *The Provoked Husband* (1727), neatly laundered an incomplete play by Sir John Vanbrugh, whose obscenity Collier had pilloried. Nine of Cibber's plays were staged in London theatres in the 1730–1 season, and over the twenty years from 1710, he was by some way the most performed living dramatist. And all of this without much that could pass for genuine originality. To those who attacked him for claiming ownership of texts that were fashioned from the work of other writers (Vanbrugh, Shakespeare, Molière, whomever), he put a simple question: 'Is a Tailor, that can make a new Coat well, the worse Workman, because he can mend an old one?',[7] and the competent transformation of Shakespeare's *Richard III* and Molière's *Tartuffe* (as *The Non-Juror*) provides at least two legs for him to stand on. No actor-manager before Garrick could mend an old coat better than Cibber, but could he make a new one? The case rests on three plays, *Love's Last Shift*, *The Careless Husband* (1704) and *The Lady's Last Stake* (1707), and the jury will probably remain a hung one.

For its first four acts, *Love's Last Shift* follows the drift of post-Restoration sex comedy. At its centre is the failing marriage of the loose-loined Loveless, who wedded his virtuous wife Amanda 'within two Women of my Maidenhead'.

LOVELESS: [T]he World to me is a Garden stockt with all sorts of Fruit, where the greatest Pleasure we can take, is in the Variety of Taste: But a Wife is an Eternal Apple-Tree; after a pull or two, you are sure to set your Teeth on Edge.
Colley Cibber, *Love's Last Shift* (1696), Act 1, Scene 1

The witty exchanges – and they are tolerably witty – follow the routines of antiromantic cynicism, but a transformation is brought about by a bed-trick that manoeuvres Loveless, unknowingly, into having sex with his wife. Clearly, the earth moves for him, and the dialogue of Loveless and Amanda in the recognition scene (Act 5, Scene 5) is conducted in the language of religious ecstasy. Incredibly, the play is then rounded off with a hymeneal masque. Given that Cibber wrote the piece as a stop-gap for Drury Lane after the defection of Betterton and the rest of the senior actors, the conclusion is as bold as it is preposterous, bold because it is preposterous.

There is nothing as formally radical in Cibber's mature work, though he continued playing the marriage tune into the new century. *The Careless Husband*, framed by a prologue and epilogue celebrating the Duke of Marlborough's recent victory at the Battle of Blenheim, is better crafted, though with a similarly sudden marital leap at the end. Sir Charles Easy is easy with himself in his amours and Lady Easy (however uneasily in personal terms) is easy on him for his unfaithfulness *until* (Act 5, Scene 5!) she discovers him and her maidservant asleep in adjacent 'easy' chairs. The sight provokes Lady Easy to an outbreak of 'point blank verse',[8] but all she does is to lay her neckcloth (steinkirk) gently on her husband's wigless head and tiptoe out. The discovery of the steinkirk is enough to convert the careless husband to a careful one: 'thou hast stirred me with so severe a proof of thy exalted virtue, it gives me wonder equal to my love' (Act 5, Scene 7). The conversion may be convincing only in the nevernever land of artificial comedy, but the steinkirk scene is undeniably charming, and Cibber was too shrewd an operator to trust much of his play to the relationship of the Easies.

The dynamic roles in *The Careless Husband* belong to Lord Foppington and Lady Betty Modish, shaped for himself and Oldfield. Foppington is the Sir Novelty Fashion of *Love's Last Shift*, now ennobled and firmer of purpose. He has married, 'to pay my debts at play and disinherit my younger brother' (Act 2, Scene 2), and perfected his style of foppishness. How does he get women? 'Why, sometimes as they get other people. I dress and let them get me. Or, if that won't do, as I got my title, I buy 'em' (Act 2, Scene 2). Foppington's malice is playful and his benevolence an accidental freak of amorality: his vital essence is theatricality. Lady Betty Modish is his sparring partner, a coquette with a heart of gold. Oldfield played the part to the hilt, and her retirement in 1730 slackened the play's long hold on the stage. It was the sheer ebullience of the acting that concealed Cibber's besetting weakness, his inability to shut up. *The Careless Husband* is too long. So, for all its lively scenes, is *The Lady's Last Stake*, which also features a mended marriage and a fizzing courtship. Cibber was not in a strong position to warn against the perils of upper-class gambling, but he does that, too. This is a play that, judiciously cut, might merit revival, but it ran for only three nights of the Christmas season in 1707: evidence suggests that Christopher Rich's staging of operas at Drury Lane drew audiences away. Cibber's surprises, the formula on which he based his dramaturgy, were becoming too predictable.

[W]e do not love to be startled into a Pleasure; as an Audience ought never to be wholly let into the secret design of a Play, so they ought not to be intirely kept out of it, you may safely leave room for the Imagination to guess at the Nature of the thing you intend, and are only to surprise them with your Manner of bringing it about.

Colley Cibber, preface to *Ximena* (1719)

When plotting *The Lady's Last Stake*, the jackdaw Cibber was well aware of the popularity of a recent play about gambling. *The Gamester* (1705) was the first real success for Susanna Centlivre (1669–1723), then writing (when not taking the politic precaution of concealing her sex) under her married name of Susanna Carroll.[9] Cibber could be shifty with rival playwrights, never more so than in 1706, when he advised against staging Carroll's *Love at a Venture* and promptly plagiarized it for his own *The Double Gallant*. Even after the passing of a Copyright Act in 1709, playwrights' control of their texts was slippery, and Centlivre, in her best plays, made free of the work of other (mostly foreign) dramatists. Even so, there was a rupture with Cibber which, despite a shared commitment to the Whig cause, was slow to heal. Quite as much as Aphra Behn, Centlivre had to contend with masculine discouragement throughout her career in the theatre, and only recently has the probability that she is the finest writer of comedy in the first half of the eighteenth century been given any credence. Her best plays are outstanding in their intense observation of 'the customs of the country'. She is not insistently witty, but her work is succinct and lucid and her plots do not surrender their momentum to verbal display. She can be quirkily particular in her dislikes (of Quakers or Tory fathers who try to master their daughters), but she drills her narrative to her purpose in a way that Cibber never could. The trio of *The Busy Body* (1709), *The Wonder: A Woman Keeps a Secret* (1714) and *A Bold Stroke for a Wife* (1718) constitutes a

Figure 7. Giuseppe Grisoni's portrait is of a young Colley Cibber, as Lord Foppington, in the elegant act of taking snuff.

body of intrigue comedies that ought to have secured for Centlivre a reputation that has been casually denied her for more than 200 years, perhaps since David Garrick made his farewell bow as Don Felix in *The Wonder*.

Despite the precedence accorded to tragedy, comedy has always been preferred by actors and audiences. Because the genre had a traditional purchase on the manners of the day, there is always something to be gained by reading the neglected comedies of this period. In the work of Mary Pix (*c*.1666–1709), for example, the transition from 'Restoration' to eighteenth-century drama is particularly clear; Steele's *The Tender Husband* (1705), ranging with ease from fashionable St James's to mercantile Lombard Street, is much better than his overexposed *The Conscious Lovers*; Fielding's *The Modern Husband* (1732) reveals the magnificent jester in serious mode, moving 'up' into an approved genre. Both tragedies and comedies were composed in five acts – proof of their belonging to the two 'legitimate' families of traditional English drama – but, particularly after John Rich inaugurated his regime at Lincoln's Inn Fields in late 1714, a significant innovation took hold. Partly to prolong the evening's entertainment, but also to shore up full-length plays that were tottering towards exhaustion, the managers of both patent houses introduced shorter 'afterpieces', altogether less predictable in form. The mischievous spirit of the solemn-sounding Augustan age expressed itself more eloquently in these 'irregular' dramatic entertainments than in the established genres of tragedy and comedy.

The irregular drama

Much of the 'regular' drama invited parody – and got it. The bourgeois dignity of *The London Merchant*, for example, must have been in Fielding's mind when he sold *The Covent-Garden Tragedy* to Drury Lane in 1732. A two-act pseudotragedy set in a brothel (Drury Lane and Covent Garden were notoriously resorts of prostitution), it is written in inflated blank verse of the kind for which Ambrose Philips's *The Distrest Mother* (1712) was frequently ridiculed. Fielding's prostitutes go about their nightly business while speaking like a simultaneous translation of Racine. The result is wickedly funny, but the incidental damage it does to Lillo's project seems to have passed unnoticed, perhaps even by Fielding himself. There is a strong vein of formal parody in many of the best-known irregular dramas of the period. *The Beggar's Opera* is the favourite example, but Gay had already deviated from the straight path before composing his 'Newgate pastoral'. *The What D'ye Call It* (1715) opened at Drury Lane as an afterpiece to Rowe's tear-jerking *Jane Shore*. Gay takes us to the home of Sir Roger (the allusion is to Sir Roger de Coverley, the best loved of the characters created by the *Spectator*), where a play is about to be performed. Because his neighbours have never seen one, the obliging country squire 'would shew them all sorts of Plays under one' – which he proceeds to do. Over two acts of Gay's typically sprightly verse, the play-within-a-play mingles the styles of tragedy, comedy, pastoral and farce, topping it off with a dash of opera. It is a slick and very funny mockery of contemporary theatrical taste, too good-humoured to offend and without the jibes at thinly disguised individuals of *Three Hours after Marriage* (1717), on which Gay collaborated with Alexander Pope and Dr John Arbuthnot. Calling their play a 'comedy' (and dividing it into five (very short) acts to prove it) was part of the joke. Getting it staged at Drury Lane and deceiving Cibber into satirizing himself in the role of Plotwell were both jokes, too.

Since 1713 Gay, Pope and Arbuthnot had been at the core of the Scriblerus Club, a loose association of Tory wits, and *Three Hours after Marriage* is one of several Scriblerus documents to mock the bad taste that applauds the work of incompetent writers. It tells of the brief marriage of an elderly, ludicrous (and, at the time, recognizable) antiquary whose young wife spends her first three hours as a bride trying to smuggle her lover into the house, and it ends with the revelation that this 'wife' is already married. The farcical, sometimes grotesque, action and the *doubles entendres* might be effective in modern performance, but the force of the personal satire is irretrievably lost. The best that can be said about the play is that its original staging demonstrates the generous willingness of the theatre to laugh at its own bad taste; the worst that can be said is that it uses farce to express its authors' contempt for the very theatre in which their work is being displayed. The whole of Gay's theatrical output is vulnerable to the charge of flippancy, whereas, paradoxically, true farce is anything but flippant about the theatre.

A rare example of a farce with political teeth is Centlivre's *The Gotham Election*, written in 1715, but denied performance in that year because its treatment of electoral misconduct was considered too inflammatory with a tense election, the first of George I's reign, in the offing. Centlivre was dead by 1724, when the Haymarket, cocking a characteristic snook at authority, staged it. Unlike Centlivre's bold play, Fielding's political forays of the 1730s, which confirmed the Haymarket as a pivotal site of political and cultural opposition, have been accorded due prominence in recent years. His stinging Haymarket medleys from *Pasquin* (1736) to *Eurydice Hissed* (1737) defy classification, but the majority of eighteenth-century afterpieces fall readily under the general heading of 'farce'. Historians of the drama have tended to neglect them, focusing instead on full-length comedies and tragedies. For actors and theatre managers, though, the popularity of farcical afterpieces was a godsend. They could prop up a fragile comedy until another one was ready for performance, or the fragile comedy itself, shorn of its main plot and two or three acts, could have a second theatrical life as a farce. Cibber, of course, wrote or filched them to order, but so did Fielding. His *The Intriguing Chambermaid* (1734), taken from the French and reshaped for Kitty Clive, a specialist in pert maids, is one of the best. But even in their own time, the value of farces was underrated until, in 1782, an enterprising Edinburgh bookseller made a collection of 'the most esteemed'.

It has long been a just complaint, that copies of FARCES and DRAMATIC ENTERTAINMENTS are difficult to be procured, even at the exorbitant charge of one shilling each, the usual shop-price; and that many of them are often not to be procured for any price: A circumstance which arises chiefly from Booksellers having little inducement to keep any regular assortment of pieces of this kind, the demand even for those of the first merit, in a detached form, being inconsiderable and uncertain. These inconveniences first suggested the design of the present publication: And as no Collection of the same kind has hitherto appeared, it is hoped this will meet with a favourable reception from the PUBLIC; and will be peculiarly acceptable to those with a good Collection of Plays, to which it will form a proper Companion or Supplement, as including the principal performances of a GARRICK, a FOOTE, &c. printed in an elegant and uniform manner, and attainable at a moderate expence.

Charles Elliot, Advertisement to the first edition of *Farces* (1782)

By 1788, when he brought out his fifth and final volume, Charles Elliot had gathered seventy-one gems of the popular drama.[10] Not surprisingly, the main beneficiaries of the taste for farcical afterpieces were 'low' comedians like Doggett and Christopher Bullock (*c.*1691–1722), both of whom composed pieces with roles tailormade for them,[11] but most actors were ready to change costume at the end of the main piece in order to resurface in a farce, and there was likely to be a section of the audience that had paid half price (normally available after the second – sometimes third – act of the full-length play) specially to see the afterpieces which are, in many ways, the special glory of the eighteenth-century theatre.

Chapter 6

Actors and acting

During the late seventeenth century major advances were made in the field of neurology. A psychological theory based on the humours and the passions was on the way to being replaced by one based on physiology. This was a development that troubled Joseph Addison, for whom the existence of an essential self was a precondition of personal and social improvement. Human interaction, he recognized, was already disfigured by pretence, but this was something the *honest* man could rise above.

> Consider all the different pursuits and Employments of Men, and you will find half their Actions tend to nothing else but Disguise and Imposture; and all that is done which proceeds not from a Man's very self is the Action of a Player. For this Reason it is that I make so frequent mention of the stage.
>   Joseph Addison, *Spectator* 370 (1712)

But if, as neurologists were beginning to imply, the body is a machine that controls the 'self', rather than the permeable shelter of that 'self', what is it that controls the controller? The evidently disinterested God who set the machine running in the first place, perhaps: the non-interventionist deity upheld by churchmen whom history has called Deists. If so, the responsibility for improvement remained in human hands, and was governed by what the Earl of Shaftesbury (1671–1713) defined as the 'moral sense'. Shaftesbury's *Characteristicks of Men, Manners, Opinions, Times* (1711), influential throughout the eighteenth century, asserted the social value of altruism in everyday life. Richard Steele's *The Conscious Lovers* (1722) is a Shaftesburian sermon with altruism as its text. It contests the neurological proposition that an altruistic act is as involuntary as a selfish one. So does Addison's *Cato* (1713). In the theatre, though, the written text is a background and the foreground always occupied by actors. Inevitably, then, the *Spectator* is much concerned with the morality of acting and with the requirement that the stage should serve as a moral guide. Actors, by virtue of the accuracy of their acting, reveal to the observers the signs of their own 'imposture', implicitly inviting them to reach down into their 'very

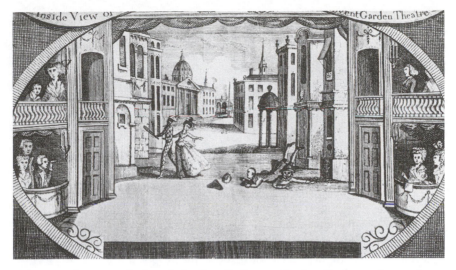

Figure 8. The stage of Edward Shepherd's Covent Garden Playhouse (opened 1732). Despite Colley Cibber's complaints, audience and actors were still in close proximity. Here (*c.*1761) the audience sees the Clown impeding a pursuer of Harlequin and Columbine during the Harlequinade of a pantomime.

selves' in order to correct *at source* this threatening falsity. It is the corollary which concerns us here: to embody behaviour accurately, the actor must reach down into the very self of the character.

> BELMOUR: Have you examin'd
>   Into your inmost heart, and try'd at leisure
>   The several secret springs that move the passions?
>   Nicholas Rowe, *Jane Shore* (1714), Act 5, Scene 2

The studying of a part 'at leisure' becomes, in this grave context, an enquiry into the sources of human action. Neurologists had, in effect, shifted the site of the soul from the 'inmost heart' to the brain. For those like Addison in pursuit of national virtue, actors were a bastion against neurology. Just how consciously actors shouldered the moral burden is another matter.

Actors in society

Christopher Rich took advantage of the 1695 defection of his major actors by shortening the forestage in order to add extra rows of pit benches to the auditorium. His concern was with the income, Colley Cibber's with the

outcome. In an often cited passage of his *Apology for His Life*, Cibber bemoans
the effect of Rich's rearrangement on styles of acting.

> When the actors were in possession of that forwarder space to advance upon,
> the voice was then more in the centre of the house, so that the most distant ear
> had scarce the least doubt or difficulty in hearing what fell from the weakest
> utterance; all objects were thus drawn nearer to the sense; every painted scene
> was stronger; every grand scene and dance more extended; every rich or
> fine-coloured habit had a more lively lustre. Nor was the minutest motion of a
> feature (properly changing with the passion or humour it suited) ever lost, as they
> frequently must be in the obscurity of too great a distance.
>
> Colley Cibber, *An Apology for His Life* (1740), Chapter 12

But Cibber's complaint needs to be read with caution. Although Rich's alter-
ations increased the capacity of Drury Lane, the auditorium retained its intimacy. The most important patrons, those in the pit and boxes, would not
have wanted it otherwise: so much is clear from Edward Shepherd's design
for John Rich's new theatre in Covent Garden (opened in 1732). Shepherd's
stage, auditorium and foyer occupied an area 36.3 metres long and 19.5 metres
wide. Standing at the front of the forestage, an actor would have been in the
audience's part of the room, separated by an orchestra pit from the eleven rows
of pit benches and the six rows available in the boxes behind the pit. Even those
spectators at the back of the two galleries, built over the foyer, would have
been no more than 17 metres from him. Shepherd's vista stage, a room about
15 metres deep by 8 metres wide behind the scenic stage, was copied from
Drury Lane. Its occasional use for grand processions gratified the demand for
spectacle. There may have been a similar facility even in the small theatre in
Goodman's Fields, also designed by Shepherd for its opening in 1732. Here
seven rows of benches in the pit were backed by five in the boxes, with the stage
and vista occupying slightly over half of a building about 27 metres long and 14
wide. While every modification of stage and auditorium in eighteenth-century
London was driven by the managerial urge to increase capacity, it was only
in the 1790s that Covent Garden and Drury Lane were rebuilt on a massive
scale.

Readers of Cibber's cavils need to know that his own voice was thin, and that
his close imitations of fashionable behaviour would certainly have benefited
from maximum proximity. But there was no need for a radical shift in styles of
acting. It remained the common assumption that an actor must feel the passion
he is expressing, and that great actors were therefore uncommonly capable of
great feeling. Even in comedy, or at least in those comedies that anticipated or
followed the fashion set by *The Conscious Lovers*, leading actors displayed an

elevated sensibility. A society that approved such largeness of heart could no longer confidently categorize such people as rogues and vagabonds.

The gradual assimilation of actors by the world of fashion, the world that was, after all, the subject of most of the plays they performed, is observable over the first four decades of the eighteenth century, particularly where Drury Lane is concerned. The members of the managerial triumvirate – Cibber, Barton Booth and Robert Wilks – had respectable pedigrees. Booth's Lancashire family was connected to the Earl of Warrington; Wilks's father had been pursuivant to the Lord Lieutenant in Dublin; Cibber benefited from his father's fame as a monumental sculptor. They were all well educated and socially adept, and Cibber in particular was a shrewd self-promoter, perhaps the first to define the upward mobility of an actor.

> If he excells on the stage, and is irreproachable in his personal morals and behaviour, his profession is so far from being an impediment, that it will be oftener a just reason for his being receiv'd among people of condition with favor.
> Colley Cibber, *An Apology for His Life* (1740), Chapter 5

The origins of their leading lady, Anne Oldfield, were humble – she was purportedly 'discovered' by George Farquhar when serving at the Mitre Tavern – but she was intelligent and she developed social grace. Her settled partnerships, first with the eminent Whig MP Arthur Mainwaring and then, after Mainwaring's death, with Brigadier Charles Churchill, (illegitimate) nephew of the great Duke of Marlborough, were not concealed, though neither man thought fit to marry her.

The first prominent man to make an actress his wife was the antiquary Martin Folkes (1690–1754), already a respected member of the Royal Society when he brought Lucretia Bradshaw's acting career to an end by marrying her at St Helen's, Bishopsgate (his mother, daughter of a knight, reportedly broke her arm by throwing herself out of a window in protest at the match) in October 1714. By the time Folkes rose to the presidency of the Royal Society (1741–53), his wife had been incarcerated in a Chelsea lunatic asylum, where she remained from 1735, a victim of religious mania, until her death in about 1755. The story of Lavinia Fenton (1710–60) is better known. Propelled to sudden stardom as Polly Peachum in *The Beggar's Opera* (1728), she captivated the miserably married 3rd Duke of Bolton (he is gazing at her in Hogarth's painting of a scene from the opera), ran away with him before the season was over, remained his mistress for twenty-three years, bore him three sons and married him soon after his estranged wife's death in 1751.

> Vain Fop, to court me to a rural Life,
> Let him reserve that Usage for a Wife.
> A Mistress, sure, may claim more Liberty,
> Unbound by Nature and by Law, she's free.
> Monster! Thy Country Cottage I disdain,
> In *London* let me live, and let me reign . . .
> Give me a *Play*, a *Ball*, a *Masquerade*,
> And let who will enjoy your lonesome Shade,
> *Lavinia* for more noble ends was made.
>
> > Verses ascribed to Lavinia Fenton, on rejecting a rich young
> > man's proposal that she live with him in a Yorkshire village
> > (1726)

Fenton was not, however the first performer to marry into the peerage. She had been forestalled by the opera singer Anastasia Robinson (d.1755), daughter of a fashionable portrait painter. Her husband was one of the most extraordinary men in England. Charles Mordaunt, 3rd Earl of Peterborough (1658–1735) was a military hero or a military menace, depending on which pamphlet you read. A prime mover in the 1688 Revolution, he was in and out of favour with every monarch from Charles II to George II, a figure whose 'history' remains so inextricably tangled with 'fable' as to make 'fabulous' a literally descriptive epithet. At least three times a duellist, he had commanded ships and land forces, mingled diplomacy with espionage and constant conspiracy and treated the House of Lords to episodes of stand-up comedy. His second marriage is part of the fable. It was kept so secret that no one knows where and exactly when (around 1723?) he and Anastasia married. The Earl was a friend of both Alexander Pope and Jonathan Swift. He bequeathed a valuable watch to Pope, with whom he shared a passion for gardens, and he maintained a lively correspondence with Swift, who wrote in his *Journal to Stella*, 'I love the hangdog dearly . . . He is the ramblingest lying rogue on earth.' Only in the year of his death, some twelve years after the deed, did he make his marriage public, but this is not conclusive proof that he was ashamed of marrying an actress. He had kept his first marriage, to a maid of honour of Charles II's wife, secret for two years. There is plenty of biographical evidence that secrecy spiced his life, but we would know more if Anastasia had not committed the widowly crime of burning her late husband's memoirs.

Such special cases as Fenton and Robinson might be seen as treatable fractures of a societal taboo that remained in place after a period of convalescence. But there was a discernible shift. An actor's social standing was most clearly demonstrated by the composition of the audience at his or her end-of-season benefit performance. The benefit system, by which the beneficiary would be awarded the proceeds of ticket sales less the fixed house charges, was well enough established, according to precedents enshrined by Elizabeth Barry, to defeat managerial attempts to curtail it. Each actor (or, for the lesser company members, group of actors) chose the playbill for the night and took on the job of drumming up an audience. The resultant income was vitally important. In 1711 Oldfield was compensated for Thomas Doggett's opposition to her joining the management team at Drury Lane by the offer of £200 per year plus a benefit clear of charges. With her contacts, she could reasonably hope to double her seasonal income on her benefit night. The same was true for Cibber, Booth and Wilks, as it would be for James Quin (1693–1766) a decade later. These were prominent among the actors with open access to aristocratic patrons. Oldfield would receive gifts, too: at her death her jewellery was said to be worth £11,000. It was not so easy for stalwart company members like John Mills (d.1736), whose annual salary was half Oldfield's and whose circle of friends included few people of wealth. Since the give-and-take of protocol inhibited actors from declining to participate in colleagues' benefits, however far their individual noses might be put out of joint, Mills was one of many actors whose favourite parts were stolen by beneficiaries. But benefits also allowed the bold to take risks, as when Quin opted to sing Macheath for his benefit performance of *The Beggar's Opera* in 1730, or when comic actors chose to defy prejudice by tackling one of Shakespeare's tragic heroes.

The rise of Shakespeare

The theatrical supremacy of Shakespeare was not fully established before Garrick's management of Drury Lane, but the early eighteenth century accelerated his climb. To be sure, the general view was that of Voltaire, that he had 'amazing genius, but no taste', and the versions of his plays seen on stage were all adaptations, in which his notorious unruliness was tamed. Nicholas Rowe's six-volume edition of Shakespeare's works (1709) presented, for the first time, a decently modernized text, together with a generally prudent, if factually naïve, biographical survey. It set in motion the scholarly study of Shakespeare and his works that would culminate in Edmond Malone's ten-volume edition (1790). Almost as remarkable as the calibre of this ferociously researched edition is the fact that it sold out in little over a year. The Shakespeare industry captured the public imagination during the eighteenth century, and Malone (1741–1812) was its first tycoon. The theatre, though, had its own rules, and Shakespeare was guilty of disobedience to them.

The preparation of Shakespeare's plays for public consumption is now generally left to directors and designers, whereas in the aftermath of the Restoration it was the business of playwrights and actors. Faced with the lack of judgement that has Julius Caesar killed at the opening of the third act of his tragedy, arbiters of theatrical taste might sagely shake their heads or, like John Dryden's patron the Earl of Mulgrave, set about correcting the lapse by reforming it into two plays, *The Tragedy of Julius Caesar* and *The Death of Marcus Brutus*. Published posthumously in 1722, Mulgrave's plays were never performed, but they speak for the eighteenth century's attitude to Shakespeare, one which combines wonder and consternation in equal measure. Viewing the shift in sensibility from the enlightened vantage point of the 1760s, Richard Hurd acutely observed that 'What we have gotten by this revolution is a great deal of good sense. What we have lost is a world of fine fabling.'[1] There is certainly good theatrical sense in Cibber's Shakespearean conflation, first performed in 1699 as *Richard III*, which displaced Shakespeare's original for most of two centuries. Cibber shaped the title role for himself, but it would later provide both Garrick and Edmund Kean with sensational material for their sudden stardom.[2] In one form or another, Shakespeare was assuming his central place in the British repertoire.

The impact on acting was not immediate. Cibber's other Shakespearean roles included Iago, Cardinal Wolsey in *Henry VIII*, Justice Shallow in *Henry IV Part Two*, and Cardinal Pandulph in his own interference with *King John*,[3] but it was as Lord Foppington that he was best remembered. Wilks played Hamlet, Othello and Prince Hal, but was most often called for by his predominantly female worshippers as Farquhar's charmingly roguish Sir Harry Wildair. Booth, essentially a tragedian, was more at home in contemporary roles – as Addison's first Cato and as Pyrrhus in Ambrose Philips's *The Distrest Mother* (1712). Doggett, clamped by nature into comedy, was a risible pantaloon as Shylock in Lord Lansdowne's remade *The Jew of Venice* (1701). It was his only notable (semi-)Shakespearean role.

This play is altered from Shakespeare's *Merchant of Venice*, and in some respects with judgment. The introduction of the feast, more particularly where the Jew is placed at a separate table, and drinks to his money as his only mistress, is a happy thought . . . In the second act is introduced a musical masque, written by his Lordship, called *Peleus and Thetis*. In this play, as Rowe remarks, the character of Shylock (which was performed by Dogget) is made comic, and we are prompted to laughter instead of detestation.

David Erskine Baker, *Biographia Dramatica* (1764)

As for Oldfield, she was probably the last 'great' actress to earn that adjective without reference to Shakespeare: it was enough that, in tragedy, she created Rowe's Jane Shore and Lady Jane Grey, and in comedy, Lady Betty Modish (in Cibber's *The Careless Husband*) and Lady Townly (in the Vanbrugh/Cibber *The*

Provoked Husband). It was on the next generation that the weight of Shakespeare began to fall.

Quin made his Drury Lane debut in 1715, but it was at John Rich's theatre in Lincoln's Inn Fields that he first played Brutus, Othello, Macbeth and King Lear (in Nahum Tate's version). He was a weighty actor, familiarly pilloried for walking in blank verse, and his favoured comic roles – Volpone and Sir John Vanbrugh's Sir John Brute among them – were positioned at the sourer, scowling edges of comedy. But his finest Shakespearean part, monumentalized in china statuettes from Bow, Derby and Staffordshire, was Falstaff. It was during the season of 1737–8, in the immediate aftermath of the Licensing Act, that Shakespeare's theatrical supremacy was finally asserted. Some responsibility for this lies with a female pressure group known as 'Shakespeare's Ladies', whose exhortations had a powerful effect on the management of the patent theatres. John Rich staged successively at Covent Garden *King John*, *King Lear*, *Macbeth*, *Much Ado About Nothing*, *Hamlet*, *Richard II*, *Henry IV* Parts One and Two, *Henry V*, *Henry VI* Part One ('At the Desire of several Ladies of Quality), *Cymbeline* and *Othello*. Drury Lane matched Covent Garden with *Henry IV* Part One ('At the particular desire of several Ladies of Quality'; Quin as Falstaff), *Hamlet*, *Richard III* (Quin as Richard), *Othello* (Quin in the title role), *Henry IV* Part Two (Quin as Falstaff), *Measure for Measure* (Quin as the Duke, Cibber as Lucio), *Julius Caesar* (Quin as Brutus), *Macbeth* (Quin in the title role), *The Merry Wives of Windsor* (Quin as Falstaff) and *Henry VIII* (Quin as Henry). The performance of *Julius Caesar* on 28 April 1738 was set aside 'Towards raising a Fund for Erecting a Monument to the Memory of Shakespear'. Seventeen of his plays were staged in London's two principal theatres during this single climactic season, by the end of which Quin may be seen as the first of an unbroken line of actors whose title to greatness is conditional on their playing of Shakespearean roles.

Actors and fairs

It was probably financial need that led a youthful Quin to perform at Southwark Fair in September 1717, since fairs were the natural preserve of 'low comedy' actors. The outstanding example is William Pinkethman (d.1725).

> Mr. *Pinkethman*, He's the darling of *Fortunatus*, he has gain'd more in Theatres and Fairs in Twelve Years, than those that have Tugg'd at the Oar of Acting these 50.
>
>   John Downes, *Roscius Anglicanus* (1708)

It was at fairs that the spirit of the irreverent popular theatre – a 'folk' drama stretching back through the Elizabethan jig and mummers' plays and forward through the nineteenth-century music halls – was most vividly preserved, and Pinkethman was shrewd enough to profit from it. Until 1708, when it was reduced to three days, Bartholomew Fair in London's Smithfield was a spectacular two-week festival,[4] never without Pinkethman's booth from 1698 until the year of his death. Ned Ward's 'London Spy' saw him there, in what was probably a travesty of Robert Greene's Elizabethan play on the Friar Bacon legend, in 1699.[5]

> [H]e kept up so true a behaviour of an idiot that it was enough to persuade the audience that he really was in nature what he only artfully represented. I could not but conclude the part was particularly adapted to his genius, or he could never have expressed the humour with such agreeable simplicity. But, I fancy, if he was to play the part of a wise man it would be quite out of his way, and would puzzle him as much as it would a common whore to behave herself in company like a virtuous woman. There was nothing in the part itself but what was purely owing to his own gesture, for it was the comedian only, and not the poet, that rendered the character diverting.
>
>   Ned Ward, *The London Spy*, Part XI (1699)

At Pinkethman's booth short plays (commonly described as 'drolls') alternated with rope-dancers, acrobats, even freaks.

Fairs were a happy hunting-ground for many low comedians. Joseph Haines (d.1701) had been prosecuted in the turbulent 1680s for staging his droll, *The Whore of Babylon, the Devil and the Pope*, at Bartholomew Fair, Doggett could rely on a good income from touring his *Hob* round seasonal fairs when the London playhouses were closed for the summer, Christopher Bullock (like his father, William) was a fairground favourite, and fat John Harper (d.1742), later a famous Falstaff with the Drury Lane company, came to prominence in 1719 for the 'drunken man' dance that he performed at Southwark Fair. His booth is featured in Hogarth's painting of Southwark Fair (1733/4). Neglected by most theatre historians, fairs and the actors who performed there were crucial preservers of a popular drama.

Provincial stirrings

Pinkethman's experience of fairground management led him on to further enterprises. He set up summer seasons in improvised playhouses in Greenwich (1709–11) and Richmond (1718–24), in the hope of attracting not only local audiences but also citizens of London starved of theatre during the summer closure of the patent houses. Other temporarily unemployed actors took to the road in touring companies, playing in provincial inns, assembly rooms or halls. The city of Norwich, whose assertive independence (the whole of East Anglia must sometimes have seemed like a separate fiefdom to nervous national governments) was traditional, upheld its equal right to control its own entertainment almost from the moment of Charles II's restoration. It was in Norwich that George Jolly sought to establish his company of players when forced out of London by the monopoly granted to Thomas Killigrew and Sir William Davenant in 1660, and it was to the Norwich authorities that, in 1663, the king granted the right to regulate the performance of plays, 'any licence from us or the Master of our Revels or any other power, liberty, matter, or thing to the contrary in any wise not with standing'.[6]

Sir Henry Herbert, Master of the Revels under Charles I, did not necessarily agree. Already deprived of income by Charles II's entrusting of censorship to Killigrew and Davenant, in March 1665 he licensed Richard Bourne to show two camels, an eagle and a vulture in Norwich.[7] The city's response to Herbert's presumption is not recorded, but Doggett took the precaution of seeking the Duke of Norfolk's patronage before, in 1697, establishing his summer company in Norwich, where he continued to perform intermittently at least until 1707. By 1710 the Duke of Norfolk's Servants were presenting a six-week winter season in the city, and by 1726 the Norwich Company of Comedians was performing regularly at the White Swan Inn as well as timing its visits to other East Anglian towns to coincide with race meetings and fairs.

Doggett's pioneering of provincial performances with a taste of London in them was matched by John Hippisley (1696–1748), another low comedian with fairground experience. Bath had built a small playhouse in 1705, mostly through subscriptions from valetudinarian visitors, and it was there that Hippisley's summer company performed in 1728. An early casualty of the Licensing Act, this playhouse was dismantled in 1737, but Hippisley had by then overseen the building of another in the Jacob's Well area of Bristol, and his company was regularly on view in Bristol and Bath until his death. Despite the Licensing Act's stipulation that no theatre in Britain could operate without a royal patent, the Jacob's Well playhouse continued to present plays, made more attractive by the regular appearance of notable London actors. Even the new theatre on its present site in Bristol's King Street ran for twelve years before receiving its royal patent in 1778. The fickle application of theatrical law is a running eighteenth-century theme.

The only active Theatre Royal outside London in the early eighteenth century was in Smock Alley, Dublin. Wilks, Booth and Quin were among the many

London actors who made their professional debuts there under the respected management of Joseph Ashbury. The Dublin repertoire, under the nose of the viceregal court, was largely determined by London taste, sometimes 'at the particular desire' of the powerful lobby of Freemasons.[8] Some few plays of local origin survive in published form, but neither they, nor any of provincial provenance elsewhere in Britain (with the curious exception of John Home's *Douglas* (1756), had any impact on the national repertoire. Eighteenth-century (and nineteenth-century) Irish playwrights abound, but the best (or best-known – masterpieces may still lie hidden) plays were written for London audiences. In the twenty-first century, British playwrights (even Alan Ayckbourn) still know the feeling.

Part Three

The theatre tamed: 1737–1789

Chapter 7

The material circumstance

The Stage Licensing Act of 1737 was, in the words of a recent historian of the period, 'the one undoubted and comprehensive victory in Walpole's extended warfare with the intellectuals of his day';[1] but the same historian also records that '[t]he British reputation for passing laws which nobody bothered to observe was so marked that it was considered an important element in the libertarian tradition'.[2] There is general agreement that the Act arrested the development of the British theatre, but such agreement should be tempered by a recognition that the letter of the law was frequently ignored, not only in London but throughout the (dis)united kingdom. Unsanctioned playhouses proliferated through the remainder of the century, and we cannot know how many unsanctioned plays they showed, since records are incomplete. Publication of licensed dramas was rapid and regular, but inconsistent, and the manuscripts now housed in the British Library are confined to those submitted for the Lord Chamberlain's approval. Performances at fairs, or in makeshift premises, have generally eluded historical enquiry, so that the possibility that a stream of theatrical subversion continued to flow has to be conceded. Even so, the weight of evidence suggests that the Licensing Act was largely successful in taming the drama. As much from prudent self-censorship as from fear of the vigilance of the Lord Chamberlain's office, playwrights of the mid-century rarely challenged the government of the day. The best of them were excellent craftsmen and shrewd observers of behaviour, but the great issues – of theology, of science, of politics – seldom surfaced. In general, managers collaborated with dramatists in the safer game of feeding off past successes. The majority of 'new' plays, many of them avowedly, were in fact 'old' ones refurbished, and popular 'characters' from the past would reappear with little more than a change of name to distinguish them. Quarantined from the infection of national politics, the theatre incubated its own anxieties, apparently unaffected by the conditions of a country almost constantly at war.

Table of events referred to in Part Three

1739	Outbreak of the War of Jenkins' Ear
1740–8	War of the Austrian Succession
1743	Battle of Dettingen
1745	Jacobite rising under Charles Stuart
1746	Battle of Culloden
1753/4	Hardwicke's Marriage Act
1756–63	Seven Years War
1760	Accession of George III. Earl of Bute becomes first minister
1763	Publication of John Wilkes's *North Briton* 45. Fall of Bute
1768	French annexation of Corsica. Foundation of Royal Academy of Arts
1769–72	Publication of the letters of Junius in the *Public Advertiser*
1773	Boston Tea Party
1775	Battle of Bunker Hill
1776	American Declaration of Independence
1777	Surrender of Burgoyne's army at Saratoga
1778	War with France: military camp established in Coxheath
1780	John Dunning's parliamentary motion on the influence of the crown. Gordon Riots
1783	Peace of Versailles
1788	George III's first 'madness'
1788–95	Trial of Warren Hastings
1789	Storming of the Bastille in Paris
1793	Execution of Louis XVI

Britain at war

Under pressure from self-proclaimed patriots, and with a king whose military ambition was dangerously inflated, Robert Walpole's pacific policy was under increasing strain. Having kept Britain out of major conflicts for twenty years, he was forced, in 1739, into declaring war on Spain by the media hype following the amputation of an English naval captain's ear. The War of Jenkins' Ear merged seamlessly with the War of the Austrian Succession (1740–8), which was itself punctuated by the internal threat of the Jacobite rising under Charles Stuart (1745–6). Either directly or indirectly, the enmity of Britain and France remained unbroken until after the Battle of Waterloo (1815), fought sometimes on battlefields in Europe, India, the West Indies or Canada, sometimes at sea, sometimes in the closed rooms of diplomacy. The wars created national heroes – Admirals Vernon, Boscawen and Hawke, General Wolfe, Robert Clive, William Pitt the Elder, eventually Nelson and the Duke of Wellington. Even George II, who led the British troops at the Battle of Dettingen (1743), was momentarily popular after that victory,[3] as was his younger son, the Duke of Cumberland, after the defeat of Charles Stuart's Highland army at Culloden (1746), until his savage reprisals earned him the nickname of 'Butcher'. Patriotic pride and the urge to empire soared during the Seven Years War (1756–63) and raged against the incompetent conduct of the campaign against the upstart Americans, with its inglorious culmination in the Peace of Versailles (1783).

An engaged theatre might have been expected to address the politics of war directly; the disengaged theatre of the eighteenth century did so only peripherally. Soldiers, particularly gentleman-officers, figure prominently in the comedies of the period, but they are soldiers on leave; sailors – Jack Tars – are mostly confined to afterpieces, where they represent the instinctive gallantry of the humbly born Englishman. Two examples may serve to make the point. In Tobias Smollett's two-act *The Reprisal; or, The Tars of Old England* (1757), staged at Drury Lane during the faltering early campaigns of the Seven Years War, a French naval captain called Champignon has captured an unarmed English vessel carrying Heartly, a true-blue Dorset gentleman, and his sweetheart Harriet. The sole concern of the plot is the rescue of Harriet, an endeavour which is aided by the active collaboration of two rebels in Champignon's crew, an Irishman called O'Clabber and a Scotsman called MacLaymore. A few routine anti-French sentiments are expressed along the way, and the chivalry of the English sailors is contrasted with Gallic baseness, but, beyond its exhortatory prologue, the play pays no attention to the specifics of this naval war, nor, for that matter, to the suggestive togetherness of Heartly and Harriet.

> What heart will fail to glow, what eye to brighten,
> When Britain's wrath arous'd begins to lighten!
> Her thunders roll – her fearless sons advance,
> And her red ensigns wave o'er the pale flow'rs of France.
>   Such game our fathers play'd in days of yore,
> When Edward's banners fann'd the Gallic shore;
> When Howard's arm Eliza's vengeance hurl'd,
> And Drake diffus'd her fame around the world.
>   Still shall that god-like flame your bosoms fire,
> The gen'rous son shall emulate the sire.
> Her ancient splendor England shall maintain,
> O'er distant realms extend her genial reign,
> And rise – the unrivall'd empress of the main.
>
>   Tobias Smollett, prologue to *The Reprisal* (1757)

In Isaac Bickerstaff's two-act *Thomas and Sally* (1760), the Seven Years War is entirely peripheral. With Thomas away at sea, Sally faithfully resists the lustful squire's approaches, despite her worldly friend Dorcas's inducements. But when Dorcas advises the squire to take Sally by force, it is only Thomas's timely return that saves her. Douglas Jerrold would fashion one of the nineteenth century's enduring favourites, *Black-Eyed Susan* (1829), out of the same simple plot. Bickerstaff (1733–*c*.1808), though, was concerned only to entertain. *Thomas and Sally* determinedly resists the pull of its latent themes – the 'pressing' into the navy of agricultural labourers with the consequent disruption of families, sociosexual exploitation in times of war, the threat of unemployment for returning combatants. Instead, he alternates tripping rhyming couplets with songs (the music arranged or composed by the maestro, Thomas Arne) in such a way as to reassure the audience that nothing serious is at stake.

> Let TOMMY ARNE, with usual pomp of stile,
> Whose chief, whose only merit's to compile,
> Who, meanly pilf'ring here and there a bit,
> Deals music out as MURPHY deals out wit.
> Charles Churchill, *The Rosciad* (1761)

What is of particular significance here is the clear disjunction between Bickerstaff's actual life as a second lieutenant in the marines and his perception of theatrical taste, which he was ambitious to flatter. In the event, *Thomas and Sally* set him on the road to fame as the first, and most fluent, deviser of a peculiarly English style of musical comedy which would culminate, most famously, in the Savoy operas of Gilbert and Sullivan.

Army and stage: the matter of John Burgoyne

Britain's colonial exploits excited much interest, not all of it sympathetic, in the second half of the eighteenth century. The first volume of Edward Gibbon's admonitory *The Decline and Fall of the Roman Empire* was published in 1776, the year of the American Declaration of Independence; the long trial (1788–95) of Warren Hastings, impeached for cruelty to the king's Indian subjects, ran in parallel with the French Revolution (which, from one perspective, had impeached a king for cruelty to his subjects); and even the choice of title for Oliver Goldsmith's second comedy, *She Stoops to Conquer* (1773), had its edge in the year of the Boston Tea Party.[4] But a man whose career better embodied both the ambiguities of empire and the remoteness of the legitimate stage from the crucial debates it fostered was John Burgoyne (1723–92).

The nephew of a baronet and – officially at least – the son of a soldier, Burgoyne was commissioned, at the age of fourteen, as a sub-brigadier in the Horse Guards. The commission was purchased for him, of course. It was the kind of appointment considered appropriate for a boy with his background. Burgoyne's biological father was more likely his mother's lover, Baron Bingley, and an easy adoption of upper-class immorality marked him as a wild card from his early years. Friendship with James Stanley, heir to the earldom of Derby, brought him into intimate contact with one of the nation's most exalted families. It may have been at the Stanleys' principal seat, Knowsley, that Burgoyne developed an interest in the stage. The Stanleys were prominent patrons of the drama and promoters of private theatricals. An ancestor (Ferdinando, Lord Strange) may well have been Shakespeare's first patron, and James Stanley's son, the 12th Earl of Derby, would make a notorious marriage to the actress Elizabeth Farren before the eighteenth century's end. In retrospect from Joshua Reynolds's profile portrait of Burgoyne, the handsome young officer had probably already a theatrical style of his own, sufficient to charm the Earl's daughter, Lady Charlotte Stanley. Like characters in a mid-century comedy, the couple eloped in 1751, married clandestinely and spent the next four years on the Grand Tour of Europe. It was not until after their return to England in 1755 that Burgoyne began to take his soldiering seriously. Having purchased a captain's commission in the dragoons, he distinguished himself in the Portuguese campaign during the Seven Years War and was promoted to full colonel.

From 1761 Burgoyne was also a member of parliament, an outspoken champion of British liberty. After the hotly contested election in Preston in 1768,[5] during which, flamboyantly theatrical as ever, he campaigned with two pistols on display, he was awarded the seat but fined £1,000 for inciting violence. Like most of his contemporaries, Burgoyne found it hard to maintain a consistent line on the colonies. As chairman of a committee investigating corruption in the East India Company, he pressed for the conviction of Clive for the fraudulent acquisition of £234,000, but he had no truck with the grievances of the American colonists. Convinced that they should be taught a lesson, he relished his 1775 appointment as fourth in line of command to General Gage in the suppression of the Boston rebels. At the inconclusive Battle of Bunker Hill, though, he was confined to the provision of artillery cover. The British army took the hill, but the plan to capture Boston was abandoned, and Burgoyne returned to England in search of higher command. A wiser man would have called it a day. That Burgoyne was the general who surrendered his army of 6,000 men at Saratoga in 1777 is well known, that he was not to blame is easily arguable; but the fact has accorded him an unenviable place in military history. Its aftermath, though, is too little known. Back in England, Burgoyne opposed the further prosecution of the war against America, voted for the legislative autonomy of the Irish parliament, campaigned for electoral reform, expressed support for the French Revolution and joined the prosecution team in the trial of Warren Hastings: the rash youth transformed into a man of principle.

Burgoyne enacted the drama of eighteenth-century England; after a comic opera youth and comedy marriage, he was caught up in the militaristic fervour of the mid-century before arriving alongside Charles James Fox [6] at a position of critical patriotism. He had the contacts, the intelligence and – crucially – the experience to challenge the age's low expectations of the drama, and in *The Heiress* (1786) he almost did. His first piece, *The Maid of The Oaks* (1774), was uncommonly site-specific. Burgoyne's house near Epsom was called The Oaks. Part of Lord Derby's estate, its grounds were the setting of a lavish *fête champêtre* in celebration of the (doomed) marriage of the future 12th Earl to Lady Elizabeth Hamilton. Burgoyne's charming two-act play, written for an amateur cast, was part of the occasion. Set in a house called The Oaks, and featuring a *fête champêtre* on the eve of a wedding, it draws constant attention to its surroundings. The plot centres on the beautiful but mysterious 'maid' who is the bride-to-be: I have been unable to discover whether Lady Elizabeth played the part, but she should have. Expanded to full length by David Garrick (like accordions, eighteenth-century plays could be pushed in or pulled out without damaging the tune) and picturesquely designed by the landscape painter and innovatory scene-designer Philippe de Loutherbourg (1740–1812), *The Maid of The Oaks* was staged at Drury Lane in November 1774.

Otherwise engaged at Bunker Hill and Saratoga, and subsequently with attempts to clear his name, Burgoyne is nevertheless thought to have collaborated with Richard Brinsley Sheridan on an eccentric 'musical entertainment', *The Camp* (1778). This hastily composed and anodynely topical piece offers sketches of life in and around the military camp at Coxheath, established in the summer of 1778 when fears of a French invasion were at their height. The play's popularity owed more to de Loutherbourg's detailed recreation of the camp than to either dialogue or music.

This petit piece is said to be the production of Mr. Sheridan, who tacked the dialogue part of it together, in order to introduce Mr. Loutherbourgh's scenic spectacle of Coxheath Camp.

> *Morning Post*, 16 October 1778

The actual authorship of *The Camp* remains in dispute, but Burgoyne's preparedness to write 'down' to theatrical taste is evident in his next play. His wife had died in 1776, and he now had a mistress – a married actress called Susan Caulfield, who would bear him four children and for whom he wrote *The Lord of the Manor* (1781). This is another play with songs, casually smuggled, like so many plays of the period, from a French original. It touches seriousness only in its concern with a perceived decline in gentlemanly behaviour.

This is a common theme in eighteenth-century comedy, reflective of widespread alarm at the pollution of manners by money. The impact of British wealth on the disposition of British society was difficult to absorb when even those who preached most vehemently against consumerism consumed. The seminal work is Adam Smith's *The Wealth of Nations* (1776), with its recognition of the wage earner, the landlord and the capitalist as the 'three great, original and constituent orders of every civilised society',[7] but the landowning aristocrat was reluctant to shake hands with the capitalist. Few plays produced in audiences the unease of William Hogarth's disconcerting *Marriage-à-la-Mode* sequence (1745), with its unrelenting portrayal of the miseries of an enforced marriage between ancient pedigree and the *nouveaux riches*, but many tried, and Burgoyne's *The Heiress* is one of the best of them. The empty-headed Miss Alscrip, a sedulous aper of fashion, is Hogarth's bride in dramatic action, and the Blandishes are sly, Hogarthian corrupters. Typically conceding to audience expectation, though, Burgoyne shrugs off the weight of the first four acts with a contrived unmasking of Miss Alscrip's rich father that releases Lord Gayville to marry the suddenly enriched Miss Clifford and his spirited and well-read (Swift, Pope, Prior, the *Critical Review*) sister to marry Miss Clifford's infinitely worthy brother. This stooping in order to conquer reached new depths in Burgoyne's regrettable final piece for the stage, his sloppily unhistorical 'libretto' for a semi-opera, *Richard Coeur de Lion* (1786). He is emblematic of a theatre that opened itself to many prominent men and a few prominent women, but discouraged them from taking it too seriously. It may be that Burgoyne's finest theatrical moment belongs, not even to *The Heiress*, but to his cameo role in George Bernard Shaw's *The Devil's Disciple* (1897). Shaw had done his research: the Burgoyne he presents is worldly wise, urbane and shockingly willing to compromise.

Theatre managers

Even a gentleman playwright like Burgoyne was dependent on the decision of a manager, and theatre management during the central decades of the eighteenth century was politically cautious, though scenically adventurous. The patent houses guarded their privilege and did their best to suppress rivals, but the discovery of new playwrights was not their priority.

Covent Garden

John Rich's long reign at Covent Garden came to an end with his death in 1761. Despite his special interest in pantomime and dance, he had maintained a balanced repertoire of plays and afterpieces while competing for actors and playwrights with Drury Lane. Financially stretched by the need to pay separate and self-sufficient troupes of dancers, singers, musicians and actors (with a further subdivision into tragedians and comedians, in some cases), as well as scores of front-of-house and backstage servants, both patent houses sought to increase their capacity in line with London's growing population,[8] but neither could guarantee full houses for untried plays. Less afraid than the Drury Lane managers of accusations of 'lowness', Rich would bring eyecatching novelty acts from the street to provide entr'acte entertainment on his stage, and this contributed to a questionable general view that Drury Lane was the home of a higher dramatic culture.

> Lord, sir, nothing so easy as to bring every living creature in this town to the window: a tame bear, or a mad ox; two men, or two dogs fighting; a balloon in the air, (or tied up to the ceiling, 'tis the same thing); make but noise enough, and out they come, first and second childhood, and everything between.
> Prompt to Lord Gayville in *The Heiress* (1786), Act 1, Scene 2

What is certain is that Rich worked hard on visual effects, at least twice in the 1750s visiting Paris to learn from French techniques, and outshining Garrick in his staging of a procession to mark the coronation of George III in 1761.

Rich bequeathed his legal rights in Covent Garden to his widow and his son-in-law, John Beard, for whom Handel had written the tenor part in *The Messiah*. By association, it was assumed that Beard favoured musical theatre, and it was certainly under his management that the immensely promising musical partnership of Bickerstaff and Charles Dibdin (1745–1814) began. *Love in the City* (1767) was their first collaboration, initially less successful than its delightful successor *Lionel and Clarissa* (1768) but in its abridged form as *The Romp* (1781) one of the favourite vehicles of the adored comic actress Dorothy Jordan. These were good years for the London theatres, and Beard was able to sell the Covent Garden patent for £60,000 to a consortium of two business-men, a playwright and the actor William Powell (d.1769). The playwright was

Figure 9. Dorothy Jordan as Priscilla Tomboy in *The Romp*. The cartoon, dated 3 January 1786, gives some impression of Jordan's comic energy.

Garrick's close friend, George Colman (1732–94), fresh from his acting management of Drury Lane while Garrick was holidaying on the Continent and now confident that his partners would leave the running of the playhouse to him. He was mistaken. Thomas Harris, a soap manufacturer, had no intention of being inactive. Above all, he was determined to promote the cause of his mistress, Jane Lessingham, on whose acting skills Colman and he disagreed. There were public ructions and eventually a lawsuit, which Colman won (by then Harris was tiring of Lessingham), but the playhouse continued to thrive, not least as a result of Colman's own writing. Particularly gratifying was the unexpected success of Goldsmith's *She Stoops to Conquer*, which Garrick had rejected for Drury Lane. Against all likelihood, it was Harris who survived, remaining as senior partner in the management of Covent Garden until his death in 1820. He had benefited from observing the working practices of a busy theatre, glimpsed for us in the *Occasional Prelude* that Colman wrote to open the 1772–3 season. Here is the diminutive Colman confirming schedules with the prompter, refusing to raise a stage carpenter's weekly wage, attempting to reason with a disgruntled playwright, patiently listening to a talentless aspirant actress's audition piece – all before his actors have arrived at the theatre: an exhausted Colman sold his share in the patent for £20,000 in 1774.

Drury Lane

Drury Lane was unstable through the late 1730s and remained so until 1747. The immediate problem was Charles Fleetwood (*c.*1707–47), who in 1734 had purchased a majority share of the patent in the hope of covering his gambling debts. Fleetwood initially entrusted the artistic management to one of the hottest-tempered actors in London, Charles Macklin (*c.*1699–1797) – a bull to mind a china shop. The outcome was predictable, though the manner of its outcoming was not: in May 1735 there was a green-room quarrel over a wig, in the course of which Macklin stabbed the actor Thomas Hallam in the eye with his stick. Hallam died the next day, and Macklin was indicted for murder. He conducted his own case skilfully enough to get off with no more than a branded hand, but his absence, like his presence, did nothing to settle the company. There were protests from within when Fleetwood tried to curry favour with his richer patrons by extending the right of their footmen to free admission for the final act of the main piece, and full-scale riots (there were many theatre riots during the eighteenth century) on 19 February and 4 March 1737 when the right was rescinded.

> This night a great number of footmen assembled together with sticks, staves, and other offensive weapons, in a tumultuous and riotous manner and broke open the doors of *Drury Lane* playhouse, for not being let into what they called *their gallery*, and fought their way in so desperate a manner to the stage door (which they forced open) that twenty five or twenty six persons were wounded in a very dangerous manner, in the fray.
>   *London Magazine*, 5 March 1737

Such events helped to ensure the passage of Walpole's Licensing Act a few months later, and Fleetwood should have been its beneficiary. But by 1739 his addictive gambling was swallowing all the Drury Lane profits, leaving nothing for replenishment of stock or refurbishment. Risking the playhouse's reputation, he followed Rich's example by employing novelty acts. His hiring of Garrick, in the wake of his astonishing 1741–2 debut at the (illegal) playhouse in Goodman's Fields, was a brilliant coup carried out in the name of novelty, but its success was short-lived. Fleetwood's actors, with Garrick as spokesman, rebelled against him in 1743, walking out *en masse*. Eventually, the Licensing Act having so reduced their options, they were forced into an ignominious return. Fleetwood had the nerve to dig his heels in by refusing to reemploy Macklin, who chose, unjustly, to make this a cause of war with Garrick! It was a managerial gesture at the gates of disaster. Fleetwood was forced to mortgage the patent, and when his raising of the admission prices in 1744 was met by riots, he sold out, for a lump sum of £3,200 and an annuity of £600, to two bankers, and fled to France.

The unsung hero of Drury Lane's revival was James Lacy (1696–1774), a minor actor and serial violator of licensing laws, whom the new patentees lured into caretaker management of the playhouse by lending him the money to buy Fleetwood's patent. It was Lacy who, at some sacrifice to his own pride, offered the much younger Garrick (1717–79) a half-share for £12,000. The model they established, over the next near-thirty years (1747–76), is not unlike the model that prevails in British theatres in the twenty-first century. Garrick was the artistic director and Lacy the financial director: they kept in touch but did not need to be intimate friends. Garrick's hand was so full of friends that he could not admit a new one without seeming to discard an old one: most of his sworn enemies were, like Macklin, former friends. When Dr Johnson called him 'the cheerfullest man of his age', he was recording Garrick's amazing gift of being good company, and it was his social skills as much as his acting, and more than his entrepreneurial dexterity, that raised Drury Lane to the level of a 'national' theatre. His retirement in 1776 (Lacy had died two years earlier) was headline news nationwide. Colman's fond 'occasional prelude' for the following season, *New Brooms!* (1776), captures the moment: 'The little man has left the house. It used to be full in his time . . . full as an egg – but he is gone off with the meat, and a whole crew of new managers are putting to sea in the egg-shell.' Garrick's was a hard act to follow, but the sheer force of his personality has left its mark on subsequent evaluations of his achievement.

To begin with, we should recognize that, of the ten most frequently performed pieces at Drury Lane during Garrick's regime, the top four were pantomimes, another four were farcical afterpieces, and only one (*Romeo and Juliet*, ninth in the list) was by Shakespeare. The remaining piece has a story to tell. In 1769 Garrick had allowed himself, with a characteristic mixture of vaingloriousness and trepidation, to become the figurehead of the English theatre's first full-scale festival of bardolatry. The small market town of Stratford-upon-Avon was to house a Shakespeare Jubilee: more a *fête champêtre* of marquees, masquerades and fireworks than a playfest, but highlighted by a street procession of Shakespearean characters in full costume and Garrick's public recital of an ode to Shakespeare that he had written for the occasion. It was unfortunate that Stratford could not accommodate the unanticipated influx of visitors. (James Boswell was famously there, dressed as a Corsican and campaigning on behalf of General Paoli, patriot hero who had led the resistance to France's annexation of Corsica the previous year.[9]) It was even more unfortunate that it poured with rain, turning the Stratford Jubilee into a muddy fiasco.

Throughout his life Garrick was obsessively afraid of appearing ridiculous. Now he did. But he had, in abundance, the admired quality of 'bottom', a word that, at the time, compressed into itself ideas of coolness under pressure, defiance of the odds, stubborn courage and self-belief. (General Burgoyne had bottom.) By the time the 1769–70 season at Drury Lane opened, Garrick had written a strange sort of play, assembling various characters in Stratford for the Jubilee and rounding it off with a procession of Shakespearean characters in full costume and the reading of his ode. Over the remaining seven years of his management, *The Jubilee* was performed – often because audiences called for it – more frequently than anything else in the Drury Lane repertoire. Why? It is not particularly well written – certainly not as well as Colman's *Man and Wife; or, The Shakespeare Jubilee*, which was designed to steal Garrick's thunder when it was staged at Covent Garden a week before the Drury Lane opening of Garrick's face-saving version. There is no answer outside the personality of the actor-manager himself. By some sleight-of-hand, not altogether dissociable from his manipulation of print through his journalistic interests, Garrick had become identified as the champion of British drama in general and of Shakespeare in particular. Yet it was at Covent Garden, not Drury Lane, over the 1747–76 period that three of Shakespeare's plays (*Romeo and Juliet*, *Richard III*, *Hamlet*) were among the ten pieces most frequently performed – and *The Merchant of Venice* was eleventh. Garrick was a pragmatist, not a snob. He would not, otherwise, have been able to ask £35,000 for his half-share of the patent.

Richard Brinsley Sheridan (1751–1816), who led the consortium that scraped together £70,000 to buy out Garrick and Lacy's son, was bolstered by the theatrical reputations of his father Thomas Sheridan (*c.*1719–88) and his father-in-law Thomas Linley (1733–95). But for his father's powerful influence, his first play, *The Rivals* (1775), might not have weathered its stormy rehearsal at Covent Garden, and his father-in-law had provided the music for the deservedly popular *The Duenna* (1775) at the same theatre. There is no doubting Sheridan's brilliance. His problem was to know what direction to point it in; and he was certainly not cut out for management. The triumph of *The School for Scandal* (1777), at the end of his first season, was complete but unrepeatable, and Sheridan's financial incompetence exasperated unpaid actors (and his sundry creditors). After 1782, he left the active management, but no funds, to Thomas King (1730–1805), a conscientious actor (creator of Sir Peter Teazle in *The School for Scandal*) who had nothing in common with Sheridan beyond an addiction to gambling. Sheridan, however, reserved the right to manage whenever he felt like it, and by 1788 the tolerant King had had enough, and John Philip Kemble inherited the thankless task of playing lieutenant to an amateur general. The troubled conclusion of Sheridan's formal management of Drury Lane belongs to the next century.

Samuel Foote and the Haymarket

Samuel Foote (1720/1–77) was a maverick, formidable in conversation and careless of reputation – other people's in particular. He chanced upon acting in 1743 after a spell in a debtors' prison, took some instruction from Macklin, and launched himself as Othello at the Little Theatre in the Haymarket, which Macklin was occupying during his exclusion from Drury Lane. Foote was no more an Othello than the Haymarket was a licensed theatre, but he enjoyed onstage power and wanted more of it. His gift was for mimicry, mostly of a reductive kind, and in 1747 he exploited it in a loosely linked anthology of monologues under the provisional title of *The Diversions of the Morning*. Renting the Haymarket, and circumventing the law by charging admission for a concert of music followed by a *free* dramatic performance, he treated his audience to a variable selection of imitations of the leading actors of the day – Quin, Garrick, Macklin and, in risible drag, Peg Woffington. For most of the next twenty years, Foote would perform at one of the patent houses during the full season and then, on the shady side of the law, at the Haymarket during the summer. Some of the idiosyncratic pieces he wrote for the Haymarket were transferable to Drury Lane or Covent Garden, but they were built round his own bizarre talent. The deployment of an effective dramatic plot was, for Foote, an unnecessary labour. All he needed was a target – hypocritical Methodists, say, in *The Minor* (1760) and *The Orators* (1762), war profiteers in one of the best, *The Commissary* (1765), men who had made fortunes through colonial exploitation and bought themselves power on their return to England in *The Nabob* (1772).[10] Terrorism like Foote's more often injures the guilty than the innocent, but there was a tarnishing element of indiscriminateness about it.

A serious accident that occurred in February 1766 led to a change in status for the Haymarket. Foote was a fellow-guest of George III's brother, the Duke of York, on the Hampshire estate of the Earl of Mexborough when he was teased into saddling a mettlesome horse. The horse threw him, breaking his leg so severely that it had to be amputated, and it may have been remorse that made the Duke agree to press his brother, through the Lord Chamberlain, to award Foote a personal patent for his summer theatre. (Foote would have preferred a year-round patent, but he settled for one operative from 15 June to 15 September.) It was granted in July 1766, by which time the one-legged Foote had resumed acting, with a custom-built 'stage' leg and to a rousing reception from a sympathetic crowd. He could have seen out a meritorious career at the newly styled Theatre Royal, but controversy was his lifeblood. Plays that *now* read quite innocently on the page carried in performance *then* a stinging mimicry of prominent London personalities. (We cannot 'read' make-up, costume and skilled mimicry.) The crunch came in 1775, with the usual puffing of his new play, to be called *The Siege of Calais*,[11] featuring a portrait of the notorious Duchess of Kingston as Lady Crocodile. The Duchess's lurid life story might raise doubts even in the credulous, and Foote's satirical version of her coincided with her prolonged trial for bigamy (she would be found guilty by her peers in 1776). At her urging, Foote's play was banned and her chaplain spread the rumour that Foote was an active homosexual. When one of Foote's servants came forward with an accusation of attempted homosexual rape, a trial was inevitable. That, ably defended by fellow-playwright Arthur Murphy, Foote was quickly exonerated made no difference. Broken in health, he sold his rights in the Haymarket to George Colman in return for an annuity of £1,600, and was dead within a year.

Colman ran the Haymarket on an annually renewable licence, and ran it very effectively until, as it was reported, 'he lost his mind' in 1789. The baton was then passed to his son, George Colman the Younger (1762–1836), under whom it continued to hold its place as London's third theatre, often assumed to be still a Theatre Royal.

Other London theatres

Despite the underlying determination of the Licensing Act to prevent their spread, new theatres were opened in or near the metropolis during the eighteenth century. Some short-term enterprises must surely have passed without leaving a trace. Nowhere in standard theatre histories, for example, is there any reference to Lacy's decision, in immediate defiance of the Act, to present performances in York Buildings in Villiers Street in the winter of 1737. He was imprisoned in Bridewell for that, but not for his building of a theatre in Ranelagh Gardens in 1740. The case of Sadler's Wells is better documented. Dick Sadler's wooden hall, opened in 1684 when he was hoping to get rich on the strength of the wells' medicinal waters, was finally dismantled in 1764 to make way for a brick playhouse. Thomas King managed it from 1771 to 1782, in parallel with his membership of the Drury Lane company, and Richard Wroughton, a regular at Covent Garden, took over when King's managerial duties under Sheridan supervened. Initially more a circus than a playhouse, the Wells was legally bound by the Minor Theatres Act (1751) to avoid spoken dialogue. There, as in other 'minor' theatres, this constraint was sometimes

INTERIOR *OF THE* LITTLE THEATRE. *HAYMARKET.*

FRONT *OF THE* ABOVE.

Figure 10. Interior and exterior of the Little Theatre in the Haymarket after 1778. It looks as if some Gothic extravaganza, with musical heightening, is in progress. No one in the audience is far from the action.

circumvented by speaking against a superfluous background of instrumental music, but even this reinforced in popular audiences the association of music (particularly songs) and drama. Provided that their cheating was negligible, minor theatres could take advantage of the freedom from censorship by staging topical pieces that would have been banned in the royal theatres. Thus it was that Sadler's Wells could greet the storming of the Bastille with *Gallic Freedom; or, Vive la Liberté* in August 1789 while Covent Garden was refused permission to stage a lost play called *Bastille*.[12]

> The first assembling of the Bourgeoisie in the Faubourg St. Martin. The Manner of their proceeding to the Assault of the BASTILLE, and their previous Conference with the Governor. The Massacre of the Citizens who passed the Drawbridge. The Cannonade and general Attack. The Skirmish with the Garde Criminelle. The forcible Entry into the Governor's House, with the Transactions which there took Place, previous to the Beheading of M. de Launay by the Mob. The actual Descent of the Soldiers and Citizens by Torch Light, into the SUBTERRANEAN DUNGEONS. The Discovery of the unfortunate Objects confined in the horrid Recesses of the Place. The affecting and happy Restoration of the several Prisoners to their Friends and Connections. And the Plundering and final Demolition of the BASTILLE by an exasperated Populace. With an ADDRESS from LIBERTY, who is represented as rising out of the Ruins of that once dreadful Prison.
>   Playbill for *Gallic Freedom* at Sadler's Wells, 31 August 1789

Sadler's Wells, just outside the village of Islington, made sporadic attempts to move upmarket, but its regular audience, the kind lightly satirized by Colman in *The Spleen; or, Islington Spa* (1776), was drawn from the City, east of Temple Bar, rather than the town, to the west.

> May not a trader who shall business drop,
> Quitting at once his old-accustom'd shop,
> In fancy thro' a course of pleasures run,
> Retiring to his seat at *Islington*?
>   David Garrick, from the prologue to George Colman's *The Spleen* (1776)

Philip Astley (1742–1814), a pioneer of equestrian display, attracted audiences across the social spectrum to his performances south of Westminster Bridge, where from 1769 he erected a succession of structures best lumped together as Astley's Amphitheatre. His hold on theatre history is secured by the development of a distinct equestrian drama, of which he was not himself either inventor or master, and by the further confusion he caused to the authorities, who found horses the thin end of a wedge of resistance to theatrical legislation. His acts of derring-do in the Seven Years War, his height (six feet or more) and strength and his bluff, uncomplicated patriotism in every subsequent clash of British arms would make of Astley an idealized figure of John Bull for those who stood for their country, right or wrong, as the eighteenth century jostled its uncomfortable way towards the nineteenth. The failure to block Astley's activities so close to the seat of government heralded the imminent proliferation of theatre building in London. The patentees had, in 1787, successfully blocked the ambitious plan to present spoken drama at the newly built Royalty Theatre, near the Tower of London, but the dam was leaking.

Provincial developments

The major contribution to the nationwide spread of theatrical provision, and to the general flowering of provincial urban culture, was made by the construction of a national road network, primarily through the Turnpike Acts (of which there were 340 between 1750 and 1770 alone). By the 1780s every region in England had a turnpike network feeding into a national system.

> 'Who would have believed, thirty years ago', says he, 'that a young man would come thirty miles in a carriage to dinner, and perhaps return at night? or indeed, who would have said, that coaches would go daily between London and Bath, in about twelve hours; which, twenty years ago, was reckoned three good days journey?'
>
>   Richard Graves, *Columella* (1779)

The new mobility enabled the establishment of regional touring circuits, more and more as the century advanced until nearly all of England, as well as parts of Wales and Scotland, could hope for seasonal visitations. It was even financially viable for companies consisting of London-based actors to tour the provinces during the summer break, and it was the London repertoire that continued to dominate. Edinburgh gained a Theatre Royal in 1769, Glasgow in 1781, but the early managers there suffered from the shortage of summer touring options. Provincial England was the major beneficiary.

The effect on the acting profession was profound. There were rich pickings for London stars on the regional circuits, as well as managerial openings unavailable in the capital. Garrick's friend James Dance, who acted as James Love after abandoning his first wife for a legally inadmissible second, had to go no further than Richmond for his investment in management: Richard Yates (*c.*1706–96), a Drury Lane stalwart, was the summer manager of the first Birmingham theatre, whose construction he oversaw, from its opening in 1774 until close to his death in old age. But the best of the regional circuits were laws unto themselves. Thomas Jefferson (1732–1807), founder of a theatrical dynasty most famous in America, ran one from a base in Plymouth for thirty years from 1765. Roger Kemble (1722–1802), whose children John Philip, Charles, Stephen and Sarah (Siddons) were theatrical leaders of the next generation, toured his company (1766–81) from Worcester to the Welsh borders. Norwich, Manchester, Canterbury, Newcastle, Exeter, even little Cheltenham acquired theatres royal during the eighteenth century, headquarters from which companies would fan out to neighbouring towns, generally timing their visits to coincide with fairs, race meetings or local festivals. By 1805, when James Winston published *The Theatric Tourist*, his illustrated précis of a countrywide survey of theatres, there was no sizable conurbation without a playhouse, most of them claiming to be 'royal', and all attached to the circuit system.[13] The best-known, because the most genially documented, circuit is the one that Tate Wilkinson created and managed in Yorkshire.

Wilkinson (1739–1803) had learnt his trade from Samuel Foote, whose methodology he adopted in his own ingenious displays of mimicry. Having prospered as a peripatetic actor, he settled in York in about 1765 and set about building his empire. Granted a patent for the York theatre in 1769, he matched it initially with Hull and eventually with Leeds (1774), Wakefield, Doncaster and Pontefract. Most of the leading actors of the age performed for Wilkinson at some time; more importantly, his company rivalled Bath's as a training ground for future stars, most notably Dorothy Jordan, whose respect for her mentor was widely shared. But Wilkinson owes his fame to his writing. The four volumes of *The Wandering Patentee* (1795) contain a wealth of advice on theatre management.

> A jaunt to London in particular, is very necessary for every manager if possible every year; it rubs up the rust of his observation, and he is sure with care to purchase novelty for his country customers.
>
> Tate Wilkinson, *The Wandering Patentee*, Volume III (1795)

But Wilkinson is a prose stylist in his own right. It is the manipulation of memory, the beguiling way in which his narrative shifts between past and present tense – silently absorbed from his reading of Laurence Sterne – that gives *The Wandering Patentee* its literary distinction: 'I make this book a matter of conversation, and only beg leave to talk' (vol. 2, p. 228).[14]

Wilkinson was the son of an Anglican clergyman who had risen to be chaplain to Frederick, Prince of Wales before blotting his copybook by conducting illicit weddings.[15] In the wake of his father's disgrace, he adopted an aggressive/defensive 'establishment' posture towards the growing evangelical challenge to the complacency of the Church of England, but his running feud with antitheatrical Yorkshire Methodists is conducted with such good humour that the seriousness of their opposition is disguised. It is one of the ironies of social history that, in their mutually exclusive assault on the hearts and minds of agricultural and industrial labourers, Methodism and popular drama used the same dialect. Excitement was its immediate object, but it was the by-product of such excitement – the empowering of the lower orders – that alarmed the leaders of Church and state. Detailed exploration of the links between Methodism, drama and political radicalism is outside the scope of this book. However, although the full impact of working-class Methodism was not felt until the nineteenth century, its eighteenth-century stirrings should not be ignored. They can be sensed in the account of his boyhood experience by the future playwright, novelist and working-class radical Thomas Holcroft (1745–1809), author of *A Tale of Mystery* (1802), the first English play to call itself a 'melodrama'.[16]

Books of piety, if the author were but inspired with zeal, fixed my attention whenever I met with them: 'The Whole Duty of Man' was my favourite study, and still more Horneck's 'Crucified Jesus'. I had not yet arrived at Baxter's 'Saint's Everlasting Rest', or 'The Life of Francis Spira'; but John Bunyan I ranked among the most divine authors I had ever read. In fact I was truly well-intentioned, but my zeal was too ardent, and liable to become dangerous.

William Hazlitt (ed.), *Memoirs of the late Thomas Holcroft* published posthumously in 1816

Chapter 8

The drama

A just estimate of eighteenth-century drama is impeded by historically enshrined evaluations. Plays by Richard Brinsley Sheridan and Oliver Goldsmith are readily available, plays by Isaac Bickerstaff, the elder George Colman, Richard Cumberland or Arthur Murphy less so, plays by Hannah Cowley and Elizabeth Inchbald have to be searched for, and the immensely popular pantomimes of Henry Woodward have sunk without trace. When John O'Keeffe's *Wild Oats* (1791) was revived by the Royal Shakespeare Company in 1976, it was received as a bolt from the blue. A pleasant enough play, it is not markedly superior to many other still-forgotten eighteenth-century comedies. Sadly, too, short farces – the vivacious afterpieces of the age – are considered too frivolous to merit reprinting. That is nothing new. Even Samuel Foote, whose hold on it was much stronger than his hold on comedy, derided farce.

> [Farce is] a kind of theatrical, not dramatic, entertainment, always exhibited at fairs, and too frequently produced at playhouses; a sort of hodge-podge, dressed by a Gothic cook, where the mangled limbs of probability, common sense, and decency, are served up to gratify the voracious cravings of the most depraved appetites: this I call farce. Comedy, on the other hand, I define to be an exact representation of the peculiar manners of that people among whom it happens to be performed; a faithful imitation of singular absurdities, particular follies, which are openly produced, as criminals are publicly punished, for the correction of individuals, and as an example to the whole community.
>
> Samuel Foote, responding to criticism of *The Minor* (1760)

Foote's contemporaries felt much the same about farce and comedy as he did. No one dared denigrate tragedy.

Tragedy

I have yet to read an eighteenth-century tragedy that I would readily recommend to anyone else. Tate Wilkinson's realistic estimate that 'tragedy is yearly decreasing in public favour . . . comedy must take the lead' is unsurprising.[1] There was no shortage of aspirants, though. Tragedy was a genre worthy enough to attract 'high culture' poets such as Edward Young and James Thomson. True to the spirit of the age, they wrote in blank verse, modelled on Shakespeare, while aiming at a wholly un-Shakespearean narrative correctness in accord with the tenets of neoclassicism. The lesson of history is that tragedies will hold the stage only if they have something serious to say about the human condition. Sedentary writers like Thomson, for whom 'courting the muse'[2] while strolling in Lord Lyttelton's Hagley Park estate was a strenuous activity, made the same mistake as Shakespeare's Richard II, that of confusing tragedy with sitting down to 'tell sad stories of the death of kings'. Because it is a play for which claims continue to be made, John Home's *Douglas* (1756) may be taken as representative of the best to be hoped for.

Home (1722–1808) was a minister in the Church of Scotland when he wrote *Douglas*, but resigned in 1757 in the face of Presbyterian outrage that a clergyman should have written a play. He had remained loyal to George II in defence of Edinburgh during the 1745 uprising, of which he would publish a *History*, dedicated to George III, in 1802, but he was insistently Scottish, part of the Edinburgh enlightenment claiming recognition in London.[3] In sending the manuscript of *Douglas* to David Garrick in 1755, he enlisted the aid of the Earl of Bute, Scottish mentor of the future George III, who was as chagrined as Home by Garrick's rejection of it. Successfully staged in Edinburgh in December 1756 and by John Rich at Covent Garden three months later, *Douglas* was to be settled firmly in the English repertoire by Sarah Siddons's playing of Lady Randolph from the 1780s until her retirement in 1812. There are good reasons for that. This is a play about the pains of motherhood, as is evident from the dying speech of its nominal hero.

> O had it pleas'd high heaven to let me live
> A little while! – my eyes that gaze on thee
> Grow dim apace! my mother – O! my mother.
>   John Home, *Douglas* (1756), Act 5

Young Norval, brought up like Oedipus by simple folk, is the lost child of Lady Randolph's secret marriage to the dead Lord Douglas, naturally noble despite his humble surroundings. Caught up in the family feud between Randolphs and Douglases, he is treacherously killed just after he and his mother have met for the first time since his birth. What can the mother do but kill herself?

> She ran, she flew like light'ning up the hill,
> Nor halted till the precipice she gain'd,
> Beneath whose low'ring top the river falls
> Ingulph'd in rifted rocks: thither she came,
> As fearless as the eagle lights upon it,
> And headlong down –
>   John Home, *Douglas* (1756), Act 5

And what, beyond pity, can be expected of an audience? There is a moment, in Act 4, when something *almost* happens on stage: the rest, admired in its time but ponderous now, is poetry. To understand the hold of Lady Randolph and Young Norval on contemporary audiences, we have to remember the emotional pull of Siddons and the statuesque beauty of her brother, John Philip Kemble. Under analysis, Norval is empty rhetoric and his mother misery festooned with similes. Garrick's letter to the Earl of Bute in explanation of his rejection of the play is absolutely right throughout, and it says more about actors and audiences than about plays that he turned out, at the time, to be absolutely wrong.

> [T]he Scenes are long without Action, the Characters want strength & Pathos, and the Catastrophe is brought about without the necessary & interesting preparations for such an Event.
>   David Garrick to the Earl of Bute, 10 July 1756

Garrick's part in the Home story does not end there. Having entered the service of the Earl of Bute in 1757, and serving as his private secretary until his fall in 1763, Home had become a force to be reckoned with in London society, and the politic Garrick subsequently staged two of his tragedies, *Agis* (1758) and *The Siege of Aquileia* (1760), without adding lustre to either Drury Lane or the genre at large. When, in 1760, the Prince of Wales ascended the throne as George III, Bute ascended with him, to the unconcealed resentment of self-proclaimed English patriots. During the early 1760s Scotsmen were more unpopular in England than at any time since the Act of Union (1707), their satiric portrayal in the drama of the period became a matter of routine, and even the mighty Garrick abandoned his promotion of Home. The new Drury Lane tragedy for the 1761–2 season was Henry Brooke's *The Earl of Essex*, starring Thomas Sheridan and glorying in *English* liberty.[4] Despite the justness of his assessment of *Douglas*, it was not always the quality of a new tragedy that determined Garrick's choice. *The Earl of Essex* is as decorously tedious as *Douglas*.

Edward Moore's *The Gamester* (1753) is not decorous. Moore (1712–57) was a bourgeois poet, best known before 1753 for his cautionary 'Fables for the Female Sex' (1744). But *The Gamester*, a domestic tragedy in prose after the rarely copied model of George Lillo's *The London Merchant* (1731), is the only reason for his name being remembered now. Gaming was the eighteenth century's fashionable drug, and its spread from the upper classes to the middling sort was particularly deplored. This is Moore's theme, pursued relentlessly through five gloomy acts and culminating inevitably in suicide. Garrick himself created the title role and must have colluded in the announcement, after the tenth night, that the cast found it 'impossible to continue acting the principal characters without some respit'.[5] Beverley is a good man, a loving husband and father, and Mrs Beverley is saintly in her support of him. For anyone with the stomach for unalleviated misery (this, at least, *The Gamester* has in common with *Douglas*), their story is a powerful parable. If Moore had had the courage of his moral convictions, he might have written a better play. As it is, instead of making gambling the enemy, he provides Beverley with a human nemesis in the person of the villainous Stukely, who corrupts his 'friend' as a means to debauching that friend's incorruptible wife.

The Gamester is the kind of play that might have gratified an eighteenth-century Methodist, if such a man could have admitted going to the theatre. It did nothing to stem the tide of gambling, which reached its height in the last quarter of the century, continuing unabated after the sensational suicide of John Damer in August 1775. Damer was an MP, part of the Devonshire House 'Circle' (Charles James Fox, Sheridan and Garrick belonged to it, too) and son of the immensely wealthy Lord Milton. He shot himself in the head after his father had refused to pay off gambling debts of £70,000. In 1773 Fox had used his father's legacy to pay off most of the £130,000 he had lost at the table, but Damer's death made Georgiana, Duchess of Devonshire shy of confessing to her husband her £3,000 debt. As for Sheridan, he was about to merge his financial problems with those of Drury Lane. In the eighteenth century *The Gamester* was always a timely play.

Sentimental comedy

Richard Steele's *The Conscious Lovers* (1722) had challenged the comic tradition of Ben Jonson and Molière by locating at its centre an *exemplary* character instead of a, perhaps correctable, *eccentric*. The popularity of that play was one source for a stream of unpalatably wholesome comedies in which virtue triumphs simply because virtue triumphs, a comfortable tautology whose application to comedy is as tenuous as its application to the stockmarket. There were other sources – Samuel Richardson's novels prime among them – before

Figure 11. Thomas Rowlandson's *A Gaming Table at Devonshire House*.
Rowlandson shows Georgiana, Duchess of Devonshire in the act of throwing the
dice. It could be Charles James Fox peering over her standing sister's left shoulder.

the outbreak, virulent through the 1760s and 1770s, of a cult of sensibility.
The impetus was provided by the publication in 1760 of the first two volumes
of Laurence Sterne's *Tristram Shandy* and reinforced by the 1761 translation
of Jean Jacques Rousseau's *Julie; ou La Nouvelle Héloise*. These were books
addressed to 'the interest . . . which men of a certain turn of mind take . . . in
their own sensations'.[6] To be a man (or woman) of feeling was to participate in
the human race. 'Let us never forget', says Harley, the eponymous hero of Henry
Mackenzie's improbably popular pseudonovel *The Man of Feeling* (1771), 'that
we are all relations.'[7]

The theatrical impact of the cult of sensibility has been so overrated as
to tar a whole century of plays with the brush of 'sentimental comedy',
almost as if this was the sole successor to 'Restoration comedy' before comedy, as a genre, went underground in the nineteenth century awaiting its
disinterment by Oscar Wilde. It is true that several plays which can be reasonably identified as sentimental comedies were staged between 1737 and
1789, but they constitute, as I have already suggested, a stream, not the

river. The point is neatly illustrated by the contrast between two plays, one staged at Drury Lane in early January 1768 and one staged at Covent Garden later in the same month. Hugh Kelly's *False Delicacy* was Garrick's choice *after* he had tinkered with the text. It is an extraordinary play by a very ordinary writer, a fantasia on a theme of delicate feeling. There are three matches to be resolved, and the main obstruction to them all is the determination of all the lovers to put themselves last: 'My heart shall break before it shall be worthless' (Hortensia Marchmont in Act 3). Performed with irony, it might be hilarious on the modern stage, as characters – one after another – fall through the holes they have dug by cutting the ground from under their own feet, but the parody of the cult of sensibility seems to have been unconscious. Despite the play's title, the delicacy that displaces self-interest is genuine, and when the tortuous negotiations yield a happy ending, the summarizing final speech concludes that 'those who generously labour for the happiness of others, will, sooner or later, arrive at happiness themselves'. (That, Wilde would point out, is what fiction means.) Garrick had rejected Goldsmith's *The Good-Natur'd Man* in favour of *False Delicacy*. Since there is no evidence that Goldsmith had had prior access to Kelly's text, we have to assume that it is only accidentally that he provides what is effectively an antidote to *False Delicacy*. Young Honeywood, the good-natured man, learns through experience that the principle of 'universal benevolence' is simply a fear of giving offence, and that the refusal to insist on either side of an argument is cowardice. In 1768, the year that saw the publication of Sterne's *A Sentimental Journey*, *False Delicacy* gained more plaudits for Drury Lane than *The Good-Natur'd Man* for Covent Garden.

Kelly (1739–77) was only briefly famous. Richard Cumberland (1732–1811) was a durable middle-of-the-road playwright, whose *The West Indian* (1771) tends now to be cited as the exemplary sentimental comedy. It reveals a wish, acknowledged in his *Memoirs*, to speak well of men belonging to frequently maligned social groups.[8] The West Indian Belcour is a nabob, a species subject to vilification from Foote but here revealed in heartfree benevolence, and the cause of true love is served by O'Flaherty, an Irish soldier released from the ridicule conventionally attached to Irishmen in contemporary comedy. In *The Fashionable Lover* (1772) there is a generous Scotsman, and in *The Jew* (1794) the tables are inventively turned on Shylock by the creation of the beneficent Shiva: 'I love my monies, I do love them dearly; but I love my fellow-creatures a little better.'[9] Cumberland was well born and well connected, and there is no doubt that he was well meaning, too, but he was a charmless man, foolishly jealous of his intellectual reputation and therefore vulnerable to Sheridan's cruel mockery of him as Sir Fretful Plagiary in *The Critic* (1779).[10]

His long career (1765–1810) as a produced playwright was decidedly uneven, and there is a discordant lukewarmness about even his friends' appreciation of him and his work. *The West Indian* is not a bad play, and *The Jew* is almost a good one, but that is because their plots are busy enough to conceal, for some of the time, the flaws of more characteristic work like *The Brothers* (1769) and *The Wheel of Fortune* (1795), a play theatrically redeemed by John Philip Kemble's weighty portrayal of the textually flimsy Penruddock. In admitting that 'Mr. Cumberland has not always the talent to make his female characters prominent', Elizabeth Inchbald was politely understating the case.[11] His handling of love scenes is embarrassing: they excite in him a heterosexual ecstasy that makes hyperbole the norm of discourse.[12]

> FREDERIC: Oh my soul's joy, my treasure, my Eliza!
> ELIZA: Frederic, what tidings?
> FREDERIC: None but of love, increasing with each moment; glowing with every beam that those soft eyes diffuse, and heightened into rapture by those charms, those graces, that each look, word, motion spread around you.
>   Richard Cumberland, *The Jew* (1794), Act 3, Scene 1

It is not that Cumberland supposed that young people were speaking to each other like this, but that, try as he might, he found no answer to the age-old problem of dramatizing goodness. This was a weakness acutely observed by Goldsmith in his 'Retaliation', and a dilemma for all sentimental writers identified by William Hazlitt.

> Here Cumberland lies having acted his parts,
> The Terence of England, the mender of hearts;
> A flattering painter, who made it his care
> To draw men as they ought to be, not as they are.
> His gallants are faultless, his women divine,
> And comedy wonders at being so fine.
>   Oliver Goldsmith, from 'Retaliation' (1774)
>
> It is not difficult to personify the passions, so as to render them natural: that is a language which men readily understand. But of the difficulty of exhibiting the passions entirely under the control of reason, of virtue, religion, or any other abstract principle, let those judge who have studied the romances of Richardson.
> William Hazlitt (ed.), *Memoirs of the late Thomas Holcroft* (1816)

The cult of sensibility had a long reach, sufficient to engulf at times writers whose natural bent was not sentimental. George Colman, for example, surrendered to it in *The English Merchant* (1767), whose title character is recklessly, if not dottily, generous in the pursuit of a contrived happy ending. It is easier, in the theatre, to accept comedy's claim that love conquers all than to endorse a playwright's argument that goodness will do the job just as well. Sentimental dramatists, when push came to Act 5 shove, were too often prepared to resort to a change of heart in the antagonist – a sudden discovery that he is a nice man really. With reference to one of the plays submitted to him during his management of the Haymarket, George Colman the Younger cites a fifth-act stage direction instructing the actor of the miser to 'lean against the wall, and grow generous'.[13]

Comedy and marriage

The fact that the promise of marriage is a conventional conclusion to comedy tends to disguise its social seriousness at a time when separation was a scandal and divorce well-nigh impossible. The marriage settlement might make or break eighteenth-century lives, and fortune hunting was a serious business. Around Ludgate Hill, within the sanctuary of the 'Rules of the Fleet Prison', clergymen imprisoned for debt (more than seventy are known to have been conducting Fleet weddings between 1700 and 1753, though some of these were frauds) would take their fees, ask no questions and conduct instant marriages.[14] Such ramshackle arrangements not only put young lives at risk, but also made it difficult to determine the facts in bigamy suits. Attempts to legislate were blocked by the Church's insistence that the regulation of marriage was subject to canon law only, and it required all Lord Chancellor Hardwicke's subtlety to carry a Marriage Bill through parliament. Hardwicke's Marriage Act became law in 1754, bringing Fleet marriages to an immediate halt by threatening felonious clergy with the death penalty.[15] The Act also stipulated that no minor could marry without parental permission, that the ceremony could only be conducted in an Anglican church, that no marriage could proceed without the public reading of the banns in the chosen church and that all marriages must be recorded, with witnesses' signatures, in the parish register.

The bill was carried into law against furious opposition, much of it predictably trumpeting English liberty, but some making the more substantial case that the real purpose was the protection of patrimony against matrimony, a shoring up of ancient privilege. Nevertheless, Hardwicke's Act went a long way towards resolving a chaotic situation, one of its by-products being a slight shifting of the focus of comedy. It did not, of course, abolish clandestine marriages. Secretive couples could have the banns published in distant churches or, in extremity, sail to the Continent or to Guernsey, where English law had no authority. More conveniently, with the improvement of the western road to Scotland, they could ride to Gretna Green.[16]

> There had I projected one of the most sentimental elopements! – so becoming a disguise! – so amiable a ladder of Ropes! – Conscious Moon – four horses – Scotch parson – with such surprise to Mrs. Malaprop – and such paragraphs in the News-papers! – O, I shall die with disappointment.
>   Lydia Languish in Richard Brinsley Sheridan's *The Rivals* (1775),
>   Act 5, Scene 1

The Clandestine Marriage (1766), jointly written by Colman and Garrick, contrasts the two daughters of a prosperous merchant. Its initial inspiration was the first plate of William Hogarth's *Marriage-à-la-Mode* sequence (1745), and Elizabeth Sterling is Hogarth's empty-headed, luxury-loving bride, longing to be 'transported to the dear regions of Grosvenor Square – far – far from the dull districts of Aldersgate, Cheap, Candlewick, and Farringdon Without and Within' (Act 1, Scene 2). Fanny Sterling, modest and, despite the authors' intentions, teetering on the edge of simpering, has secretly married her father's clerk. The concealment and final acceptance of this clandestine marriage is the main business of the plot, in the course of which the prospect of Elizabeth's marrying the sympathetic Lord Melvil vanishes. Despite the promise of its title, *The Clandestine Marriage* adds no new features to the familiar map of the vexed union between wealth and birth. In this respect it falls short of John Burgoyne's *The Heiress* (1786). It has, though, the advantage of Colman's absorption in contemporary issues, whether of taste or of commerce, and of Garrick's intuitive grasp of comic timing. My abiding memory of a performance at the surviving (miniature to modern eyes) Georgian theatre in Richmond, Yorkshire[17] is of the older-generation comic eccentrics, the gross Mrs Heidelberg, the good-hearted fop Lord Ogleby and old Sterling himself, fanatical about his garden and a sworn enemy of straight lines.[18]

> Ay – here's none of your straight lines here – but all taste – zigzag – crinkum-crankum – in and out – right and left – to and again – twisting and turning like a worm, my lord.
>   Mr Sterling to Lord Ogleby in *The Clandestine Marriage* (1766),
>   Act 2, Scene 2

It is a sign of weakness (the authors' quite as much as mine) that I have no recollection of the quartet whose task it was to carry the plot.

The playwright who best expresses the felt life of the eighteenth-century marriage market is the sadly neglected Hannah Cowley (1743–1809). Garrick recognized the quality of her first play, *The Runaway* (1776), submitted anonymously. Having embellished it (he always 'improved' new plays), he staged it at Drury Lane and found himself embroiled in controversy. Tackling the iniquity of arranged marriages from a woman's perspective, Cowley had let her runaway challenge the wording of the marriage vows: 'I won't hear of it, "love" one might manage that perhaps, but "honour, obey"! 'tis strange the ladies had never interest enough to get this ungallant form amended.' The subsequent debate, conducted in newspapers and salons, might be said to have culminated in the publication of Mary Wollstonecraft's *A Vindication of the Rights of Woman* (1792). Feminism is never strident in Cowley's plays, but it is pervasive. Her women have most of the best lines and an independent spirit that can overpower her men in the muscular dialogue that marks her superiority over an established playwright like Cumberland. Unlike Cumberland and many other comic dramatists, Cowley had the dexterity to compose comic plots without recourse to the convenience of villains. In *The Belle's Stratagem* (1780), Letitia Hardy has to work to help Doricourt become worthy of her. She loves him unreservedly, but suspects him, justly, of indifference. Her 'stratagem' is to make herself repugnant to him '[b]ecause 'tis much easier to convert a sentiment into its opposite, than to transform indifference into a tender passion'. And it works – through the device of a masquerade, one of many such social occasions in her plays.

Through these artfully staged 'polite' gatherings, Cowley both displays and criticizes eighteenth-century attitudes. The success of *The Belle's Stratagem*, following that of the crafty two-act farce *Who's the Dupe?* (1779), had given Cowley an entrée to London society, and her quizzical observation of the *ton* at play in the marriage market is a peculiar strength of the excellent *Which Is the Man?* (1783). Her comedies address the issue of social change more seriously than her audiences realized, and although arranged marriages are her bugbear, they are not the exclusive object of her feminist concern. Her last play, *The Town Before You* (1794), arraigns men for devaluing women's creativity. The sculptor Lady Horatia Horton owes something to Anne Damer, widow of the suicidal gambler whose death shocked London in 1775. Like Cowley, Damer constantly struggled against male prejudice in exhibiting her work. If this is not Cowley's best play, it is conclusive evidence of her determination to take comedy seriously.

Richard Brinsley Sheridan

Having borrowed enough to buy out the ageing Garrick, Sheridan entered into management of Drury Lane at the beginning of the 1776–7 season and, to his discredit, immediately shelved Cowley's *The Runaway*;[19] a backhanded recognition of a rival talent, at least. He was only twenty-five, and had an eighteen-month-old dramatic reputation to confirm. *The Rivals*, *The Duenna* and the two-act farce *St. Patrick's Day* had all been produced at Covent Garden in 1775, and Sheridan enjoyed being the talk of the town. He had fashioned *The Rivals* by stretching a single joke – 'my father wants to force me to marry the girl with whom I'm planning to elope' – across five acts, in the course of which he both mocks (through Lydia Languish) and indulges (through the dreary Faulkland) the cult of sensibility, but he could produce wittier lines than any playwright since William Congreve, along with a stream of show-stopping mangled words from the fatuous Mrs Malaprop: 'she's as headstrong as an allegory on the banks of Nile', 'he is the very pineapple of politeness', 'female punctuation forbids me to say more'. *The Duenna* is better, more busily plotted than anything by Bickerstaff, but honouring his innovatory style of music theatre. It was announced as a comic opera, but is closer in form to the twentieth-century musical. Like Cowley's, Sheridan's was a fresh voice in a theatre largely occupied by revivals of familiar plays. The *London Packet* reviewer credited *The Duenna* with 'rescuing the stage from that state of lethargy, and melancholy madness, into which Cumberland and his sentimental compeers had lulled it' (22 November 1775). What few people, perhaps not even Sheridan himself, yet knew was that this new playwright was a politician in the making.

In late adolescence Sheridan had been caught up in the furore provoked by the letters (1769–72) of the mysterious 'Junius'[20] in the *Public Advertiser*. Ferociously critical of the government at large and the king in particular, these letters carried further John Wilkes's notorious assault in *North Briton* 45 (1763) and anticipated the passing in parliament of John Dunning's motion that the 'influence of the crown has increased, is increasing and ought to be diminished' (1780). These early stirrings of rationalizing radicalism would become more widespread after 1789, when Sheridan, while opposing the execution of Louis XVI, would rage against his acting manager's decision to close Drury Lane on 24 January 1793 in commemoration of the 'murdered' French king. Like his grandfather, George III was a jealous guardian of the royal prerogative. The Earl of Bute had been *his* choice as chief minister, and no change of government could take place without his imprimatur. A succession of ministers rose and fell with the tide of royal favour, and the Sheridan who now found himself in command of London's premier theatre was certain to intervene in some way or other. When it came, though, the intervention was unorthodox.

Cleverly camouflaged, *The School for Scandal* (1777) is a play about politics. The control of scandal is the control of power, just as, since Robert Walpole, the screening of crime had been the privilege of power. The climactic revelation (Act 4, Scene 3), after Charles Surface has toppled the screen concealing Lady Teazle, enforces a moment of stillness which is a tableau of exposed political chicanery. Laughingly encouraged by the taste-setting Duchess of Devonshire, who claimed to *be* Lady Teazle, contemporary audiences viewed the play as a *pièce à clef*; for some, Charles Surface was the profligate John Wilkes, and his brother Joseph anyone from Wilkes's ultra-respectable rival for the chamberlainship of the City of London, Benjamin Hopkins, to Lord North, the prime minister, or even George III himself. It is the contrast between the two brothers that sustains the plot of *The School for Scandal*. Joseph Surface presents himself as a 'good' man, employing the language of sensibility as a cover for his selfish schemes, whereas Charles conceals his inward goodness under the outward appearance of a philandering wastrel. That the play is an active counter to sentimentalism like Cumberland's is true, but its importance lies much more in its marrying of comedy and politics, a cause that even Sheridan quickly abandoned. He was not, as some said, written out; rather, uncertain of the future of a political theatre, he increasingly devoted his skills as a wordsmith to what he liked to see as the great causes of liberty. When he broke a two-year silence with the very funny rehearsal play *The Critic* (1779), he gave the opening speech to Dangle as a representative of theatregoers' lack of interest in affairs of state.

> DANGLE: [*reading a newspaper*] 'BRUTUS to LORD NORTH.' – 'Letter the second on the STATE OF THE ARMY' – Pshaw! 'To the first L dash D of the A dash Y.' – 'Genuine Extract of a Letter from ST. KITT'S.' – 'COXHEATH INTELLIGENCE.' – 'It is now confidently asserted that SIR CHARLES HARDY.' – Pshaw! – Nothing but about the fleet, and the nation! – and I hate all politics but theatrical politics. – Where's the MORNING CHRONICLE?
>
> Richard Brinsley Sheridan, *The Critic* (1779), Act 1, Scene 1

Laughing comedy

'Laughing comedy' was the ungainly term used by Goldsmith (*c.*1730–74) to distinguish the play he had just written, *She Stoops to Conquer*, from the

Figure 12. David Garrick and Mrs Pritchard in *The Suspicious Husband*. Francis Hayman's depiction of the slimline young Garrick with the more substantial Hannah Pritchard in her voluminous dress makes the intended rape look ambitious.

sentimental comedy then in vogue. His partisan essay 'On the Theatre' appeared in the *Westminster Magazine* (January 1773) a few weeks before the play opened at Covent Garden. It promotes the cause of comic laughter against the taste for sympathetic tears, arguing in effect that sentimental comedy is neither true comedy nor even good drama. In this he spoke for most discerning critics of the contemporary stage: Dr Johnson's *Dictionary* definition of comedy reads, 'a dramatick representation of the lighter faults of mankind, with an intention to make vice and folly ridiculous'. Most, even of the forgotten eighteenth-century comedies, are in the laughing tradition, which is not to say that their humour has survived the passage of time. The example of one of Garrick's favourite plays is revealing.

Garrick was friendly with the Hoadly brothers, sons of a controversially outspoken Bishop of Winchester,[21] and an occasional participator in their amateur theatricals. Although generally ascribed to the older Benjamin (1706–57), *The Suspicious Husband* (1747) was probably the product of sibling collaboration. Between its first staging and his retirement, Garrick played the part of Ranger more often than any other in his repertoire. It is difficult to know why, unless he found Ranger's assertive masculinity an effective counter to the vocal minority who accused him of effeminacy. Ranger is peripheral to the main plot, though he provides some assistance towards the clearing of obstructions to the courtship of two friends. He is a rake in the Restoration tradition, a charmer whose favourite leisure activity is seducing women or, where seduction is insufficient, raping them. For eighteenth-century pornogaphers, and *The Suspicious Husband* borders on pornography, the female body was 'Merryland'.[22] During the great set piece of Act 3 – a foiled elopement, disguises, identities mistaken, concealments, frenzied exits and entrances and the vital properties of a rope ladder and a dropped hat – Ranger tries, as the action twice pauses for breath, to take two women by force. And yet, in the shamelessly sexist world of the Hoadlys, we are supposed to *like* the man. Fifty years later, in *Wives as They Were and Maids as They Are* (1797), Elizabeth Inchbald (1753–1821) has the virtuous Lady Priory divert the lust of the would-be rapist Bronzely (a character fashioned in Ranger's image) by knitting: an act of detumescent improvisation far subtler than anything the Hoadlys could have imagined. Inchbald's plays are too often burdened with an admonitory feminism to match Cowley's controlled ambivalence, but she is prominent among the playwrights who carried eighteenth-century laughing comedy into the nineteenth century.

Beyond a revival of *All in the Wrong* (1761) at the Orange Tree Theatre, Richmond in 1998, Arthur Murphy (1727–1805) has suffered much the same neglect as Cowley and Inchbald. Lawyer, biographer, poet, pamphleteer, translator and journalist, he was a versatile dramatist and, like George Colman, one of the finest craftsmen of comic afterpieces: *The Apprentice* (1756), *The Upholsterer* (1758), *The Citizen* (1761) and the scintillating *Three Weeks after Marriage* (1776). It was Murphy's championship of unpopular causes that threatened to blight his theatrical career then,[23] but he stands now as a fair representative of a theatre that knew well how to refashion French comedies for the English stage. Originality was no more a requirement at the end of the century than it had been in the age of Colley Cibber. Even *She Stoops to Conquer*, among the funniest comedies ever written, is composed of purloined episodes and characters.

Goldsmith, Irish like Sheridan and Murphy, had an outsider's insight into the class divisions that were taking shape in England as an industrial economy began its inroads into the agrarian establishment.

> Ill fares the land, to hastening ills a prey,
> Where wealth accumulates and men decay;
> Princes and lords may flourish, or may fade;
> A breath can make them, as a breath has made.
> But a bold peasantry, their country's pride,
> When once destroyed, can never be supplied.
>
> Olwer Goldsmith, *The Deserted Village* (1770), ll.51–6

The endlessly blundering Young Marlow of *She Stoops*, victim of Tony Lumpkin's disinformation, is already the sexual victim of his own snobbery. An expert chatter-up of serving wenches, he is tongue-tied in the presence of women of his own class ('They freeze, they petrify me'). His mistaking, under Lumpkin's prompting, of the home of his prospective bride for a country inn plays into the hands of comic actors. Not only is Marlow three characters in one – shy suitor, insolent upper-class guest, ladykiller – but so is Kate Hardcastle – sentimental romantic, witty lady, pert maid. In their own performances, they span the range from high to low comedy, gathering the audience with them as they move from one style to another. The immense good humour of the whole piece need not blind us to the fact that, as in all good comedies, something serious is being said. Marlow's journey through the play, insouciantly aided by Lumpkin as a mischievous but ultimately benevolent Puck, harks back to a Shakespearean pattern. Like Rosalind and Celia in *As You Like It*, and like the lovers in *A Midsummer Night's Dream*, Marlow has to go deep into the country to discover who he really is.

Chapter 9

Actors and acting

David Garrick, either in person or by reputation, dominated the London stage throughout the third quarter of the eighteenth century. Except by an iconoclastic minority, his supremacy was taken for granted. The fact that audiences believed that he had revolutionized acting is inescapable, the nature of that 'revolution' much more elusive. We can conveniently date it from 1741, a year which began with Charles Macklin's novel interpretation of Shylock at Drury Lane and ended with Garrick's crowd-pulling Richard III at the temporarily licensed playhouse in Goodman's Fields. Garrick, still a wine merchant by profession, had been spending off-duty time with Macklin, impressed by the Irishman's revisionary approach to rhetoric: first practise the lines as you would speak them in normal conversation, Macklin advised, and only then elevate them for performance. Before undertaking Shylock, he had read Josephus's *History of the Jews* and paid observational visits to London's Jewish quarter. His Shylock, played opposite a bemused James Quin's Antonio, was not the conventional comic grotesque. Macklin probably deserves the credit for being the first professional to envisage a systematic training for actors, and Garrick, to begin with, was his acolyte. The revolution was initially based on a new approach to elocution: as Garrick grew in confidence, it would evolve into a promotion of the sensuous above the merely aural.

Garrick or Quin?

Quin was nearing fifty when Garrick made his debut, and the conclusion of their vaunted rivalry looks, in retrospect, foregone. Quin was Rich's leading tragedian at Covent Garden when Garrick began his long association with Drury Lane, and Charles Churchill (1732–64) was recording the general memory when he wrote (in 1761, ten years after Quin's retirement) that 'No actor ever greater heights could reach / In all the labour'd artifice of speech' (*The Rosciad*, ll.949–50). By contrast, connoisseurs of the voice found fault with Garrick. Laurence Sterne has fun with one such connoisseur in *Tristram Shandy*.

> And how did Garrick speak the soliloquy last night? – Oh, against all rule, my Lord, – most ungrammatically! betwixt the substantive and the adjective, which should agree together in *number*, *case* and *gender*, he made a breach thus –; and betwixt the nominative case, which your lordship knows should govern the verb, he suspended his voice in the epilogue a dozen times, three seconds and three-fifths by a stop-watch, my Lord, each time.
>
> Lawrence Sterne, *Tristram Shandy*, Volume III (1761)

And yes, Garrick punctuated blank verse lines in a way that would have been anathema to Quin. He had an irresistible impulse to animate everything he touched. Richard Cumberland, in a famous recollection of their first appearance together, at Covent Garden in *The Fair Penitent* in 1746, contrasted the heavy-paced Quin with the young Garrick, 'light and alive in every muscle and in every feature'.[1] The novelty may have been more straightforward than has been generally admitted. As an old-school rhetorician, Quin would have considered it indecorous to move his feet while delivering his lines. The Garrick revolution may have been expressed by his moving about the stage when delivering set speeches, and doing it so naturally that few observers felt impelled to comment.

Much critical energy continues to be expended on a quest for the theory that underpinned eighteenth-century acting, Quin's as well as Garrick's. In Quin's case it is fairly clear that there was none. He spoke and acted, give or take physiological variations, as Barton Booth and Thomas Betterton had done before him. With Garrick the position is more complex. As early as October 1745, he was trying to borrow a copy of Francis Hutcheson's *Essay on the Nature and Conduct of the Passions and Affections* (1728),[2] and the extensive private library that he accumulated during the years of his prosperity contained a few volumes, the weightiest in French, that might broadly be termed theoretical; but his own *Essay on Acting* (1744), intended primarily to forestall attacks on his performance as Macbeth, adds nothing to received opinion on the portrayal of human passions, and only a few professional hints – delightfully in his advice to the actor of Macbeth after he has murdered Duncan.

> I hope I shall not be thought *minutely circumstantial*, if I should advise a *real* Genius to wear *Cork Heels* to his Shoes, as in this Scene he should seem to *tread on Air*.
>
> David Garrick, *An Essay on Acting* (1744)

The paradox of Garrick – the difference between his guileful preparation and the guilelessness of his reception – is neatly encapsulated here. This is the actor who used a system of wires to make Hamlet's hair stand on end when confronted by his father's ghost.

'No actor pleases that is not possess'd'

For Robert Lloyd, from whose 'The Actor' (1760) this subheading is culled, the golden secret of acting was to 'learn to FEEL'. Lloyd's poem pays homage to 'feeling Garrick', who, in tragedy, 'marks th' internal woe' with 'a single look', and, in comedy, provokes 'the laugh of sense'. Lloyd's formidable friend Churchill emphasizes the same quality in *The Rosciad*: it is the sting in the tail of his admiration for Quin's voice.

> Speech! Is that all? – And shall an actor found
> An universal fame on partial ground?
> Parrots themselves speak properly by rote,
> And, in six months, my dog shall howl by note.
> I laugh at those who, when the stage they tread,
> Neglect the heart, to compliment the head;
> With strict propriety their care's confin'd
> To weigh out words, while passion halts behind.
> To syllable dissectors they appeal,
> Allow them accent, cadence, – Fools may feel;
> But spite of all the criticising elves,
> Those who would make us feel, must feel themselves.
>
> Charles Churchill, *The Rosciad* (1761)

It was on his ability to convince audiences that he suffered or rejoiced *with* the characters he portrayed that Garrick built his fame. Ironically, though, it was Garrick who provided Denis Diderot with the clinching evidence of 'the paradox of acting' – that a skilled actor can make audiences experience emotions that he himself is not experiencing. Diderot (1713–84) was a polymath whose interest in actors, like Joseph Addison's before him, was part of a wider study of human behaviour.[3] His *Observations sur Garrick* (1770) arose from the English actor's impromptu performances in Parisian salons during his continental tour of 1763–5. Diderot would later incorporate them in his *Paradoxe sur le Comédien* (unpublished until 1830).

> Garrick will put his head between two folding doors, and in the course of five or six seconds his expression will change successively from wild delight to temperate pleasure, from this to tranquility [*sic*], from tranquility to surprise, from surprise to blank astonishment, from that to sorrow, from sorrow to the air of one overwhelmed, from that to fright, from fright to horror, from horror to despair, and thence he will go up again to the point from which he started. Can his soul have experienced all these feelings, and played this kind of scale in concert with his face?
>
> Denis Diderot, *The Paradox of the Actor* (c.1770)

Given the critical expectations of his age, it was in Garrick's interest to sustain the pretence that he *felt* what he was required to express on stage. To some extent, no doubt he did: certainly he found the daily repetition of tragic roles tiring, and increasingly avoided it. But we must always take account of Garrick's professionalism. No one worked as hard as he to win for actors a place among the professions in the nascent world of urban commerce, and few actors have been more successful at persuading audiences that they are seeing what they came to see.

Because theatre historians have devoted more attention to tragic than to comic acting, Garrick is most often placed in the great tradition of tragedians. There was, perhaps, too much mischief in him to remain there safely. Finding French actors too rigid, he protested that 'there must be *comedy* in the perfect actor of tragedy', though he was unprepared to go so far as to admit the humours to the domain of the passions.[4] Garrick's versatility was uncommon and much envied. Among major actors, only John Henderson, who died untimely in 1785, shared his ease in both comedy and tragedy, but Henderson was less prepared to compromise his reputation by acting in farce. Garrick, the all-rounder, not only played in farces but also wrote several. The comic trick was to locate the quirks of an allotted role and play them to the hilt. When Macklin was asked 'what is character?', his answer was that 'the alphabet will tell you. It is that which is distinguished by its own marks from every other thing of its kind'.[5] Garrick delighted Robert Lloyd because he was as happy in the possession of a humour as of a passion.

Garrick and society

From early in his career, Garrick enjoyed the friendship of the Cavendish family, in particular that of the Marquis of Hartington, heir to the dukedom of Devonshire. Hartington had married the daughter of Lord and Lady Burlington, whose ward Garrick's Austrian wife had been when they first met. His own marriage, not accomplished without initial opposition from Lady Burlington, lifted Garrick a step on the social ladder. He would advise the aspirant William Powell to cultivate friends in high society – and 'never let your Shakespeare be out of your hands, or your Pocket'.[6] It was advice that he himself followed assiduously. The editors of his letters have calculated that one-twelfth of his extant correspondence was addressed to people of title, and he confessed to Lord Lyttelton that 'It is my utmost pride and ambition to deserve the kind thoughts of the great and good.'[7] Not that the traffic was all one way. Garrick had a rare gift for being good company, and he returned his entertainment lavishly at the villa in Hampton that by 1754 he was rich enough to purchase. George III was a guest in September 1768, and Garrick hosted there a particularly splendid *fête champêtre*, with fireworks by Giovanni Torré, in August 1774.[8] By the 1770s the Garricks were regulars on the summer circuit of aristocratic country houses and counted as friends by political heavyweights such as the Earls of Halifax, Sandwich and Camden.

There were important, though more volatile, friendships with the cultural elite, too. Dr Johnson, Garrick's boyhood tutor in Lichfield, had his doubts, and his celebrated pupil's election to the inner circle of Johnson's literary club was delayed until 1773. Partly because he was sensitive about his own writing, Garrick's relationships with writers were fractious. The rejection of plays submitted for performance made enemies of playwrights, and there was a temporary breach even with George Colman, until then his closest theatrical ally. With painters – William Hogarth, Francis Hayman, Johann Zoffany, Benjamin Wilson, Thomas Gainsborough – Garrick was more relaxed. He was a discriminating collector of prints and pictures, something that needs to be borne in mind when assessing his transformative approach to the theatrical event.

In all of this Garrick was the great exemplar of an actor's legitimate access to the corridors of cultural power. It was only during his management of Drury Lane that the theatre became a necessary journalistic concern. Aaron Hill's *The Prompter* (1734–6) was a forerunner, but now that every new journal featured reviews of London productions, actors were public property. Their private lives were exposed in the notorious 'tête-à-tête' articles in the *Monthly Mirror* and the *Town and Country Magazine*, and Churchill's *The Rosciad* (1761), an imitation of Alexander Pope's *The Dunciad* but focusing only on actors, was greedily consumed by a reading public enamoured of theatrical gossip in whatever form. 'Actors, as Actors, are a lawful game', Churchill asserted in 'The Apology' (1761), his riposte to the published protests of some of the victims of his satire, and he continued to occupy his favourite seat in the front row of the pit at Drury Lane and Covent Garden, only a few feet from players whose efforts he had resoundingly mocked. There was always something of the bear-pit about eighteenth-century playhouses.

A visual theatre

Unstated but implicit in the debate about the relative merits of Quin and Garrick is an opposition of the aural and the visual: have you *heard* Quin? have you *seen* Garrick? Stage spectacle assumed an overriding importance during the second half of the eighteenth century, until by 1800 it accounted for the majority of Richard Brinsley Sheridan's expenditure at Drury Lane. Under Garrick's early management actors' salaries accounted for two-thirds of the annual outgoings, but it was, nevertheless, he who oversaw the development of a visual theatre attuned to a pictorially driven age. The Royal Academy of Arts, founded under George III's patronage in 1768, was a symptom of a developed taste. Its first librarian, Francis Hayman (1707–76), had begun his artistic career as a scene-painter, and his involvement with theatre continued alongside his activities as an easel artist.[9] It was Hayman whom Garrick asked to paint him as King Lear and Othello. His letters of advice to the artist reveal his painterly approach to theatre.

> Suppose Lear Mad upon the Ground with Edgar by him; His Attitude Should be leaning upon one hand & pointing Wildly towards the Heavens with his Other, Kent & Fool attend him & Glocester [*sic*] comes to him with a Torch; the real Madness of Lear, the Frantick Affectation of Edgar, and the different looks of Concern in the three other Characters will have a fine Effect; Suppose You express Kent's particular Care & distress by putting him upon one Knee begging & entreating him to rise & go with Gloster [*sic*].
>
>   David Garrick, letter to Francis Hayman, October 1745

What Garrick is here envisaging is closely comparable with the approved style of history painting (see, for example, John Singleton Copley's *The Death of Major Peirson* (1783) in Tate Britain, a picture which amply demonstrates the stage's return effect on painters). Actors of tragedy, it should be noted, were regularly urged by 'theorists' to look to history painting for inspiration, and Garrick's Shakespearean productions interspersed busy action with such tableaux. They contributed to the sensuousness of his own performances, in comedy as well as tragedy. When Laurence Sterne's narrator turns on the stop-watch connoisseur at the end of the passage quoted earlier in this chapter, it is the failure to use his *eyes* that condemns him.

> Admirable grammarian! – But in suspending his voice, was the sense suspended likewise? Did no expression or attitude or countenance fill up the chasm? Was the eye silent? Did you narrowly look? – I looked only at the stop-watch, my Lord. – Excellent observer!
>
>   Laurence Sterne, *Tristram Shandy*, volume III (1761)

It was during Philippe de Loutherbourg's decade at Drury Lane (1771–81) that Garrick's pictorial ambitions came closest to realization. De Loutherbourg had already established his reputation as an easel artist in Paris before his

Figure 13. John Singleton Copley's *The Death of Major Peirson*. Copley has
grouped his figures like a stage crowd around a featured actor.

arrival in London, and he continued to exhibit there almost until his death
in 1812. His work was characterized by the ferocity of his lighting effects and
the contrasting impact of a gloomy mass of rocks and hillsides seeming to
threaten human habitations, as in his *Coalbrookdale by Night* (1801), now
on show in London's Science Museum. They characterized his wildest stage
designs, too, adding overtones of the Gothic to the admired picturesque style.
Garrick had enlarged the capacity of Drury Lane in 1762 – as far as was possible
without demolition – but it was still an intimate theatre. De Loutherbourg's
innovatory lighting techniques – achieved through the play of coloured silks
in front of pivoted lanterns – were received, from pit to gallery, as magical.
He was an inventive machinist as well, ingeniously enacting the defeat of the
Spanish Armada for Sheridan's *The Critic* (1779). Above all, he had the vision
to translate landscape from canvas to stage. *The Wonders of Derbyshire* (1779),
of which de Loutherbourg was effectively the author, married pantomime to
travelogue, eleven of its twelve scenes having originated in on-the-spot sketches,
among them two (Gothic) caves, Matlock Tor at sunset, Dovedale by (Gothic)
moonlight. The progress towards the pictorial exhibitionism of the Victorian
stage was unstoppable after de Loutherbourg. It affected playwrights' choice

Figure 14. Philippe de Loutherbourg's *Coalbrookdale by Night*. It was with atomospheric scenery in the chiaroscuro style of this famous painting of industrialized Britain that de Loutherbourg advanced scenic art at Garrick's Drury Lane.

of subject and their conduct of dramatic action. Even so simple a stage direction as the one that opens Cumberland's *The Wheel of Fortune* (1795) harks back to de Loutherbourg: '*The cottage of PENRUDDOCK, seated in a group of trees, with a forest scene of wood and heath*'. Cottage and trees must be three-dimensional, the forest scene two-dimensional. Such an affecting mixture was brought about by de Loutherbourg's mechanical skill and visual imagination. Melodrama germinated on his enchanted stage.

A theatre for actors

The intimacy of the actor/audience relationship, as well as its metatheatrical range, continued to be exploited in prologues and epilogues. Garrick was at his entrepreneurial best in writing and delivering prologues, though he might concede the epilogue to a favoured actress whose flirtatiousness was designed to make the men in the audience feel good about themselves before leaving. More equal than the others Garrick may have been, but there were many who attracted public attention in an age of personality. The sudden vogue for theatrical portraits accompanied the proliferation of art exhibitions open to the public from about the middle of the eighteenth century. Anyone lucky enough today to get into the Garrick Club, where actors cover the walls like posters in a student bed-sit, will come away with a sense of surfeit. Minor artists (Gainsborough Dupont and Samuel de Wilde, for example) earned their living by portraying actors in role. Zoffany was at Garrick's beck and call, and even the great Sir Joshua Reynolds, whose potential clientele included the whole of wealthy London, had no evident sense of stooping when he chose theatrical subjects. Actors were perceived as representative public figures whose individuality could be captured on canvas and whose vices and virtues were as open to debate as those of politicians or preachers.

Garrick's queens of tragedy were Susannah Cibber (1714–66) and Hannah Pritchard (1711–68), though Pritchard was versatile enough to play comedy, too. They were unlike each other in almost every way. Born into the musical Arne family, Cibber was trained as a singer. Handel gave her the contralto role in the first performance of his *Messiah* (1741), but her preference was for acting. Always frail, she was better suited to Ophelia than to Lady Macbeth, a melter, rather than a seizer, of hearts. She and the slimline young Garrick[10] were physically compatible; plausible casting as Viola and Sebastian in *Twelfth Night*, had the male role been longer and stronger. Pritchard was much more robust, perhaps the finest Lady Macbeth before Sarah Siddons, but admired also for her Rosalind in *As You Like It* and her Beatrice in *Much*

Ado About Nothing. Taller than Garrick, whose lack of inches nagged at him constantly, she was undeterred by her increasing weight, which was about the only fault her detractors could find with her.

> Figure, I own, at first may give offence,
> And harshly strike the eye's too curious sense:
> But when perfections of the mind break forth,
> Humour's chaste sallies, Judgment's solid worth;
> When the pure genuine flame, by Nature taught,
> Springs into Sense, and ev'ry action's Thought;
> Before such merit all objections fly;
> PRITCHARD's genteel, and GARRICK six feet high.
>   Charles Churchill, *The Rosciad* (1761)

Her happy marriage, equability and blameless private life delighted Garrick, whose own marriage had been precipitated by a felt need to unsow the wild oats of his early manhood, not least his well-publicized liaison with the beautiful Irish actress Peg Woffington (*c.*1720–60), in order to bolster the respectability of his profession. Appearing for the first time in the 1749–50 Drury Lane season as Benedick opposite Pritchard's Beatrice in *Much Ado About Nothing*, Garrick announced to his public that he, like Benedick, was a bachelor no longer. This was the new, the *married* man.

Cibber was different, though largely blameless. Her 1734 marriage to Colley Cibber's yapping son Theophilus had been a mistake, the outcome of paternal pressure on both sides. Theophilus was in it for the money, *her* money, and when funds ran low he effectively sold her to the wealthy William Sloper while continuing to share house and board with the adulterous couple. Eventually – the *ménage à trois* had lasted at least eighteen months – Susannah moved out with her lover, and Theophilus immediately abducted her, later suing Sloper for alienating her affections. In separate lawsuits the court granted him £10 (he had asked for £5,000) and £500 (he had asked for £10,000). Not until his death by drowning did she and Sloper, himself a married man, finally shake Theophilus off, and by then her health was failing. The scandal of her life was painful to Cibber, who felt excluded from polite society by it. Society, though, was surprisingly forgiving. Hers was an unusual case, in which the stage persona was believed to be truer than the biography.

Garrick shared dominance of the comic stage with women more than men, though Henry Woodward (1714–77) should be better remembered. Dashing as Mercutio in *Romeo and Juliet*, he was celebrated for his eccentric Bobadil in Ben Jonson's *Every Man In His Humour* (1598) and acknowledged to be the finest Harlequin, often in pantomimes of his own devising, since John Rich. In their own low-comedy line, Edward Shuter (*c.*1728–76) and Thomas Weston (1737–76) followed the popular tradition of James Nokes, Joseph Haines, Thomas Doggett and William Pinkethman. There is an intriguingly continuous line, unbroken even by the closure of playhouses from 1643 to 1660, from such anarchic Elizabethan clowns as Richard Tarleton and Will Kemp to Shuter, Weston and beyond.[11] It is a line that passes through fairground booths, and that was (arguably) broken in England by 1855, when Smithfield's Bartholomew Fair, which had nurtured the talents of both Shuter and Weston, was discontinued. Shuter was one of many famous 'funny men' to be afflicted by melancholy in a private life that contradictorily mingled Methodism with alcohol. His oscillation between George Whitefield's tabernacle in Tottenham Court Road and a Drury Lane tavern became a journalistic joke, but audiences relished his (?drunken) habit of abandoning the text to address them directly. Weston, a chronic alcoholic, was different. It was his onstage absorption in a part that captivated.

The parts in which [Weston] excited such uncommon emotion, were those of low humour. He was the most irresistible in those of perfect simplicity: his peculiar talent was the pure personification of nature. I do not think it possible for an actor to be less conscious than Weston appeared to be that he was acting. While the audience was convulsed with laughter, he was perfectly unmoved: no look, no motion of the body, ever gave the least intimation that he knew himself to be Thomas Weston . . . I doubt if Garrick, or any other actor, had so complete a power of disguising himself.

    Thomas Holcroft, *Theatrical Recorder* (1806)

Literary scholars tend to forget that it was (to some extent still is) more often actors than plays that drew people to the theatre.

It was certainly Peg Woffington, supreme in breeches as George Farquhar's Sir Harry Wildair, who assured for *The Constant Couple* (1699) a place in the repertoire. Woffington and Kitty Clive (1711–85) were formidable women who could hold their own in any company. The fiery end of their relationship in 1745 kept Garrick and Woffington apart. She acted at Covent Garden while he, as manager of Drury Lane, sparred, generally good-humouredly, with Clive. A real thorn in Garrick's side was the temperamental Frances Abington (1737–1815), with whom he would have dispensed were she not indispensable. On and off stage, she played the lady of fashion, and the interaction of theatre and society is evident in her trend-setting adoption of the 'Abington cap' and loose, flowing gowns – almost negligées. Under new management, she was the logical choice for the role of Lady Teazle in *The School for Scandal* (1777), but Richard Brinsley Sheridan found her no easier to deal with than had Garrick,

Figure 15. Thomas Rowlandson's *Mrs. Abington on a Couch.* A lady of fashion in comfortable retirement.

and willingly released her to Covent Garden in 1782. By that time he had found her successor in the elegant Elizabeth Farren (1759–1829).

Rumblings of reform in society and theatre

Farren was the next actress to marry into the peerage. After a prolonged, and reportedly chaste, courtship, she became Countess of Derby in 1797, when the Earl's first wife died. Such matches are of more than idle interest. They tell us something about the changeable status of both theatre and aristocracy at a particular time. If actresses were seen as fair game by one side, an aristocracy in decline was a legitimate target for the other. The spirit of reform was strengthening, becoming for the first time sloganized, in the 1780s, partly as a shocked response to the destructive anti-Catholic Gordon Riots in London (1780) and partly in the disputatious aftermath of the American war – Britain's first recent taste of decisive defeat. In France the ancient power of the aristocracy was being challenged, and in England upper-class misbehaviour was more openly attacked than ever before: Charles James Fox's gambling habit, some argued,

Figure 16. Johann Zoffany's portrait of Elizabeth Farren as Hermione in *The Winter's Tale*. Unlike Thomas Lawrence, whose eye is on Farren as siren, Zoffany presents us with Farren the graceful actress.

rendered him unsuitable for political leadership, and as for his womanizing, was it not time for the law to stamp out adultery?

As they generally have, the 'top people' carried on regardless. Through the late eighteenth century and onward into the Regency period, society hostesses were not above doing a little on-the-sly procurement for their friends and relations. The Duchess of Devonshire, Fox's political ally, introduced the actress Mary Robinson (1758–1800) to four of the prominent men she slept with (they included Sheridan and Fox as well as the Duchess's brother-in-law, Lord George Cavendish). Robinson's better-known relationship with the future George IV was independently negotiated, but it was Fox's aunt, the Duchess of Leinster, whose special interest in Farren secured the friendship of the Earl of Derby. Thomas Lawrence's seductive portrait of Farren in 1789 shows her as she was seen by a susceptible man at the height of her stage career, and two years into her discreet but not secret relationship with her future husband. It was a time of hot gossip for society's upper crust. George III experienced a first bout of 'madness' in the autumn of 1788, thrusting before parliament the possibility of a regency and thus bringing his high-living eldest son into focus. Such close friends of the Prince of Wales as Sheridan assisted in the concealment of his marriage to the Catholic Mrs Fitzherbert,[12] in preparation for his assuming of high office, and the king's recovery in the spring of 1789, while greeted with public rejoicing, was privately regretted by the Prince's Whig adherents, among whom Fox and Sheridan were leaders.

The toast of the theatrical town, meanwhile, was Dorothy Jordan (1761–1816), a comic actress in the boisterous line of Kitty Clive. She had made her London debut in 1785 after learning the tricks of the trade on Tate Wilkinson's Yorkshire circuit, and she brought into Sheridan's Drury Lane an unfamiliar blend of the artful and the unsophisticated. Her qualities were perfectly suited to the part of Miss Prue in William Congreve's *Love for Love* (1695), in which she first caught the eye of the king's third son, newly created Duke of Clarence. Theirs is a story of 'virtual' marriage, during which she bore him ten children between 1794 and 1807, all of whom survived her and all but one him.[13] It was a love match; but royalty has its prerogatives. When Jordan had grown stout through childbearing, and when the possibility of the Duke's succeeding to the throne (which he eventually did as William IV in 1830) had become less remote, she was pensioned off. Her impoverished death in France might furnish the text, shared with Lola Montez, for a sermon on the incompatibility of stage and throne.[14]

Jordan was one of a new generation of actors whose careers flourished amid the ferment of the Age of Reform, with herself and John Bannister (1760–1836) at the forefront of comedy and Sarah Siddons (1755–1831) and her brother John

Philip Kemble (1757–1823) at the forefront of tragedy. Garrick had done his best to bring discipline to the random stage, but old habits died hard. Rehearsal remained haphazard, legitimizing the elder George Colman's complaint about his *Polly Honeycombe* (1760) that 'The first night's representation, like most other first nights, was nothing more than a Publick Rehearsal.'

[T]he Comedy [Arthur Murphy's 1760 *The Way to Keep Him*] will require four or five regular Rehearsals at least, and tho *You* may be able to appear with two, Yet I am afraid the rest of the Dramatis Personae will be perplex'd and disjointed if they have not the advantage of your Character to Rehearse with them.

David Garrick to Susannah Cibber, January 1760

It was at the Haymarket under the managements of Colman and his son, rather than at either of the patent houses, that something like ensemble performance was first discernible. It is, then, no surprise to read in Thomas Holcroft's diary entry on 25 June 1798 that 'Mr. Stoddart came to me from the play-house, to inform me, that the piece [Holcroft's *The Inquisitor*] had on this second performance, been well received; that the actors, who played vilely the first night, were greatly improved, and that his opinion of it was very much changed.'[15] And that was at the Haymarket!

Part Four

Theatre in the Age of Reform: 1789–1843

Chapter 10

The material circumstance

Before the 1780s, the use of the word 'reform' (rather than 'reformation') as a noun was uncommon. Over the half-century that led to the Representation of the People Act (1832), it was part of every thinking person's vocabulary. The act itself is generally known as the Reform Act, and the parliament that passed it as the 'Reform Parliament', but to see it as a culminating response to the demands of pressure groups is to forget how small its extension of the electorate actually was, and how little it changed the social composition of the House of Commons. The urge to reform the ways in which England, Scotland, Wales and (after the 1800 Act of Union) Ireland were governed was not halted but further encouraged by the events of 1832. My concern in Part Four of this book is to explore the effect on theatre of the reform ethos, but that is something that cannot be viewed in isolation.

Table of events referred to in Part Four	
1789	Storming of the Bastille
1792	Royal proclamations against seditious publications and vice
1793–1815	Near-continuous wars against France
1795	The Two Acts (Treason and Seditious Meetings)
1798	Irish rebellion
1800	Act of Union with Ireland
1807	George III's dismissal of the 'ministry of all the talents' – to prevent Catholic Emancipation. Abolition of the slave trade
1811–20	The Regency
1815	Victory at the Battle of Waterloo
1819	The Peterloo massacre
1820	Death of George III
1820–1	George IV and Queen Caroline in open hostility
1824	Repeal of Combination Acts
1829	Catholic Relief Act
1830	Death of George IV. Accession of William IV
1832	Reform Act
1833	Dramatic Copyright Act

1837	Death of William IV. Accession of Queen Victoria
1838	People's Charter presented to parliament. Emancipation of slaves completed
1843	Theatres Regulation Act

The French Revolution and its aftermath

The storming of the Bastille, viewed as a people's outcry against oppression, was greeted with enthusiasm by many of the English radicals who would speak out against 'Old Corruption' in their own country over subsequent decades. The response enforced on a reluctant George III and his ministers a recognition that preservation of the status quo could not be taken for granted. The argument, essentially Edmund Burke's in his famous *Reflections on the Revolution in France* (1790), that measures of (moderate) reform might avert revolution held force even in conservative circles, but the radical voice was Thomas Paine's in *The Rights of Man* (1791). Charged with sedition, Paine fled to France, but his work was discussed in the clubs, societies and associations that proliferated during the last quarter of the eighteenth century. William Godwin's *Enquiry Concerning Political Justice* (1793) expresses, not entirely naïvely, the anarchic utopianism of the reform movement. This seminal work concerns itself with matters outside the immediate range of politics, matters, in fact, that also attracted the attention of single-issue campaigners, like those calling for the abolition of the slave trade.

In 1787, the year in which the London Abolition Committee was founded, the Haymarket staged a play by the manager's son, George Colman the Younger. *Inkle and Yarico* is no kind of clarion call for abolition, though it might have been seen as mildly supportive of the Committee's campaign. Colman had gleaned the plot from Richard Steele's contribution to the *Spectator* 11 (1711): Thomas Inkle, a Bristol merchant shipwrecked on a desert island, is preserved by a noble savage/native princess, Yarico, whom (business before pleasure) he sells as a slave when the rescue ship reaches the West Indies, upping her price when he discovers that he has made her pregnant. In Colman's good-humoured version, Inkle redeems himself by changing his mind about Yarico, allowing the piece to end with a rousing eight-part sung finale. For William Wilberforce and the Abolition Committee, resolution was not so easily achieved, but national support for the movement was widespread. The 10,000 signatures on Manchester's 1788 petition had risen to 20,000 by the time of its successor in 1792. Despite opposition from interested ports such as Liverpool and Bristol, the trade was formally abolished in 1807 and slavery finally outlawed in all British territories in 1834.

Examples of 'reform' issues, 1789–1843

Medical practice (having gained independence from barbers in 1745, surgeons were granted their own charter of incorporation in 1800; Thomas Wakley's radical *The Lancet* was founded in 1824)

The slave trade (the trade was formally abolished in 1807, and slavery itself in 1834)

Payment of Church tithes

Costs and delays of the law

Conduct of lunatic asylums

Criminal sentences (including capital punishment)

Catholic Emancipation in Ireland

Maintenance of a standing army

Prison conditions

Workhouses and poor relief

Conditions in the navy

The Corn Laws

Working conditions of agricultural and industrial labourers

When the French Revolution degenerated into the 'reign of terror', the engine of reform stalled, and the years between 1792 (when a royal proclamation against seditious publications was issued) and 1795 (when the 'Two Acts' – against treason and seditious meetings – were passed) were, broadly speaking, counter-revolutionary. Thomas Holcroft, quietly spoken as a playwright but articulate in reformist political associations with his close friend Godwin, was one of those brought to trial for treason (and therefore for his life) in 1794. His crimes, if there were any, were his membership of the Society for Constitutional Information and his continuing support for the aims of the French Revolution. The case collapsed, and a sympathetic crowd cheered the released prisoners, but Holcroft's dramatic career was adversely affected.

If any person be desirous of having an adequate idea of the mischievous effects which have been produced in this country by the French Revolution and all its attendant horrors, he should attempt some legislative reform, on humane and liberal principles. He will then find, not only what a stupid dread of innovation, but what a savage spirit it has infused in the minds of many of his countrymen.

Samuel Romilly writing in 1808, *Memoirs of the Life of Sir Samuel Romilly* (1840)

Paradoxically, the wars against revolutionary and then Napoleonic France revitalized reformist politics. To meet the military costs the government deployed up to 30 per cent of the national income, fuelling complaints that 'Old Corruption' was making the rich richer while the poor (including wounded or demobilized soldiers and sailors) starved. Fear of invasion brought about militarization on an unprecedented scale.[1] The evangelically led Society for Bettering the Condition of the Poor, founded in 1796, was one kind of response to crisis; the naval mutinies at the Nore and Spithead in 1797 were another, more ominous. It was the impact on the rural population that turned William Cobbett (1762–1835) – a supporter of the government in the 1790s – into an agitator for reform. His *Political Register* would be a long thorn in conservative flesh from the day of its founding in 1816.[2] Euphoria following the victory at Waterloo in 1815 was short-lived. Castlereagh's brilliant diplomacy in the subsequent peace negotiations helped to postpone major European wars for a century, but did nothing to prevent the popular disturbances at home that were a feature of the Regency years (1811–20).

'Old Corruption'

John Wade (1788–1875) published the first cheap instalments of *The Black Book, or, Corruption Unmasked!* in 1819, the year of the Peterloo 'massacre' in Manchester, when local magistrates employed cavalry to disperse a peaceful crowd, leading to eleven deaths and more than 500 wounded. A highly readable catalogue of the abuses of a predominantly aristocratic elite, *The Black Book* became a weapon in the hands of militant reformists.[3] Wade, who had started his adult life as a journeyman wool-sorter, was one of a new breed of working-class journalists whose mission was to promote a fairer society by exposing the state parasites who pocketed the profits of the people's labour. Although *The Black Book* approaches economic details cavalierly, Wade's view that the landed elite had enhanced their wealth and position since 1780 has been upheld by subsequent study. The figure of the grasping landlord, who threatens the livelihoods of countless heroines (and not a few heroes) in nineteenth-century melodramas, was a reality throughout the British Isles. In Scotland the Highland clearances – the eviction of crofters and their replacement by sheep – had been underway since the 1790s; in Ireland Protestant landowners (absentees in some cases) continued to control the lives of their Catholic tenants after the crushing of armed rebellion in 1798; and in England grievance regularly erupted into violence, not least in protest against the protectionist Corn Law (1815), which had the effect of raising the price of the poor's essential commodity, bread. Exploitation of the labour force was more often assumed than politically contested in the theatre: a commonplace rather than an incendiary issue. Even so mild a radical as Frederick Reynolds (1764–1841) made it a theme of his comedy *Begone Dull Care* (1808). Here the villainous Danvers is shocked to find the employees of the St Albyn copper-works 'some dancing! – some at cricket![4] And none employed upon the works.' He is answered by Solace, superintendent of the mines: 'Aye; – honest lads! they have done full six days' work in five. – And they be not slaves – or if they were, why only rule their hands? Why not be master of their hearts? and gain by willing toil what force could never earn?' Solace is one of those salt-of-the-earth countrymen entrusted by dramatists with the responsibility of expressing the true English spirit.

> [T]hough we were all intended to aid, and benefit each other, yet selfishness do so creep in, that one half of the world, to load themselves with luxuries, do deprive the other of, almost, necessaries.
> Solace in Frederick Reynolds's *Begone Dull Care* (1808), Act 5, Scene 1

The lavishness and loose morals of high society were a cause for concern to George III and some of his ministers. Had not similar failings in France created the conditions for revolution? But the 1792 royal proclamation against vice rebounded on the king: James Gillray's cartoon of 'Vices overlooked in the Royal Proclamation' convicts George III and Queen Charlotte of avarice and their three eldest sons of, in chronological order, drunkenness, debauchery and gambling. The conduct of the pleasure-driven Prince of Wales was a source of particular anguish for his dutiful father and an easy target for hostile propagandists. It could hardly be denied that he squandered public money on women, racehorses and architectural projects (Carlton House and, later, the Brighton Pavilion among them), and only the privileged few knew of his educated interest in the arts. First as Prince of Wales, then as Prince Regent, and finally as George IV, he thrived on the exclusiveness of royalty and relished the elitism with which the Regency period is particularly associated. 'Old Corruption' was out in force at Almack's (the fashionable members-only club in St James's Street, founded 1765, but in decline after 1832), where admission to concerts and balls was tightly controlled, and at the opera.[5] Comparably with Restoration rakes, Regency bucks disported themselves in London's hotspots, opening themselves to the derision of reformists. They were like Nero, fiddling while the poor starved. The 'fancy' and the 'flash' mingled with the fashionable: the negative effects can be read in the lives of prominent men from Charles James Fox and Richard Brinsley Sheridan to Lord Byron and Edmund Kean, but it was the monthly publication of Pierce Egan's *Life in London* (1820) that caught the public eye. Taking as his model Ned Ward's *The London Spy*, Egan has Corinthian Tom introducing his country cousin Jerry Hawthorn to the pleasures of the city. Tom's indiscriminate delight in high or low entertainment is conveyed in the racy slang of the 'fancy', and Egan leaves critical response to the so-inclined reader. Watching drunkards from a distance, though, is a sobering experience.

The prolific William Moncrieff (1794–1857) cashed in by adapting *Life in London* for the stage. His *Tom and Jerry* (1821) was a sensational success at the Adelphi – it may have been the first play to achieve a continuous run of 100 nights – despite (or because of) the fact that complaints of its immoral tendency were made to the Lord Chamberlain. Sprinkled with songs, in compliance with the law that confined spoken drama to the patent theatres, and with its dialogue enlivened by Moncrieff's close adherence to Egan's slang, the play depended on the artistry of the scene-painters. It provided spectators with a tour of London,but it also exposed the emptiness of a daily round of mindless activities: 'Drinking, dancing, prinking, prancing, / Milling, billing, wetting, betting, / Playing, straying, bumbling, tumbling, / Smoking, joking, swagg'ring, stagg'ring', as one of its songs proclaims.

List of London scenes in *Tom and Jerry* (1821)

> The Burlington Arcade (for assignations or pick-ups)
> Tattersall's (for horse sales)
> Hyde Park Corner (to find a cab[riolet])
> Almack's ('brilliantly illuminated')
> Tom Cribb's parlour/gymnasium (Cribb had been a boxing champion)
> Temple Bar (the City side)
> Fleet Street (near St Dunstan's)
> Interior of the watch-house in St Dunstan's (where a constable is on duty)
> A fashionable 'Hell' (gaming house)
> The slums of St Giles
> Jackson's Rooms (for sporting gentlemen)
> Mr Mace's Crib in the East End (punningly known as 'All Max in the East')
> Chambers in the Albany
> Interior of a whistling shop (debtors' prison)
> Leicester Square

During the 1820s a language of class warfare was developing, aided by the repeal of the Combination Acts (1824) which allowed trade unions to declare themselves openly. Francis Place (1771–1854), an architect of the repeal, was another of the self-made men who spoke and wrote articulately in the dialect of the people. After apprenticeship to a breeches-maker (and, in 1791, leadership of an ineffective strike of breeches-makers), he prospered as a tailor in Charing Cross, where his shop became a meeting place for radicals. Place's meticulous amassing of evidence – on the conduct of lunatic asylums, on London's beggars, on education, and so on – would be of service to parliamentary committees, but it is his interest in the theatre that is of significance here. As a vehement promoter of 'rational recreation' for the working class, he recorded instances of abuse in order to challenge the privileged status of the patent theatres. It was in the interest of 'Old Corruption', Place argued, to reserve high art for the elite, but the national interest demanded open access. That the argument for art had political force was acknowledged in the Reform Parliament, by Sir Robert Peel (1788–1850) among others. The conservative claim that the patent duopoly sustained the national drama fell apart under Place's scrutiny and the critical gaze of theatrical connoisseurs. English drama was sinking in the ocean of privilege: how could liberation make it worse? Had French art declined when Paris opened the Louvre to the nation in 1793? Where was London's national gallery?

> In the present time of political excitement, the exacerbation of angry and unsocial feelings might be much softened by the effects which the fine arts [have] ever produced upon the minds of men.
>   Sir Robert Peel speaking in parliament, 23 July 1832

Interventionist drama

In his evidence to the 1832 Select Committee, John Payne Collier, deputy examiner of plays in the Lord Chamberlain's office, reported that the chief examiner – none other than George Colman the Younger – had instructed him to 'strike out or object to any profaneness, immorality, or anything political, likely to excite commotion'. Inevitably, such swaddling of the drama in nursery clothes impeded its growth. It is the basic joke of Reynolds's most popular comedy, *The Dramatist* (1789), that the title character should make the mistake of fashioning his plays out of 'real-life' incidents, in eventual acknowledgement of which he pretends that his latest effort is, just like a high proportion of 'new' English plays, 'from the French'. But France had also supplied a revolution, in the wake of which, however reluctantly, the old dispensation of 'enlightenment' England developed cracks. Some redefinition of royalty, aristocracy and the patriotic principle was inevitable, and, despite the endeavours of the Lord Chamberlain's examiners, the theatre was not impervious to the impulse for reform. Gillian Russell has provided fascinating evidence of the felt need for military control in provincial playhouses during the French wars, and George Taylor has located a discernible shift in London's dramatic taste – towards

Gothic terror and melodramatic polarities – in response to the revolution.[6] Russell and Taylor find in the ferment of the times a reason for both the writing and the popularity of Sheridan's *Pizarro* (1799), a play which by any other reckoning is an aberration. That Sheridan had a political motive for staging it cannot be seriously doubted: he was engaged at the time in a fierce struggle for power, in which his patriotism, and that of Fox's Whig faction, was being disputed. The speech given to Rolla, the heroic general defending Peru (= Britain) against the marauders from Spain (= France), is Sheridan's parliamentary rhetoric inserted into a dramatic text. They *say*, he is protesting, that we Foxite Whigs are republicans: no, we stand foursquare behind a *patriot* king.

> THEY [the Spanish/French], by a strange frenzy driven, fight for power, for plunder, and extended rule – WE, for our country, our altars, and our homes. – THEY follow an Adventurer whom they fear – and obey a power which they hate – WE serve a Monarch whom we love – a God whom we adore . . . They call on us to barter all of good we have inherited and proved, for the desperate chance of something better which they promise. – Be our plain answer this: The throne WE honour is the PEOPLE'S CHOICE – the laws we reverence are our brave Fathers' legacy . . . Tell your invaders this, and tell them too, we seek no change; and, least of all, such change as they would bring us.
>
> Rolla in Richard Brinsley Sheridan's *Pizarro* (1799), Act 2, Scene 2

It required the nerve of a Whig politician to say 'We seek no change' while striving to unseat the Tory government of William Pitt, and to hope to gratify George III himself[7] with the equivocal claim that 'The throne we honour is the people's choice.'

Patriotic sentiment, whether homespun or grandiose, was always acceptable to the Lord Chamberlain. Voices of protest on the domestic front were not. But his control over the minor theatres was much less assured – a grey area of the law – than his control of the patent houses' repertoire. It was at the Surrey, located south of the Thames on the busy Blackfriars Road, that John Walker's anomalous *The Factory Lad* was staged in 1832. Walker is a mystery; just possibly he was related to the outspoken and persecuted radical, Thomas Walker of Manchester, friend of Thomas Paine. *The Factory Lad* is certainly informed by its author's knowledge of working conditions in the Lancashire cotton mills, a setting unfamiliar to London audiences. The play is unusual in other ways, too. It lacks the happy ending already traditional in melodramas, and the near-demented anger of the firebrand Will Rushton, whose courtroom murder of the heartless mill owner brings down the curtain, seems to be shared by his creator. Walker was the first playwright to treat the industrial enmity of mill owner and labourer in class terms, and *The Factory Lad*'s portrayal of a proletariat on the brink of armed struggle is unique. Between it and John Galsworthy's judiciously measured *Strife* (1909), scarcely more than a handful of plays champion the workforce against the captains of industry.[8] Douglas Jerrold's *The Factory Girl* (1832), first performed at Drury Lane nine days before the Surrey opening of *The Factory Lad*, conceals its social criticism behind a conventionally pathetic plot.

Jerrold (1803–57), like his friend Charles Dickens, owed his brand of humane radicalism to personal experience. The son of a struggling provincial actor and theatre manager, he volunteered for the navy at the age of ten, first serving on a guardship at the Nore, and witnessing at first hand the brutality of naval discipline. His *The Mutiny at the Nore; or, British Sailors in 1797* (1830) was designed to alert audiences still infatuated with Lord Nelson to the harsher realities of life at sea. In this it contradicts the jolly jargon of his best-known play, *Black-Eyed Susan* (1829), which merits its popularity at the same time as reminding us that men like Jerrold – men and women like virtually all nineteenth-century dramatists – wrote plays to make money rather than to change the world or establish a literary reputation. His *Fifteen Years of a Drunkard's Life* (1828), one of a number of such cautionary plays, made its small contribution to the proliferation of temperance societies through the 1830s, but the most serious of his dramatic interventions, by virtue of its timing as well as its theme, was *The Rent Day* (1832). It was in domestic melodramas of this kind that a link between national and 'village' politics was forged.[9]

Jerrold's immediate inspiration was two genre paintings by David Wilkie (1785–1841). The painter had collided the tenant farmer's consciousness of an inability to pay with the nightmare prospect of eviction in frozen images which it was Jerrold's project to cajole into dramatic life. He must also have had in mind the recent exploits of 'Captain Swing' in the grain counties of eastern England, the violent expression of the rural poor's sullen hatred of the rural rich. Parliament had responded inadequately to the hardship years following the end of the French wars, when the agricultural labour market was flooded by thousands of demobilized soldiers. It was in Kent, on 28 August 1830, that the Swing rebellion started: a threshing-machine was destroyed. Over the next months there were also burnings of hayricks, attacks on overseers, riotous assemblies demanding the reduction of rents and tithes and an increase in wages and, to add a touch of the melodramatically sinister, the delivery to selected victims of anonymous threatening letters signed by 'Swing', or sometimes 'Captain Swing'. The rural cause was promoted in London by Richard Carlile (1790–1843), a defiant working-class radical who had leased the concert hall of the Rotunda in Blackfriars Road. A friend of Place and a publisher of vigorously subversive journals, Carlile varied his programme of political meetings with occasional

Figure 17. Sir David Wilkie's *The Rent Day*. Wilkie wrote a letter to the Drury Lane management, expressing his admiration for the way in which this first picture had been realized by the opening tableau and the second (Figure 18) by the curtain tableau at the end of Act 1.

Figure 18. Sir David Wilkie's *Distraining for Rent.*

theatrical events, one of which featured 'John Swing'.[10] An audience of close to a thousand crowded into a hall with an official capacity of 500. Violence spread from Kent to Sussex, Surrey, Hampshire, Wiltshire and further north through Essex, Bedfordshire and Cambridgeshire to Suffolk and Norfolk. Well into 1832, while Drury Lane was staging *The Rent Day*, Captain Swing continued his sporadic forays, and convicted agricultural labourers – the innocent along with the guilty – were being transported to Tasmania and elsewhere by the boatload. *The Rent Day* is not an incendiary play, nor even a manifestly angry one, but its opening in the first month of 1832 was at least a timely reminder to parliament of the urgency of reform.

William Cobbett continued his rural rides throughout the Swing rebellion: he was even accused of inciting it. More to our point, he wrote a play in defence of the equal rights of the labouring poor in rural England. *Surplus Population and Poor-Law Bill* (1831) was never performed[11] – there was no theatre manager brave enough to stage Cobbett – but it was (and is) thoroughly performable. Typically combative, Cobbett took issue, not so much with Thomas Malthus's population theory as with contemporary applications of Malthusian doctrine.[12] Why, the play asks, should the rural poor rather than the London rich be pressurized into marrying late (thus reducing the period of procreation), or reduced to poverty in order to make them ineligible for marriage? Squire Thimble, delighted by the recent reduction in poor relief, argues that impoverished couples should be separated 'upon the same principle that farmers separate rams from ewes and boars from sows', and the dastardly (there is no other word for him!) Sir Gripe Grindum plots to prevent the marriage of Dick and Betsey by kidnapping her and incarcerating her in London for his own uses. It is left to Farmer Stiles to defend the rights of those who work the land. There are, he admits, too many idle people in England: 'too many pensioners,[13] sinecure-people, place-men, stock-jobbers; too many parsons; too many who live on our labour; but, not a man too many of those who work; and not enough in harvest time . . . Why not check the breeding of those swarms of drones; why want to check the breeding of the bees only?' For Cobbett, the economic reality is that 'Old Corruption' costs the nation far more than its notional 'surplus population'.

> Why, there's the Hanoverian officers and their families, swallow up as much as the poor of one county; Saxe Coburg as much as the poor of another county; and Sir James Graham has told us that 113 place-men swallow up as much as the poor of six great counties; and the pensioners and other idlers, maintained out of the labour of the people, swallow up twice as much as all the poor put together.
>
> Farmer Stiles in William Cobbett's *Surplus Population* (1831),
> Act 1, Scene 6

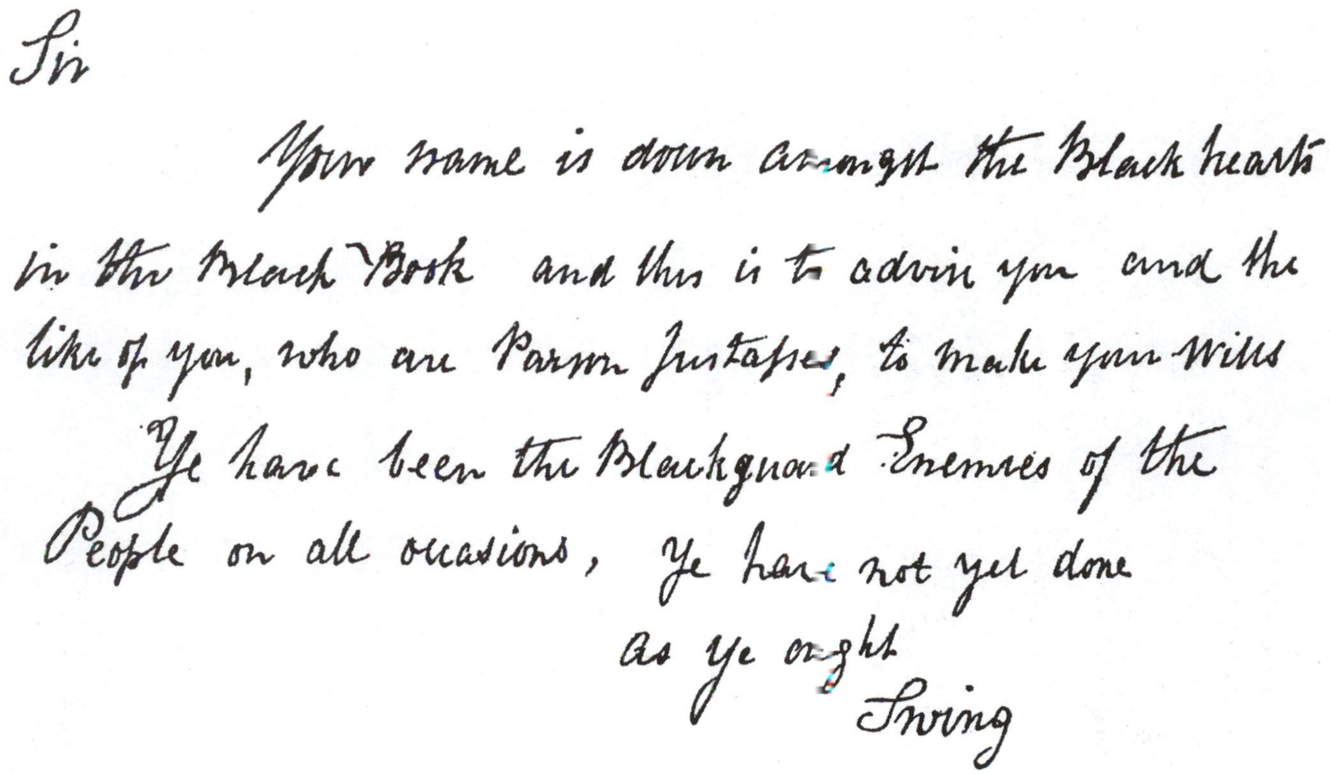

Sir

Your name is down amongst the Black hearts
in the Black Book and this is to adwis you and the
likes of you, who are Parson Justasies, to make your Wills

Ye have been the Blackguard Enemies of the
People on all occasions, Ye have not yet done

As ye ought

Swing

Figure 19. A 'Swing' letter.

Figure 20. 'Is this a rattle which I see before me?' One of many anti-Kemble cartoons brought out during the running battle of the Old Price Riots.

Set against Cobbett's muscular analysis, and despite its promising title, Moncrieff's *Reform; or, John Bull Triumphant!* (1832), staged at the Coburg in anticipation of the Reform Act, is vapidly nostalgic.

The Old Price Riots: 1809

Overwhelmed by the likely cost of maintaining the newly rebuilt Covent Garden, the acting manager John Philip Kemble fronted a decision to raise the price of seats. What followed was simultaneously a theatrically unprecedented demonstration of people power and, for the government, ominous evidence of the capacity of the underclasses to discipline their resistance to authority. The bare facts are these. Kemble elected to open the vast new playhouse on 19 September 1809 with *Macbeth*. Already costumed for the title role, he delivered the prologue through catcalls, hisses and boos (rattles, drums and brass instruments would be added later) which continued throughout the performance (afterpiece and all). Beyond the front rows and boxes close to the stage, the actors were inaudible – but they ploughed on. Such uproars were not new, and braving it out was part of an actor's 'bottom'. Wait till tomorrow – and tomorrow – and tomorrow . . . The protests were sustained for a further sixty-six nights, and Kemble (on behalf of the management) was forced finally to surrender to the public will. The details of the Old Price Riots are the subject of an excellent book-length study, which distinguishes between spontaneous popular outrage, orchestrating leadership (principally by the radical barrister Henry Clifford) and back-room support (by, among others, the Charing Cross tailor Place).[14] My interest here is in the man whom the rioters believed had provoked the storm of which he became the principal victim.

   Kemble had earned himself a place among the elite. Crowned at last, George IV would remember him as 'one of my earliest friends'.[15] The defiant dignity with which he confronted the rioters inside the theatre was received as provocation – an actor in the costume of 'Old Corruption'.

> The Throne of Taste a gloomy tyrant held,
> Who scorned his subjects meek, their claims repell'd,
> Forgot, inebriate with unbounded sway,
> That those who gave the crown, can take away,
> And full adopting, in prescription strong,
> That glorious maxim, 'King can do no wrong'.
> Impos'd new taxes, yet alledg'd no cause,

> And hir'd the Law to violate the Laws:
> This moved the Town, this imp'd its vengeance on
> To dash the diadem from the brows of John.
> Anon., *The 'Old Price'-iad* (1809)

It was, of course, unfair to single out Kemble. He had only a one-sixth share in the patent, and there is some gallantry in his shielding of Thomas Harris, the principal shareholder. Furthermore, there were sound reasons for financial retrenchment, and it might have been possible to argue that the new prices were being imposed within the terms of 'reform'. Instead, the rioters hijacked the language of the age. 'Reform' was acceptable, even necessary: 'innovation' was anathema – and this was innovation. Kemble and the management fell foul of an ambiguity at the heart of the reform movement: for every one reformist who sought radical change, there were ten John Bulls who associated reform with a return to the sturdy values of 'old' England.[16] It was no advantage to Kemble that Covent Garden was the only patent house in London in late 1809. Sheridan's Drury Lane had been destroyed by fire in February, and his company was to be temporarily housed at the Lyceum. The Old Price Riots focused public attention on the responsibility of a theatre that boasted possession of the national drama. Did Covent Garden belong to the management or to the nation?

Questions of ownership are fundamental to the age of reform, and confusion about the ownership of the national drama contributed to the progressive decline of Drury Lane and Covent Garden between 1789 and 1843. The value of the patents was affected by the speculative trading in shares that was a by-product of the French wars, and the patentees found themselves in open competition with the 'illegitimate' theatres that served the growing population of industrial London. Among those close to the patent houses were the Lyceum (1794), the Sans Souci (1796), the Sans Pareil – from 1819 renamed the Adelphi (1806), the Olympic (1813), the Strand (1830), the St James's (1835) and the Princess's (1836); south of the river, and familiarly called 'transpontine', were the well-attended Surrey (1809) and Coburg – later the Old Vic (1818); in the East End the Whitechapel Garrick (1830), the City in Cripplegate (1831), the City of London (1835), the Britannia in Hoxton (1841) and other short-lived ventures. The protection afforded by the patents during the eighteenth century was too fragile to be relied on in nineteenth-century courts, and the duopoly was an anachronism decades before its legal termination in 1843.

If you can't beat them, join them

Laws governing theatrical performance were moderately clear on one thing: only the 'royal' theatres could stage 'straight' plays – 'straightness' being defined by the *absence* of music rather than by the *presence* of anything valuable in its own right. Common usage, rather than any hard-and-fast legal formula, distinguished between 'legitimate' drama and 'legitimate' theatres and their 'illegitimate' rivals. This might have served the interests of Drury Lane and Covent Garden had it not been for two things. Firstly, financial need (or greed) had transformed the intimate playhouses of the eighteenth century into capacious stadiums: Sheridan's rebuilt Drury Lane (1794) could accommodate more than 3,500 and the new Covent Garden (1809) 3,000. The human voice is hard-pressed to command such spaces, and their monopoly of the spoken drama was a dubious asset. Secondly, popular preference for gaudier entertainment reduced the appeal of 'legitimate' plays, particularly new ones. Audiences might clamour to see Sarah Siddons as Lady Macbeth or George Frederick Cooke (if drunk, so much the better) as Richard III, but what was so special about Thomas Holcroft's new comedy, *Love's Frailties* (Covent Garden, 1794)?[17] There is no commercial advantage in holding a monopoly on products you are ill-equipped to sell, and it is in this context that the chorus of contemporary complaints about the decline of British drama should be assessed.

Bucking the trend has rarely been a practice of theatre managers, and it is unsurprising that the repertoire of the patent houses during the Age of Reform moved closer to that of the illegitimate theatres. Reynolds's melodramatic *The Caravan* (1803) brought crowds to Drury Lane, not because of its merits, but because the management found the right dog to perform the leap from a rock into a raging torrent to rescue a drowning child. Reynolds would later recall Sheridan's nomination of the dog as guardian angel and preserver of Drury Lane.[18] And one of the worst plays by the biddable Moncrieff, *The Cataract of the Ganges*, was the sensation of Drury Lane's 1823–4 season purely on the strength of its final scene.

Bramins seize Zamine – she shrieks and struggles – Iran and Jahrejahs break through the burning brushwood in the back ground, and drive Mokarra and Bramins off – Zamine rushes into Iran's arms – the burning trees fall on all sides, and discover the terrific Cataract of Gangotri, supposed to form the source of the Ganges – the Emperor and the Bramin's troops appear, pouring down the rocky heights around the Cataract in every direction.

William Moncrieff, *The Cataract of the Ganges* (1823), Act 2, Scene 6

The spectacle is capped when Zamine, the heroine, mounts her lover's horse and rides up the cataract to safety. By 1823 Drury Lane was in the hands of the unshamable Robert Elliston (1774–1831), whom Charles Lamb dubbed the 'Great Lessee', and who had cut his managerial teeth at the illegitimate Surrey and Olympic. The downmarket drift of the patent houses was met by an upmarket drift at some of the minor theatres, where the inclusion of music as a legal requirement (at least five songs per act was Colman's rule of thumb) was frequently ignored.

By 1832 – the reform year – the situation was blatantly in need of redress, and Edward Bulwer MP (always a believer that he was the man for whom the hour cometh) proposed the establishment of a select committee on the theatre. Bulwer (1803–73)[19] had probably determined the committee's conclusions before its first meeting: the patent monopoly should be abolished, playwrights should be protected by a strengthening of dramatic copyright and the powers of the Lord Chamberlain should be redefined. The committee questioned playwrights, managers and interested parties (Place, by now two years married to a Covent Garden actress, among them[20]), carried its proposals through the House of Commons – and had them rebuffed by the House of Lords. Bulwer's personal response was to launch himself as a playwright in an attempt to halt – singlehanded if necessary – the decline of the drama in the face of the conditions that, he believed, had brought about that decline. His plays, particularly *Richelieu* (1839) and *Money* (1840), are among the age's best in their different kinds. When the Theatres Regulation Act was eventually passed in 1843, it authorized *one* of the recommendations of Bulwer's Committee: the patent monopoly over the spoken drama was ended. It was a watershed of a kind, but the signature on the royal assent was Queen Victoria's. A new age was in its infancy.

I say you're free to act where'er you please.
No longer pinioned by the Patentees,
Need our immortal Shakespeare mute remain,
Fixed on the portico of Drury Lane;
Or the nine Muses mourn the Drama's fall,
Without *relief*, on Covent Garden's wall.
Sheridan now at Islington may shine;
Marylebone echo 'Marlow's mighty line';
Otway may raise the waters Lambeth yields,
And Farquhar sparkle in St. George's Fields;
Wycherley flutter a Whitechapel pit,
And Congreve wake all 'Middlesex to Wit'.
    J. R. Planché, *The Drama at Home; or, An Evening with Puff*
    (1844)

The new age

Victoria came to the throne only seventeen years after the death of her grandfather, George III, but hers was a very different country from any he had known. The grip of the aristocracy was altogether looser, John Debrett's *Peerage of England, Scotland and Ireland* (1803) and his *Baronetage of England* (1808) notwithstanding, and the royal prerogative, if used at all, had to be used sparingly. When George III dismissed the 'ministry of all the talents' in 1807 – to forestall the emancipation of Catholics – it was the last such exercise of regal authority. By 1829 George IV – equally opposed to Catholic Emancipation – recognized the need to surrender his assenting signature to it. The inauspicious start to his reign, when popular outrage over his treatment of Queen Caroline, brilliantly orchestrated by Cobbett, turned him into a figure of fun and loathing, went some way towards disempowering him, and the quasi-personal monarchy of George III was very different from the constitutional monarchy of his successors. It was not Queen Victoria but the government that the Chartists targeted after 1837. The People's Charter, which, after its presentation to parliament in 1838, continued to gather adherents during 'the hungry '40s', was the fiercest expression of working-class grievance that those in authority had ever encountered. Police surveillance of East End theatres, particularly Samuel Lane's Britannia in Hoxton, suggests that the Charter was at least tacitly endorsed in their repertoire, as it surely was among the exclusively working-class audiences of London's generally unrecorded penny gaffs.[21] The spirit of Walker's *The Factory Lad* must have been released into the theatres of the 1840s. If it has remained, for the most part, invisible, that reflects the alertness of the Lord Chamberlain's Office to the risk of insurrection. It also conceals the power of the actor to express more than the text.

One 'innovation', at least, proved irresistible. The illuminating properties of coal gas had been confirmed before the end of the eighteenth century. For the opening of the 1815–16 season, Covent Garden's playbill announced that the exterior and foyer 'will be illuminated by gas', and in August 1817 the Lyceum audience was promised that 'The GAS LIGHTS will this Evening be introduced over the whole Stage.' After that, the Haymarket was the only one of London's theatres to procrastinate. In 1833 Alfred Bunn, the new lessee of Covent Garden, noted his theatre's employment of 1,200 gas burners, and the greater brilliance of limelight was everywhere available before 1840. It is as difficult to imagine as it is to overstate the effect of gaslight on actors and audiences. What is certain is that it gave a new dimension to onstage action. Instead of performing *in front of* the scenery, actors could move visibly *inside* it. The idea of the moving picture, literally exploited by Jerrold in *The Rent Day* and sensationally by Moncrieff in *The Cataract of the Ganges*, had come into material being.

Chapter 11

The drama

Anxiety about the quality of the national drama reached new heights during the Age of Reform, when attention was repeatedly drawn to reliance on continental plots as the source of 'English' plays. The virtues of invention, vaunted by critics, were neglected by working dramatists. Let Thomas Holcroft be our example. The self-taught son of a shoemaker, Holcroft forced himself to learn French, German and a smattering of Italian in order to earn a living through translation and by writing 'English' plays. *The Maid of the Vale* (*c.*1778) was snatched from Goldoni, *The German Hotel* (1790) and *Love's Frailties* (1794) from minor works of the German *Sturm und Drang* school, *A Tale of Mystery* (1802) from the French of Pixérécourt. The list could be prolonged. Most famously, in late September 1784 Holcroft went to Paris solely in order to pirate Beaumarchais's *Le Mariage de Figaro*, which he achieved by repeated attendance at performances during which he surreptitiously recorded the dialogue. Under the title of *The Follies of a Day*, his version opened at Covent Garden within a few weeks of his return to England. And yet Holcroft, the persecuted radical, was recognized even by his political enemies – primarily on the strength of his highly derivative comedy, *The Road to Ruin* (1792) – as one of the most original of contemporary playwrights. Knowing his views, it is possible to read 'reform' into some of his lines, but more honest to acknowledge how carefully (much more carefully in his plays than in his novels) he stuck to the middle of the road.

Middlebrow drama

Holcroft is one among many who might have written better plays for a different theatre. If an audience had been asked, in 1800, to nominate the major active playwrights, the list would certainly have included George Colman the Younger, Frederick Reynolds and Thomas Morton (1764–1838). Freer thinkers might have added Holcroft and Elizabeth Inchbald. The relegation of all these people to the minor leagues of dramatic history reflects a shift in taste which was more or less complete by 1843. Rather than rocking the eighteenth-century boat, they rowed it; but they rowed it into a few new inlets, and they deserve to be better remembered. Their common problem was the control of language during a period when the time-honoured assumptions about appropriate diction were being programmatically unsettled.

> The majority of the following poems are to be considered as experiments. They were written chiefly with a view to ascertain how far the language of conversation in the middle and lower classes of society is adapted to the purposes of poetic pleasure.
>
> William Wordsworth, advertisement to *The Lyrical Ballads* (1798)

The playwrights who provided the best of the 'middlebrow' drama were good writers, but, anxious to gratify audience expectation, they imposed on their characters acceptably distinct modes of speech rather than letting them speak for themselves. This is a problem from the outset of Colman's extraordinarily moovy (and which ought also to have been extraordinary popular) *The Mountaineers* (1793). Here we have two Christian prisoners of the Moors in dialogue. One is the Spanish Count Virolet and the other Captain Kilmallock – a stage nobleman and a stage Irishman. The Count has a secret to impart.

> VIROLET: Come, I will trust thee. I do know thee brave;
> And in the breast where fire-eyed Courage rears
> Her rugged throne, sure honour must inhabit.
> Yet, dare I trust thee?   *(Wavering)*
> KILMALLOCK: Dare you? Look you, Count Virolet! you dare do much! – for you are the first that ever dared tell me to my teeth, he held my honour in doubt. Och, fire and oons, and Saint Dominick, to boot!
>
> George Colman the Younger, *The Mountaineers* (1793), Act 1, Scene 1

And the pairing of Shakespearean pastiche and stage-Irish vernacular stumbles on for four more minutes of audience time. Only rarely, during the whole course of the three acts, are two characters speaking the same language to each other.

There are, of course, alternative approaches to this kind of schematic mismatching. We can find it bathetic and contemptible, or we can relish it. Colman was as good as anybody at approximating Shakespeare's blank verse, and better than most at writing comic songs. The taste of the time allowed him to combine his talents at random. There is, for example, a show-stopping moment at the end of Act 2, Scene 2. Count Virolet and his Moorish sweetheart Zorayda take shelter from the approaching army of vengeful infidels ('the next bank, o'ercanopied with trees, / Must now, perforce, be thy rude lodging, sweet'), leaving Kilmallock to keep silent watch. In total defiance of the plot's urgent demand for concealment, our gallant Irishman bursts out with a (very funny) comic song, detailing the disasters of his first bout of love back in Tipperary. Spilled equally casually into *The Mountaineers* are episodes of Gothic gloom, tub-thumping Christianity and patriotic diatribes. It is a play totally out of touch with seriousness, despite its crusading 'conversion of the Moors' theme. Colman – it is probably his saving grace – could never be serious for long. When he dramatized William Godwin's political novel *Caleb Williams* (1794) as *The Iron Chest* (1796), he left the politics out, producing a Gothic melodrama interspersed with jolly songs. When he delved (unstrenuously) into history with *The Battle of Hexham* (1789) and *The Surrender of Calais* (1791), he produced the same kind of mix-and-match hodge-podge, with characters designed to suit the strengths of his Haymarket company. It was, you could argue, writing by numbers; but the numbers added up in ways that have always produced theatrical satisfaction.

Colman's strongest claim on posterity is probably *John Bull; or, The English-man's Fireside* (1803). 'To know the temper of the times with accuracy', wrote Inchbald in her edition of the play, 'is one of the first talents requisite to a dramatic author.' That Colman's John Bull should be so resolutely middle class as the provincial brazier Job Thornberry is expressive of 'the temper of the times', and the scene of his confrontation with 'Old Corruption' in the person of Sir Simon Rochdale (Act 5, Scene 2) is a fine one. Colman had studied (unstrenuously again) for the law, and the quarrel over the proper administration of justice is cleverly layered. It is, as so often in post-Restoration drama, in its exaggerated language of love that *John Bull* falters. The young lovers – and love itself – crumble under the weight of their vocabulary. This is not a problem confined to the drama – it afflicts novelists from Walter Scott to Charles Dickens – but it raises questions about audience expectation within the *real* time of theatrical performance. How was a sentence like this of Frank Rochdale's spoken? 'By acceding to this match, in obedience to my father, I leave to all the pangs of remorse, and disappointed love, a helpless, humble girl, and rend the fibres of a generous, but too credulous heart, by cancelling, like a villain, the oaths with which I won it.' And how was it received? With their clauses in apposition, their similes, parentheses and alliteration, such speeches *may* both look and sound carefully composed, but they are universal, not particular. Main-plot lovers are carelessly undifferentiated. They speak an imaginary language, in which the final word of a sentence is already determined before the first word is uttered, and in this they cut themselves clear of the fumbling, felt experience of every lover in an audience.

John Bull is one of Colman's rare ventures towards the classic genre of five-act comedy. Much more characteristic are the middlebrow 'mixed dramas' which he helped to popularize, and of which Morton's *Speed the Plough* (1800) is a riotous example. Morton was an unfailingly affable pilferer of plots and characters who, like Colman, escaped from the burden of legal training into the theatre, where he settled for providing audiences with more of the same, whatever particular 'same' he had in mind at the time. Nothing implausible was outside his dramatic grasp. Children, wives and brothers are lost like safety-pins only to be rediscovered just where the audience must have hoped they were. In *The School of Reform* (1805), which ought by its title to have been a political play, Lord Avondale corrects his callousness when he discovers that his secretary is his lost son and his lost wife lives near by. The 'reform', that is to say, is nothing more than a fifth-act change of heart partly prompted by the 'evidences of my shame' concealed in a box (we might have expected a peer of the realm to have the sense to dispose of the incriminating cloak, mask and pistol).

The School of Reform is one of many plays staged in England after 1790 to have drawn on the German of August von Kotzebue (1761–1819). Emotional excess, still sometimes confused with Romanticism, was Kotzebue's stock-in-trade.[1] Richard Brinsley Sheridan stole *Pizarro* (1799) from him, and Benjamin Thompson's adaptation of his *Menschenhass und Reue* as *The Stranger* (1798) provided John Philip Kemble with one of his most famous roles (Kemble could mingle aloofness, gloom and pathos like nobody else). The Gothic main plot of *Speed the Plough* was borrowed from Kotzebue, too, but Morton threw into it almost everything else that he or his intended actors liked – including, in the homely ambience of Farmer Ashfield's family, the kitchen sink. Preposterous it may be, but the resultant play is a glorious piece of theatrical mayhem. To read it is to encounter most of the dramatic styles of the age – melodrama certainly, but also farce, spectacle, pantomime and comedy (both sentimental and 'laughing'). To see it fully staged by a major company with an unrestricted budget would be, for audiences able to free themselves of intellectual snobbery, a revelation.[2]

It would not have pleased Edward Bulwer to find himself included under a 'middlebrow' heading, but his comedy *Money* (1840) and the young Dion Boucicault's *London Assurance* (1841) are the best available evidence of the shift in taste that had made Colman and his contemporaries seem old-fashioned by 1843. *Money* is written in a wholly recognizable idiom, and every incident has a bearing on the unifying plot at the same time as illustrating its thematic *raison d'être.* That theme, which the play unexpectedly fails to contradict, is that wealth, not worth, is what society respects. It is a defect that this point is already established at the end of the superbly crafted first act. At the beginning of the act, Sir John Vesey's factotum Alfred Evelyn is so insignificant that nobody (except, of course, the audience – he is, after all, being played by the actor-manager William Charles Macready) notices his entrance. At the end, having inherited the riches of the man whose will his 'betters' have assembled to hear read, he is centre-stage. Bulwer's clever conduct of the plot (there is another example of outstanding dramatic craftsmanship in the 'Crockford's scene' (Act 3, Scene 3), in which Evelyn apparently gambles himself towards bankruptcy) ensures that he remains at the centre from then on, but there is no significant variation on the theme. *Money* was successfully revived by the Royal Shakespeare Company in 1982 and the Royal National Theatre in 1999, though with some necessary editing of the still-indigestible language of love.

> There, it is decided! A few days, and we are parted for ever – a few weeks, and another will bear his name – his wife! Oh, happy fate! She will have the right to say to him – though the whole world should hear her – 'I am thine!' And I embitter their lot – I am the cloud on their joyous sunshine! And yet, O Alfred, if she loves thee – if she knows thee – if she values thee – and, when thou wrong'st her, if she can forgive, as I do – I can bless her when far away and join her name in my prayer for thee!
>
>   Edward Bulwer, *Money* (1840), Act 3, Scene 1

It is Evelyn's destined 'true love' Clara Douglas who (having evidently swallowed an out-of-date dictionary) is speaking here. It is only because they have been infected with Hugh Kelly's 'false delicacy' that the lovers take so long to discover their mutual passion, and their scenes together are weighed down by punitive altruism. Bulwer, who had an ear for snappily 'modern' dialogue, was still as dependent on the cloyingly conventional rhetoric of love as he was on the convention that allowed characters to speak their thoughts aloud – and sometimes to be conveniently overheard while doing so. Although touched by naturalism, *Money* is not a naturalistic comedy.

London Assurance has been more easily accommodated in the modern repertoire largely because Boucicault (1820–90) found a way of evading the excesses of troubled love. *Money*, despite the supposed stranglehold on spoken drama of the patent theatres, had been staged at the Haymarket, and was still running when *London Assurance* was brought out at Covent Garden. It was the first triumph of a young man who would become a power in the Victorian theatre. Looking back on it later, Boucicault remembered[3] that Charles Mathews, joint-lessee with his wife Madame Vestris, had invited him to write 'a five-act comedy, depicting London fashionable life as it exists today'.[4] The young novice did just that, setting *London Assurance* 'in London and Gloucestershire in 1841'; but he was a slippery customer, and the play, for all its boasted modernity, has a Regency feel. As James L. Smith observes, the finished piece looks like a Georgian comedy of manners: 'a witty and satiric prose play in five acts, about the love intrigues of a few stock characters from the leisured classes, tinged with rural sentimentalism and resolved by moral criteria'.[5] Dazzle, the part tailored for the spectacularly relaxed Mathews, is one of the 'flash', brazenly crashing a party of the fashionable, and Sir Harcourt Courtly is a superannuated fop after the school of Sir John Vanbrugh and Colley Cibber. There is never much doubt about the outcome, and the narrative is sustained by the fatuous behaviour of the characters who cavort around it. Various subplots are neatly threaded onto a main plot which brings about the engagement of the initially untouchable Grace Harkaway to the initially unlovable Charles Courtly. When the flimsily floating comedy threatens to sink, Boucicault bales it out with farce.

Where *Money* offers to locate a fundamental fault in contemporary values, *London Assurance* makes fun of marginal foibles – an excessive love of hunting, a slavish adherence to the dictates of the London 'season' (from late April to early July – before the fashionable exodus to Bath or Brighton), the current cult of 'dandyism' and so on. If the excessive regard for wealth is the theme of Bulwer's play, Boucicault's questions the efficacy of metropolitan suavity (London 'assurance'). It is a quality fingered by the perceptive Lady Franklin in *Money*: 'A man of fashion in the last century was riotous and thoughtless – in this he is tranquil and egotistical' (Act 1). Dazzle is Boucicault's epitome of this new man, justly rebuked, along with Charles Courtly, in the play's final speech: 'Barefaced assurance is the vulgar substitute for gentlemanly ease, and there are many who by aping the *vices* of the great imagine that they elevate themselves to the rank of those whose faults alone they copy.'[6] And it is notable that the resolution of both plays is reached only when a legacy is finally bestowed on the two people whose love provides the happy ending, a pointer to the fact that most nineteenth-century plots – of melodrama as well as comedy, of novels as well as plays – boil down to struggles over the rightful possession of money. True love deserves the swag, and poverty is its death-knell.

There are two significant footnotes to *London Assurance*. Firstly, its five acts are unbroken by subdivision into scenes.

The French method of occupying the stage with only one scene per act was, it is believed, introduced to the English stage on this occasion. But the extravagance of innovation was reached when the author suggested that a *carpet* should be

used in the drawing-room. 'What next?' murmured John Cooper, the stage-manager. 'He will be asking for real flowers and real sunlight in the garden.'
Dion Boucicault, 'The Debut of a Dramatist' (1889)

The detail of Boucicault's recollection is not to be trusted, but it contains matter of importance. To sustain the action in a single location for thirty minutes required a new approach to dramaturgy, paving the way for the 'realism' of Tom Robertson, Arthur Wing Pinero and Henry Arthur Jones. And its corollary – the second footnote – is picked up by the '*carpet*'. The Vestris/Mathews management was famous for the care it took over the furnishing of its plays. With only five scenes (four if Acts 4 and 5 are played in the same drawing room) to provide, they could afford to indulge their taste. Wings, borders, sliding screens and painted backdrops facilitated rapid changes of location, but where rapidity was unnecessary (and with audiences tolerant of long *entr'acte* intervals), scene-designers – the well-established Grieve family in the case of *London Assurance* – could provide something more solid. The box set, which encased most British plays for a century from the 1860s, was embryonic in the Covent Garden production of *London Assurance*, and the 'Decorations and Appointments' (by Mr W. Bradwell) were an applauded feature.

Drawing-rooms were fitted up like drawing-rooms, and furnished with care and taste. Two chairs no longer indicated that two persons were to be seated, the two chairs being removed indicating that the two persons were not to be seated.
Charles Dickens Jr, *The Life of Charles James Mathews* (1879)

Highbrow drama

Seven months after staging *London Assurance*, Vestris and Mathews premiered *Old Maids*, a comedy by James Sheridan Knowles (1784–1862). It is in blank verse throughout: Knowles was jealous of his reputation as a poetic playwright in the great tradition. Posterity's verdict that he was overpraised, perhaps spoiled by praise, in his own time is a fair one.[7] At various times a vaccinator, schoolteacher, actor, journalist and itinerant evangelist, he was always an overreacher within the nineteenth century's peculiarly introverted style of overreaching. But he is not a *bad* playwright, just an out-of-date one. *Virginius* (1820), which catapulted him to fame, borrows its blank verse from Elizabethan drama without surrendering its contemporaneity. It is a tragedy about middle-class fatherhood, decked out in, but not disguised by, trappings of ancient Rome. John Webster (with Thomas Heywood) had treated the same story in *Appius and Virginia* (*c*.1608), but the change of title advertises a change of focus. Appius, a place-proud decemvir, lusts after a centurion's daughter. For Webster, the horror is the brutal abuse of power which causes the centurion to save his daughter by killing her. For Knowles, the horror is the father's anguish. The 'fate worse than death', which is a threat regularly averted in melodrama, can be averted in tragedy only by death itself. We have to accept Knowles's verdict that Virginia has no say in the matter.[8] The fifth-act focus is on her father's descent into madness. Knowles is here at full stretch to do something different with blank verse. The language reaches a mid-point between bathos and Robert Browning, and although there are resonances from King Lear, the texture is nineteenth-century.

> I did dream
> That I had murder'd her. 'Tis false! 'twas but
> A dream. She isn't here, you say. Well, well!
> Then I must go and seek her elsewhere. Yet
> She's not at home – and where else should I seek her
> But there or here? Here, here, here! Yes, I say,
> But there or here – I tell you I must find her –
> She must be here, or what do you here?
>
> James Sheridan Knowles, *Virginius* (1820), Act 5, Scene 3

In order to represent ideal paternity, Knowles has amalgamated *King Lear* and *Coriolanus* into a domestic drama.

Like Bulwer, Knowles was theatrically nurtured by Macready (1793–1873), who was behind many of the highbrow ventures of the mid-century stage, and whose portrayal of suffering fathers had deep autobiographical roots. On the page, a thirteen-word speech may be unspectacular, but, spoken by Macready, it shook Covent Garden's vast auditorium: 'I never saw you look so like your mother / In all my life!' (Act 4, Scene 1). Fathers vied with mothers at the pathetic centre of nineteenth-century fiction, but Knowles never matched the success of *Virginius*. *William Tell* (1825), written at Macready's suggestion, is a limply predictable paternal period-piece, and the most interesting thing about *Alfred the Great* (1831) is its published dedication to William IV, 'A Patriot Monarch', who will 'rescue a devoted people from the ravages of the worst of invaders – Corruption'. If Knowles is ever to undergo a revival, it is more likely through such comedies as *The Love-Chase* (1837) and *Old Maids* than through his attempts at tragedy. Slowed down by verse, they are nevertheless neatly plotted.

William Hazlitt was not alone in thinking Knowles 'the first tragic writer of the age', but there were many other aspirants, some of them fine poets. (It was

still through tragedy that the redemption of literary drama was anticipated.)
William Wordsworth and Samuel Taylor Coleridge both tried their hand.[9] So
did Charles Lamb and John Keats.[10] But the great white hope was George, Lord
Byron (1788–1824), whose brief membership of the Drury Lane subcommittee
of management (1815–16) was more than token. Byron's tragedies, particularly *Marino Faliero* and *Sardanapalus* (both 1821), are more neglected than
negligible. 'My dramatic simplicity', he would claim, 'is studiously Greek', in
conscious opposition to 'the wild old English drama' (letter to Lady Byron,
14 September 1821). A problem of which, in Italian exile, he may have been
only half aware was the possession of the London stage by the wild *new* English
drama, and his defensive protest that he was *not* writing for the stage is unbe-
lievable. Byron would have loved recognition as a dramatist, and the bisexual
Sardanapalus is one of historical fiction's most resonant creations. Overwordy
the play may be, but it is surprising that a 'national' theatre has not seen fit to
employ a competent dramaturg to shape it for performance.[11] It is an accident
of history (and a product of temperamental flaws) that Edmund Kean did not
play the title role in *Marino Faliero* when it was staged at Drury Lane in 1821,
and a sign of the times that Byron's most melodramatic (and probably worst)
play, *Werner*, was – in Macready's staging (1830) – the only one to establish
a place in the national repertoire. The great white hope was some years dead
before actors (Macready, Charles Kean, Charles Dillon, Samuel Phelps, Henry
Irving) found ways of using him.

Equally unsuccessful in the theatre of her time was the persistent Joanna
Baillie (1762–1851), one of the few contemporary playwrights whom Byron
admired.[12] Her long-term project was to compose a sequence of parallel comedies and tragedies, each concentrating on a single ruling passion. Her *De Mon-
fort* (ruling passion, 'hatred'), reluctantly revived by Edmund Kean in 1821,
was first performed at Drury Lane in 1800 (Kemble and Siddons starring).

> Every care was taken in the decoration of De Monfort. [William] Capon painted a
> very unusual pile of scenery, representing a church of the 14th century with its
> nave, choir and side aisles, magnificently decorated; consisting of seven planes in
> succession. In width this extraordinary elevation was about 56 feet wide, 52 in
> depth, and 37 feet in height. It was positively a building.
>
>   James Boaden, *Memoirs of the Life of John Philip Kemble* (1825)

Between 1798 and 1836, Baillie wrote and published plays (mostly in com-
edy/tragedy parallel, and in blank verse) on love, hatred, ambition, fear,
remorse, jealousy and (a 'serious' musical drama) hope, but it was not until the
final 1836 volume of *Miscellaneous Plays* that it became the critical custom to

Figure 21. Charles Kean set about rescuing Byron for the theatre by his lavish staging of *Sardanapalus* at the Princess's Theatre in 1853.

praise her. What is most significant about her lonely venture is its transference to literature of a psychological theory that originated in acting: Kemble, in particular, disciplined his performances in tragedy by determining the ruling passion of the character he was playing. It was probably Kemble who fired Baillie's ambition.

The most widely praised now of nineteenth-century verse tragedies, Percy Bysshe Shelley's *The Cenci* (1819), remained unperformed until 1886, and had no effect on the British stage. Francesco Cenci, the brutal father who simultaneously hates and lusts after his daughter, is the polar opposite of Knowles's Virginius, and the pairing of the two plays at Covent Garden in 1820 was briefly contemplated – but incest was taboo, and the censors were not tested. Also unstaged, and more remarkable than Shelley's play, was *Death's Jest-Book* (published in 1850). Its author, Thomas Lovell Beddoes (1803–49), had much in common with Shelley (1792–1822), whom he admired: radicalism bordering on revolution, a lyrical gift, periods of voluntary exile from an England he despised, fascination with the occult, absorption in the darker world of Jacobean drama. But where Shelley might flirt with death, Beddoes was infatuated with it. *Death's Jest-Book*, with which he was still tinkering between his first suicide attempt and his second (successful) one, finds eroticism in eschatology. It is, perhaps, the most remarkable dramatic poem in English, 'a monumental failure, more interesting than many facile triumphs'.[13] It might be staged, as *The Cenci* was by Antonin Artaud in 1935, in a hallucinatory scenario designed to expose the secret world of the nineteenth century.

Macready would have had no time for Beddoes, though he solicited plays from less talented writers, and strove to make a playwright out of Robert Browning,[14] all in the name of restoring the drama to its former greatness. But his only lasting success was with Bulwer, whose *Richelieu* (1839) stands, along with a few other plays of the period, at the intersection between the highbrow and the middlebrow. This is a drama built round a series of theatrical moments, all featuring the indomitable Cardinal Richelieu. Bulwer's ambition, though, is evident from the historical footnotes he provided for the first published edition. He had planned, not a tragedy, but a history play to rival Shakespeare's. But the climax – when the failing Richelieu casts off death to resume control of France – owes more to the theatre of thrills than to historical truth. Like all successful nineteenth-century dramatists, Bulwer conceded primacy to the actor; in the case of *Richelieu* to Macready. That he has opposed him with a group of outstandingly inept conspirators is just one example of the play's defective dramaturgy. In its time, and for a further fifty years, it was great theatre. It was never a great drama.

Melodrama

As early as Act 2, Scene 2 of *Richelieu*, the page François is entrusted with the care of a secret document. We have to believe (and, in the present tense of the theatrical event, might truly believe) that the faction which possesses this document controls the future of France. Its whereabouts are in doubt until almost the end – and the fact is that it does not matter (but we are not supposed to think that!). This is the typical hokum of melodrama – 'the play not disguised as literature'[15] – but Bulwer was sufficiently distinguished to deceive Macready, the audience and (almost certainly) himself into believing that *Richelieu* was a literary triumph. It was, after all, this play that introduced to the English language the optimistic cliché 'the pen is mightier than the sword' (Act 2, Scene 2).

As a genre obedient to its own rules, melodrama belongs to – presides over – the nineteenth-century theatre, though it is older than the witches in *Macbeth* and Desdemona's handkerchief (power lies with the possessor of the 'document') in *Othello*. It declared itself in England with Thomas Holcroft's *A Tale of Mystery* (1802), but the motifs were part of the common stock: guilty secrets, usurping villains, threatened virtue, rightful heirs, echoing castles, sinister caves, marauding bandits (or poachers, pirates, smugglers), nature and climate out of human control – and a part for the popular star of low comedy. Sing sorrow, sorrow – but good win out in the end. It was in melodrama that the collaborative craft of theatre supremely expressed itself: lesser actors came into their own, along with scene-painters, stage-carpenters, pit orchestras (melodramas were as dependent on musical heightening as films are now) and machinists. Real water, easily available for nautical spectaculars at Sadler's Wells, could be piped into Drury Lane for *The Cataract of the Ganges* (1823); advances in technology could produce more effective fires and explosions; and new machines could reinforce with stage magic the magical mystery that melodrama shared with pantomime. As the provincial manager D. P. Bustle boasts in R. B. Peake's *Amateurs and Actors* (1818) of his 'stage crash', 'With this machine we knock down towns and towers, break bridges, and upset tilburies', and we can be sure that anything Bustle could do, London could do better.

Melodrama was swept into the English theatre by the entertainment boom of the 1790s, carrying with it the popular delight in being frightened by Gothic horror. After Horace Walpole had set the standard with his novel *The Castle of Otranto* (1764),[16] the trade in Gothic excess was bound, sooner or later, to reach the stage. It was fed from France and Germany, too. Nor was it confined in its appeal. Coleridge's 'Kublai Khan' is a stage-setting waiting for a melodrama, and his Ancient Mariner is blood-brother to Edward Fitzball's Flying Dutchman (1826). Byron's Turkish tales, from 'The Giaour' to 'The Corsair', are plotted like melodramas, Shelley's *The Cenci* occupies some of the same sadistic ground as Matthew 'Monk' Lewis's sensation-seeking novels and plays,[17] and Mary Shelley's *Frankenstein* (1818) is a brilliant teenager's sensitive response to the temper of her times. The Romantic movement, that is to say, exploited Gothicism's extension of the emotional scope of literature. Melodrama used it to attack the nervous system of its audience before soothing it with a happy ending. As the nineteenth century advanced, the novels of Scott and (what could be easier?) Dickens would be routinely melodramatized, with the descriptive passages replaced by gestural acting and scenic art. Sensation novels (of which Dickens's are supreme examples), serialized before being brought out in two or three volumes, kept their readers on melodramatic tenterhooks. Their authors owed much to the theatre.

There is something endearingly straightforward about melodrama. It never tries to be clever. Villains behave villainously, heroes heroically, heroines pathetically – and the comic man, often paired with a comic woman and having precious little purchase on the plot, brings us down to earth with the reminder that laughter, too, has a place in the world of the gasp. This is *story* theatre: what happens matters more than who it happens to. Today we have lost the nineteenth-century delight in sheer story, and good audiences for melodrama are hard to find. Most of the available early examples are crude, certainly – less texts than pretexts for scenic and histrionic display. Isaac Pocock's *The Miller and His Men* (1813) was the favourite piece for toy theatres[18] precisely because it has no subtlety. It had a gloomy cavern, a climactic explosion – and John Liston (1776–1846) as the easily frightened comic man – and that was enough. The same is broadly true of such popular pieces as James Robinson Planché's *The Vampire* (1820), in which the vampire trap[19] was first deployed and which featured John Harley as the bibulous comic Scotsman M'Swill, and Fitzball's *The Flying Dutchman* (1826), whose text consists mostly of knockabout comedy but whose eerie special effects thrilled Adelphi audiences. Thomas Potter Cooke (1786–1864), clearly a master of melodramatic pantomime, created the demonic (and *silent*) title roles of both these pieces, as well as that of the *silent* monster in Peake's scanty dramatization of *Frankenstein* as *Presumption* (1823), but his enduring image was that of the sailor hero. His naval service in the French wars was used in the promotional advertising for his Long Tom Coffin in Fitzball's *The Pilot* (1825), a skeletal adaptation of James Fenimore Cooper's 1823 novel, and was firmly established before the opening of Douglas Jerrold's *Black-Eyed Susan* (1829). There was no need for Cooke to add to his repertoire after that. He continued to play Long Tom Coffin and Jerrold's William for the rest of his long career.

Black-Eyed Susan is a domestic play, free of exotic Gothic or 'oriental' trappings, and it was in its domestic mode that melodrama would most substantially embody the nineteenth-century values that we think of as 'Victorian'. John Baldwin Buckstone (1802–79) wrote several between *Luke the Labourer* (1826) and his proleptically cinematic *The Green Bushes* (1845), an all-action play which ventures from rural Ireland to a valley of the Mississippi and back to the streets of Dublin. However sugar-coated with a happy ending, these melodramas expose the hardship of poverty and the iniquities of inherited or appointed authority. It is the trick of melodrama – one which it shares with the Christian narrative that underpins it – to make tragedy unavoidable and then avoid it. From this perspective, tragedy is melodrama with 'the nick of time' removed. The abyss of human desolation and the havoc created by crime are common to both, presences that permeate nineteenth-century art and literature. Any society that works so hard to preserve the appearance of confidence must be suppressing a profound anxiety, and anxiety is the legitimate territory of melodrama. We should not underrate its theatrical scope.

Dramatic all-sorts

The difficulty of categorizing much early nineteenth-century drama has exasperated literary critics, most of whom have responded by ignoring it, thus implicitly denigrating the taste of audiences who did not, and theatre managers who knew better. The surest banker at Christmas or Easter[20] remained, as it was for David Garrick, pantomime, by which was understood a two-part entertainment loosely plotted around the frustrated pursuit of fugitive lovers. A rudimentary text would establish, in the first part, the 'real life' of the characters, who would be transformed, for the second-part chase, into Harlequin, Columbine and (the antagonistic authority figure) Pantaloon.[21] Even more than in melodramas, the unsung heroes of these seasonal spectaculars were the scenic artists, machinists, costumiers and property-makers, but pantomime created its own star performers from Joseph Grimaldi (1778–1837) at Sadler's Wells and Covent Garden to George Conquest (1837–1901) at the Grecian and Dan Leno (1860–1903) at Drury Lane. Grimaldi's Clown – generally silent, but given to patter-songs – embodied the subversive subculture of the Age of Reform. Attached to the enemy camp as part of Pantaloon's household, he is a kleptomaniacal mischief-maker, randomly humiliating anyone who crosses his path – old women or representatives of the law, cripples or custodians – and

Figure 22. John Everett Millais's *The Order of Release*. A wife has procured her Scottish husband's release from prison by selling her body. This painting is a frozen melodrama, one which no dramatist would have dared to write.

himself subject to humiliation. And all this in vividly expressive white-face. Grimaldi might linger over a leg of mutton or execute an acrobatic pratfall, sometimes reducing the human body to the status of an automaton. His Clown survives, still representing something subversive of the spectacle it adorns, in the circus.

There is cultural subversion, too, in the burlesque. Any favoured opera or drama was liable to appear, grotesquely relocated and with the wind taken out of its sails, in an afterpiece at a rival playhouse. Six months after its opening at the Surrey, for example, Jerrold's *Black-Eyed Susan; or, All in the Downs* resurfaced at the Olympic in Frederick Cooper's *Blackeyed Sukey; or, All in the Dumps*, and anyone who missed the London opening of Carl Weber's vastly admired *Der Freischütz* at Covent Garden in 1824 could see it burlesqued at two other theatres before the end of the year. Weber's opera belongs with melodrama, a perilously easy subject for burlesque, but Shakespeare was a regular target, too. John Poole's *Hamlet Travestie* (1810), like W. S. Gilbert's *Rosencrantz and Guildenstern* (1891), has an honourable place in the rich history of nineteenth-century humour.

In the overlapping network of dramatic categories, burlesque and travesty are not easily distinguishable from extravaganza, which shares a bed with pantomime. William Moncrieff's *Giovanni in London* (1817) is too independent of its Mozartian source to be confined to burlesque and too dependent to qualify as extravaganza. Its greatest significance was in introducing Madame Vestris (1797–1856), breeches-clad in the title role, to London audiences at the Drury Lane revival of 1820. It was under Vestris's pioneering management of the Olympic (1830–8) that a distinct style of extravaganza[22] emerged. Its principal purveyor was Planché (1796–1880), a theatrical jack-of-all-trades who has – except by students of heraldry[23] – been shamefully neglected. *Olympic Revels* (1831), which opened the Vestris management, is closer to burlesque than are the fairy extravaganzas. Beginning with *Riquet with the Tuft* (1836), these are Planché's seminal contribution to comic drama. The theatrical trick was to present fairy tales in quirkily rhyming couplets that could accommodate puns and topical references[24] and cheerfully descend to doggerel, in elegant settings and tasteful costumes and through actors who gave the appearance of taking them seriously. Later writers of outrageously punning Victorian pantomimes owed much to him. So did W. S. Gilbert (1836–1911), whose fiercely but hilariously ironic *The Palace of Truth* (1870) takes fairy extravaganza into the realms of social satire. Planché belongs, with R. H. Barham (1788–1845), author of the *Ingoldsby Legends*, at the whimsical end of the 'nonsense' tradition, before Victorians such as Edward Lear and Lewis Carroll added anxiety to its jocularity.

It was the novelty of the Vestris/Planché venture that attracted fashionable audiences to the Olympic: the combination of contained irreverence and a feeling for decor which spread from the stage to the auditorium. At the Coburg, according to a current joke, a voice from the gallery had jeered, 'We don't want no grammar, but you might jine the flats': at the Olympic they had grammar *and* joined-up flats. Novelty – distinct from originality – was paramount in the new era of mass consumption. The Age of Reform was the heyday of the 'infant prodigy', the most remarkable of whom was 'Master' Betty (1791–1874). Betty was thirteen, and beautiful, when, after a triumphal provincial tour, he took London by storm in 1804, playing such classic roles as Hamlet and Young Norval in *Douglas*. He had been well coached for exploitation, but Bettymania is ultimately explicable only by the public hunger for novelty.[25] Hippodramas at Astley's Amphitheatre were in vogue from 1807, and given a new boost there from 1823 by the brilliant equestrian Andrew Ducrow (1793–1842). Whatever was novel had a *prima facie* hold on the growing number of consumers of entertainment. Why else would the journalist Gilbert A'Beckett have written a play called *The Siamese Twins* (1838) so soon after the second visit to England of Chang and Eng, the original Siamese twins?[26]

Mass consumption of new plays demanded their mass production, and it is unsurprising that dramatists such as J. H. Amherst and Henry Milner, who furnished Ducrow with his hippodramas, have vanished with him. But there is much to be learnt about the nineteenth century from its minor drama, and the challenge of the Age of Reform can be found in unexpected places, few more surprising than in Thomas Haynes Bayly's *The Spitalfields Weaver*, staged at the St James's in 1838. Bayly (1797–1839) was well connected (one of his cousins was an earl) and, until an investment failed in 1831, wealthy; an unlikely egalitarian. But this one-act play ('from the French', but utterly English) is a trenchant attack on the snobbery of fashion. Brown, a simple weaver, has married a 'lady' after inheriting her uncle's wealth. Her good-hearted attempts to sophisticate him are mocked by her fashionable friends, particularly by her would-be seducer and dandified cousin Darville, and Brown takes comfort in the company of his unashamedly rough-mannered former workmate, Simmons (heart of gold and salt of the earth, of course). Their conversation is finely crafted by Bayly, and, emboldened by it, Brown turns on Darville in a speech that expresses the discernible difference between the England of George IV and the England of Victoria.

I am no gentleman, you say; granted, you *are* one. Mark the difference. I ask you to my house, I share with you all the advantages I possess; *you* – press my hand, you call me friend, and when least I suspected it, you repay me by attempting the seduction of my wife; but mark me, sir, there is one requisite in the character of a gentleman, which you seem to have forgotten. HONOUR – without it, *you* are none, and standing before you now, throwing your vile scrawl in your face, I feel that *I*, the uneducated workman, look down with scorn upon a scoundrel!

Thomas Haynes Bayly, *The Spitalfields Weaver* (1838)

Chapter 12

Actors and acting

The fact that playwrights sometimes dramatized pictures tells us something about acting styles, as well as painting styles, in the nineteenth century.[1] While Jean Géricault's massive *The Raft of the Medusa* was attracting 40,000 paying visitors to London's Egyptian Hall in 1820, at least two plays cashed in by depicting the plight of the survivors of the shipwrecked French frigate. Decency precluded a theatrical reproduction of the painting itself, but James Robinson Planché's *The Brigand Chief* (1829) notably incorporated onstage tableaux from three paintings by Charles Eastlake (1793–1865). *A Brigand Wounded* is a particularly vivid pointer to the gestural semaphore of emotional peaks in melodrama. Mezzotints of Eastlake's brigand sequence were, Planché tells us, on display in all the printshop windows, and their realization on stage was frozen until the audience had applauded it. David Wilkie's canvases were so well known in 1832 that they inspired both Douglas Jerrold's *The Rent Day* and John Baldwin Buckstone's *The Forgery* that year. When playwrights dramatized novels, they regularly used the illustrations to those novels to capture a climactic encounter. Alternatively, they might set moving the narrative embedded in a dramatic moment frozen on canvas. In 1842, for example, the watercolourist Sarah Setchel (1813–94) exhibited *The Momentous Question*. Engraved by Samuel Bellin, this enigmatic portrayal of a prison visit was sufficiently familiar to the theatregoing public to tempt Fitzball into providing a 'momentous' answer. A stage direction towards the end of Act 1 of *The Momentous Question* (1844) specifically calls for a tableau of the 'Celebrated picture'. Whether or not Edward Fitzball consulted Setchel's source in George Crabbe's *Tales of the Hall* (1819), his mundane conclusion is that Rachel, though she loved the poacher, was right to marry the gamekeeper.

Something of great importance to our understanding of nineteenth-century plays – the style of acting and the taste of audiences for which they catered – is encapsulated in the enduring vogue for story-painting from Eastlake to (its supreme master?) John Everett Millais (1829–96).[2] The quality of the work of art matters less than the quantity of the emotional response that it evokes.

Figure 23. Sir Charles Eastlake's *A Brigand Wounded*. The Pollock's Toy Theatre version of *The Brigand* reproduced the gestures of Eastlake's painting.

The ability to engineer a narrative that allowed actors to signal – and to hold in tableau – pathetic peaks was crucial to the wrighting of plays, just as the skill to make the most of them was the mark of the true actor. These were the actor's 'points': those moments scattered through a performance that would elicit from responsive audiences repeated rounds of applause (Edmund Kean might get as many as nine).

Pictorial acting

The debate provoked by Edmund Burke's distinction between the beautiful and the sublime[3] lasted into the nineteenth century. Beauty may please us, Burke argued, but we are so overwhelmed by the sublime that we submit to it. For Uvedale Price, sublimity 'produces astonishment by stretching the nervous fibres beyond their usual tone'.[4] Such submission and astonishment combine in William Hazlitt's recollection of Sarah Siddons as Lady Macbeth.

We can conceive of nothing grander. It was something above nature. It seemed almost as if a being of a superior order had dropped from a higher sphere to awe the world with the majesty of her appearance. Power was seated on her brow, passion emanated from her breast as from a shrine; she was tragedy personified.

William Hazlitt, *Characters of Shakespear's Plays* (1817)

This was the actress whom Joshua Reynolds depicted as the Tragic Muse. Both Siddons and her brother John Philip Kemble were associated with the sublime by contemporary reviewers, though in Kemble's case the association some-times furnished detractors with evidence of the gap between aspiration and achievement. Agile and graceful in youth, Kemble was reduced to comparative immobility under the affliction of asthma, and many of those who saw him only in his later, nineteenth-century years, particularly in the Roman parts (Cato, Coriolanus, Brutus) in which he was unrivalled, described him as statuesque. The impression has been reinforced for subsequent generations by Thomas Lawrence's grandiose portraits of him in role. At a time when history paint-ing was rated above all other kinds, Kemble may, in pursuit of the sublime, have pictorialized himself as history – his admiration for the baroque grandeur of Nicolas Poussin's canvases certainly affected his staging of *Coriolanus* and probably of *Julius Caesar*, too – but his conscious concern was always to identify and then to embody the ruling passion that brought his character into conflict with circumstance. Leigh Hunt, not an admirer, conceded that 'no player . . . understands his author better'.[5] Appreciation of Kemble, even before the Old Price Riots of 1809, was measured compared with the exaltation of Siddons. In his patrician style he took too little account of the new age. It is probable, too, that the vastness of the rebuilt patent theatres was ill-suited to his method of mounting gradually towards an explosive climax.

Inevitably in the enlarged patent theatres, the sublime was paraphrased as the spectacular, and it was spectacular acting that threatened Kemble's more reasoned approach to the dramatic text. When he moved from Drury Lane to Covent Garden in 1803, he had immediately to negotiate his relationship with the wayward George Frederick Cooke (*c.*1756–1812), tactfully playing Antonio opposite Cooke's Shylock and Richmond opposite his Richard III. It was to Kemble's advantage that Cooke, even when not drunk, was erratic. He either pulverized audiences or alienated them. Kemble could never have dappled malignancy with humour as Cooke did, but he was far more disciplined and still strong enough to wear down his adversary. That was no longer true by 1814, when Edmund Kean (1787–1833) made his legendary debut as Shylock at Drury Lane. 'We wish we had never seen Mr. Kean,' wrote Hazlitt in the *Examiner* (27 October 1816). 'He has destroyed the Kemble religion and it is the religion in which we were brought up.'[6]

Kean reached the London stage after years of provincial poverty and two months after the death in squalor of his elder son. A bitter resentment at the way the world had treated him from childhood must have contributed to the mess he made of his life after the sudden acquisition of wealth and fame. Kemble – a theatre manager in London and the son of just such a provincial theatre manager as had exploited him for so long – belonged among the oppressors, and here was an opportunity to eclipse him. Even in adversity, Kean had been naturally adversarial. Acting for himself, he was also acting against a society that had scorned him. Inner fury amounting frequently to paranoia fuelled his finest performances and made them dangerous to a degree unrivalled on the English stage. He found points of identity with Shylock, and it was at these points that he thrilled Regency audiences. 'The character never stands still,' wrote Hazlitt in a review of the second night (*Morning Chronicle*, 2 February 1814). 'There is no vacant pause in the action; the eye is never silent.' For critics close up in the pit, Kean's eyes were always a feature, but he was a people's actor too, celebrated in the upper gallery as Kemble rarely was. His voice, reputedly weak in the upper register, resonated in Drury Lane. He would continue to abuse it until it cracked under the strain, forcing him to hold back for most of a performance to preserve energy for its peaks. The famous transitions from the rhetoric of high passion to the startlingly conversational may have owed as much to necessity as to art, and he was envious of the vocal strength of Kemble's heir, Charles Mayne Young (1777–1856). Sober, he acknowledged the quality of Young's musical voice; drunk, as he generally was by 1823, he would rant to James Winston about having to act with 'that bloody thundering bugger'. Smaller even than David Garrick, Kean was an extreme physical contrast to the tall, straight-backed Kemble, and he had none of Kemble's interest in the totality of the stage picture. He was a soloist whose performances were self-portraits, often with startling distortions after the manner of Henry Fuseli (1741–1825). Perhaps the best visual capture of a Kean 'moment' is Fuseli's pen-and-wash drawing of a scene from *Richard III*, just before the encounter with Lady Anne. There is some significance in the fact that Fuseli's actual inspiration was Garrick, who, like Kean, knew how to attract the focus. And Kean, it should be remembered, had the benefit, for much of his career, of gaslight. He could search out the most advantageous spot on the stage.

Who can forget the exquisite grace with which he leaned against the side-scene while Anne was railing at him, and the chuckling mirth of his 'Poor fool! What pains she takes to damn herself!' It was thoroughly feline – terrible yet beautiful.
    G. H. Lewes, *On Actors and the Art of Acting* (1875)

Figure 24. Henry Fuseli's drawing from memory of David Garrick as Richard III.

Romantic Shakespeare

Primarily through its essayists and public lecturers – Charles Lamb, Leigh Hunt, Hazlitt, Samuel Taylor Coleridge – the Romantic movement infiltrated Shakespeare into the new spirit of the age. Not the Elizabethan Shakespeare, of course, but the superpoet at work on the 'Science of Man'.[7] It was to Lamb that Hazlitt dedicated his *Characters of Shakespear's Plays* (1817), a volume which is implicitly a manual for actors as much as it is explicitly a teach-yourself-Shakespeare for readers. It was always a problem for Hazlitt that his delight in actors threatened his conviction that the sublime Shakespeare was out of their reach.

> We do not like to see our author's plays acted, and least of all, HAMLET. There is no play that suffers so much in being transferred to the stage . . . Mr. Kemble unavoidably fails in this character from a want of ease and variety. The character of Hamlet is made up of undulating lines; it has the yielding flexibility of 'a wave o' th' sea'. Mr. Kemble plays it like a man in armour, with a determined inveteracy of purpose, in one undeviating straight line, which is as remote from the natural grace and refined susceptibility of the character, as the sharp angles and abrupt

starts which Mr. Kean introduces into the part. Mr. Kean's Hamlet is as much too splenetic and rash as Mr. Kemble's is too deliberate and formal.

William Hazlitt, *Characters of Shakespear's Plays* (1817)

Nor can it have been easy for actors to find themselves measured against some projected absolute – a completed 'character', already more expressive of the human condition than they could ever be, and yet awaiting their interpretation. Kemble's way was to study and reflect (he has been plausibly posited as the first actor to set about producing a *play* rather than just a performance), Kean's to seize a part by the throat and let the whole go hang. What tends to be forgotten is the way in which major actors reshaped Shakespeare's plays to fit both their own talents and the scenic and musical requirements of the contemporary stage. It was in Colley Cibber's version, slightly adjusted, that Kean played out his Mephistophelean Richard III, and there was no Fool to provoke or comfort his (and Nahum Tate's) King Lear. His favoured roles, which also included Shylock and Othello,[8] were in those of Shakespeare's plays which could most readily be camouflaged as melodramas, and thus elicit the immediacy and magnitude of response that gratified both actor and audience.

In his pomp Kean possessed the actorly quality of 'gusto', so highly prized by Hazlitt. When he was at his best, Drury Lane was fervent, but his reign was a brief one, and his fall from grace almost as savage as Lord Byron's. However profligate the manners of Regency society, it did not 'do' to be found out. Kean's drunken 'benders' were partially concealed from his public, and rumours of his wildness fed the cult so long as they remained rumours, but his health was already suffering when he embarked on an American tour in 1820. More significantly, his affair with the passionate Charlotte Cox, wife of a London alderman, had already begun. The tour, which started triumphantly, ended in ignominy after Kean declined to perform before a Boston audience which he considered too small, and press reaction converted a tantrum into an international insult. Even at Drury Lane the reception on his return was comparatively cool and, faced with the prospect of sharing the stage with the rising star William Charles Macready in 1823, he did what he nearly always did when under extreme pressure: he bolted (this time to the estate he had bought on the Isle of Bute). There was no escape from Charlotte Cox, though. When their affair had ended in mutual recrimination, the previously complaisant alderman sued Kean for criminal conversation with his wife, and the case of *Cox* v. *Kean* was heard in January 1825 amid prurient public excitement.

Although he struggled on for a further eight years, through a controversial second tour of America and several equally controversial provincial tours in England, Kean never recovered from the setback of the Cox trial, and the years of glory, preceded by abjection, ended in abjection. But the myth of Kean as the embodiment on stage of Romantic individualism lingers. Less than three years after his death, Alexandre Dumas *père* chose him as the subject of a play. *Kean* (1836) glorifies the rebelliousness of a flamboyant actor who, like the mythical 'bad' Lord Byron, refused to be subdued by the moral constraints of a repressively stuffy English establishment. The image has proved historically persuasive, despite its lack of substance.

Kean was as tangential to the new aesthetic of Romanticism as the Byronic hero, whose erotic appeal had fluttered fashionable bosoms since the publication in 1812 of the first two cantos of *Childe Harold's Pilgrimage*. But we should not underrate the cultural significance of Byron's Childe.[9] Kean's Richard III was as illicitly thrilling as any of Byron's smouldering isolates.

> There was a laughing devil in his sneer,
> That raised emotions of both rage and fear;
> And where his frown of hatred darkly fell,
> Hope withering fled, and Mercy sighed farewell!
> Lord Byron, *The Corsair* (1814)

Eroticism, Gothicism and a melodramatic sensibility fed into the Romantic revolution, and it was to these comparatively superficial aspects that Kean's Shakespearean performances adhered. Neither he, nor any other actor, grappled with Coleridgean notions of organic growth and the nice distinction between fancy and imagination. It is just possible that if Kean had ever been granted the authority over Drury Lane that he craved, but did not merit, his unruliness would have expressed itself in theatrical innovation. Fine scene-painters such as Clarkson Stanfield (1793–1867) were certainly capable of realizing the Romantic vision of natural grandeur, but actors were still too hidebound by the unremitting demands of a constantly changing repertoire to envisage the possibility, or submit to the discipline, of allowing any of Shakespeare's plays to grow afresh through exploratory rehearsals. It was hard enough to entice Kean to attend rehearsals at all. In the circumstances, it has to be sufficient that he came close to staging the Byronic hero.

Early actor-managers

Garrick's dexterity in both pandering to and leading the taste of his public had set a precedent in actor-management which was a spur to ambitious successors, but the complexity and financial burden of the enlarged patent theatres limited the scope of even so patrician a figure as Kemble. At Drury Lane he was subservient to Richard Brinsley Sheridan's unpredictable whims, and at Covent Garden (1803–17) he had still to negotiate with managerial partners. But, as the Old Price Riots conclusively proved, final authority was the audience's. The problem was to identify that audience. A full house of 3,000 or so was never univocal, and the patent houses were expected to cater to many tastes, operatic and balletic as well as dramatic. Covent Garden, though always associated with Kemble during his tenure, was never identified with him.

If the true mark of the actor-manager is total control of the company's repertoire, this was never attainable at the reactive, and at times reactionary, patent houses; it was in the smaller, illegitimate theatres that adventurous actor-managers came closer to establishing a model for their Victorian successors. Charles Dibdin's musical entertainments at the Sans Souci (1796–1805) brought his extraordinary theatrical career to a distinguished end. Having quarrelled with almost every theatre manager, Dibdin had little alternative but to go it alone, and he was probably surprised when – threatened by the renewal of hostilities with France in 1803 – Addington's government commissioned him to produce and publish monthly morale-boosting patriotic songs, and even awarded him a pension of £200: a rare recognition by the nation's rulers that the theatre might contribute to the war effort. Dibdin, who had first established his celebrity as a collaborator (with Isaac Bickerstaff), was by now essentially a soloist.

Jane Scott (1779–1839), by contrast, began as a solo entertainer – singing her own compositions to her own piano accompaniment – and ended as the collaborative manager of the Sans Pareil. From 1809 to 1819 she also provided that theatre with most of its dramatic material: operettas, melodramas, pantomimes – any fare that could be plausibly included under the amorphous category of 'burletta', for which the playhouse was licensed. Only after her retirement, when the Sans Pareil was renamed the Adelphi, did this theatre on the Strand develop its particular reputation as a home to melodrama. During her highly profitable management, it was responsive to the shifting tastes of the volatile new public. Even Scott, then, aimed to feed rather than challenge an increasingly assertive public.

Independent women like Scott have often dropped through the cracks of theatre history, and it is only recently that the provincial management of the actress and puppeteer Sarah Baker (*c*.1736–1816) has been credited. Baker properly belongs with Tate Wilkinson among the group of managers who raised the standard of theatre outside London. That she did so in the face of patriarchal prejudice is her distinction, that she presided over the Kent circuit of playhouses for more than forty years (*c*.1772–1815) is evidence of her feisty durability, and that she exploited her proximity to London by enticing metropolitan stars to make brief guest appearances in Canterbury, Rochester or Maidstone – and paying them in full – demonstrates both shrewdness and success. According to her will, her wealth at death amounted to £16,000.

It was quite otherwise with the most famous of pioneering actress-managers, Madame Vestris. Her tenure of the Olympic (1831–9), latterly in association with her actor-husband Charles James Mathews (1803–78) and always in collaboration with James Robinson Planché, was notable in many ways, not least in its approach to ensemble acting, but she and Mathews were constantly plagued by debt.[10] They were, to be sure, monetary bunglers, but their problems are representative of the financial crisis that afflicted provincial as well as London theatres in the years surrounding the 1843 Act. One answer – and it was one that Vestris/Mathews tried at the Olympic and in their subsequent managements of Covent Garden (1839–41) and the Lyceum (1847–53) – was to extend the run of successful plays. Economic trends demanded it, but audiences clamouring for variety were resistant. So, in many instances, were actors, who valued their off-duty nights.[11] The exemplary actor-manager of the period, Macready, was one such.

Macready was already a bourgeois Victorian before Victoria's accession. The son of a provincial theatre manager, he had been sent to school at Rugby in preparation for a respectable career at the bar or in the Church, and his commitment to the theatre was a reluctant response to his father's sudden near-bankruptcy. His fascinating *Diaries* read like those of a country vicar, conscious of a sacred mission but tormented with a sense of failure, bludgeoned by a conviction of his own frustrated potential and resentful of the tawdriness of the institution he serves. No one tried harder to elevate the profession he often despised. His values, though, were conventional, and his aspiration was less to revolutionize theatre than to restore Covent Garden (which he managed from 1837 to 1839) and Drury Lane (which he managed from 1841 to 1843) to a mythical grandeur, founded on the conscientious staging of great plays, ancient and modern.

Mortified to discover Covent Garden's financial links with neighbouring brothels, Macready cancelled the deals and bankrupted the theatre. A bare cupboard was better than one with skeletons in it. Committed to a changing repertoire *and* to expenditure on scenery by artists as fine as Stanfield (*Henry V* in 1839; *As You Like It* in 1842) and William Telbin (*King John* in 1842), he profited little from success. His cultivation, sometimes obsequious, of a literary circle which included Dickens, Thomas Talfourd and John Forster as well as James Sheridan Knowles, Edward Bulwer and Robert Browning, aimed to create a better drama, but the results were mixed, and Macready's fellow-actors were antagonized by the attendance at rehearsals of the manager's literary lions.

> Morning after morning there sat, close to the prompter's table, Messrs. Browning, Bulwer, Dickens, Maclise, Forster, and others, to our great horror and disgust. Mrs. Humby was especially annoyed at Forster's, 'roaring out, when I miss a word, "Put her through it again, Mac, put her through it again", as if I were a piebald mare at Astleys!'
>
> James Anderson, *An Actor's Life* (1902)

But at least Macready, like Vestris, was insistent on systematic rehearsals, to the certain advantage of his theatrical successors. At the benefit dinner after his retirement from the stage in 1851, Forster intoned a sonnet by Alfred, Lord Tennyson.

> Thine is it that our drama did not die,
> Nor flicker down to brainless pantomime,
> And those gilt gauds men-children swarm to see.
> Farewell, Macready; moral, grave, sublime;
> Our Shakespeare's bland and universal eye
> Dwells pleased, through twice a hundred years, on thee.
>
> Alfred, Lord Tennyson, 'To W. C. Macready' (1851)

By then Macready had concluded his professional diary with an italicized flourish, '*Thank God!*'.

Solo acts

Samuel Foote and Wilkinson were personality performers and mimics rather than actors, at their best when directly in contact with audiences. Their stock-in-trade was the satiric impersonation of living celebrities. Dibdin took solo performance in a different direction by specializing in comic and patriotic songs, with patter serving primarily as a link, and the first significant *actor* to stage an original one-man show was John Bannister, for so long Dorothy Jordan's preferred comic partner. *Bannister's Budget* (1807) was an offshoot of the actor's association with George Colman the Younger at the Haymarket. Its source was the first scene of Colman's occasional prelude to the 1795 season there, *New Hay at the Old Market*, in which Bannister as an out-of-work actor pointlessly endeavoured to exhibit his talents to an unacted playwright. As *Sylvester Daggerwood* (the name of the out-of-work actor), this piece remained popular with comedians until at least the end of the nineteenth century. Henry Irving's friend J. L. Toole contrived twenty or more imitations of his contemporaries when performing it in the 1880s. But when Colman assisted in the compilation of the *Budget* in 1807, mimicry was only one constituent of a programme that was designed to exploit Bannister's versatility in the creation of character 'types'.

Engraved by R. Cruikshank.   Pub.d by Sherwood, Jones & C.o Sep.t 1824.

The King, at Home, or, Mathews at Carlton House.

Figure 25. This extraordinary capture of the Prince Regent observing Charles Mathews the Elder 'At Home' in Carlton House shows the future George IV's cultural alertness as well as the actor's popularity.

This quick-fire succession of monologues, featuring rapid costume changes, was further developed in the monopolylogues of Charles Mathews the Elder's *At Homes*. From 1817 until his death, Mathews (1776–1835), father of Vestris's future husband, was the beloved master of the one-man show. He had made his name as a character actor, but felt, with some justification, that specialists in comedy were consigned to the lower ranks of the theatrical hierarchy. The *At Homes*, constantly changing, gave him up to three hours alone with an audience, using material of his own and others' composition. The nineteenth-century 'character', later to be developed in the pages of *Punch* and Dickens and in music halls, came to life in Mathews's expertly differentiated performances. Audiences found him accurate as well as funny, less concerned with the mockery of eccentricity than with the physical and vocal detail – regional accents a speciality – of its manifestation. Surviving texts, though often banal on the page, open themselves up for mind's-eye performance to an alert reader. Mathews has an important place in the history of nineteenth-century humour.

Writing for actors

By 1805 Frederick Reynolds could earn himself £500 with a five-act comedy by negotiating special deals with Thomas Harris at Covent Garden before selling the text to him and to a publisher. But even Reynolds, who marketed himself much more effectively than most playwrights could, was unable to make a secure living solely by writing plays. Until 1833 there was no copyright law that specifically addressed the drama, no financial benefit to authors from performances of their work at theatres other than the one with which they had initially contracted, and no easy access to legal protection. Nor did the 1833 Dramatic Copyright Act, of which Bulwer had high hopes, greatly improve the situation. With the outcome of legal proceedings so uncertain, there was still more to be lost than gained by recourse to the law. Unsurprisingly, then, most of the new plays staged in London (and restaged in the provinces) were written by amateurs,[12] prepared to take a long shot but not dependent on hitting the target, and happy to sell their commodities to an interested manager for £50 an act. The intelligent option was to create parts well suited to particular actors: Reynolds, after all, owed much to William Lewis (*c.*1746–1812) who had created Vapid, the title role of *The Dramatist*, and whose elegant deportment had earned him the nickname of 'Gentleman'.

If there is a countryman, it must be adapted to EMERY; if an Irishman, to JOHNSTONE; if a gabbling humourist, it must be copied from nothing but the manner of FAWCETT . . . The loss of LEWIS, for instance, whose gaiety of limb

Figure 26. Charles Mathews the Younger. Every inch the gentleman.

Figure 27. John Liston as Paul Pry. This Bloor Derby porcelain of Liston as Paul Pry was marketed on the strength of both actor and role. There were rival figures from Staffordshire, Enoch Wood & Son and Rockingham potteries.

is of so much benefit to modern comedy, would be a perfect rheumatism to Mr.
REYNOLDS; and the loss of MUNDEN, who gives it such an agreeable variety of
grin, would affect him little less than a lock-jaw.
     Leigh Hunt in *The Examiner* (1808)

Lewis's line in the gentlemanly roles of comedy was inherited by Charles Mathews the Younger, but where Lewis was rapid in speech and movement ('the
greatest comic *mannerist* that perhaps ever lived', in Hazlitt's view[13]), Mathews
was nonchalant, even languid. The difference was reflected in the more leisurely
style of single-theme comedies, like Bulwer's *Money* (1840), that came to the
fore in Victorian London. Earlier in the century, comedy was a more ramshackle
commodity, with characters drafted in to exploit the popularity of particular
actors. One of the great 'hits' of the period, John Poole's *Paul Pry* (1825), for
instance, owed its success to two actors only flimsily connected to its double
plot: Vestris, whose singing of 'Cherry Ripe' and 'The Lover's Mistake' was
always encored, and John Liston in the title role. Paul Pry is nothing other than
a meddling neighbour, but with his vast bottom stuffed into striped trousers
and his calculated insouciance, Liston convulsed the Haymarket audience. Pry's
'I hope I don't intrude' became a catchphrase for at least two generations.

Go where you would 40 years ago, you could not, by any means, avoid Paul Pry;
the stern Puritan, by some means or other, knew his face as well as the inveterate
playgoer . . . And his constantly recurring phrase 'I hope I don't intrude' became a
constant element in the 'chaff' of the London street-boy.
     The Times, 31 August 1866

And all this a decade before Liston's outstanding contributions to Vestris's
Olympic seasons.

It is not much use, of course, to remind twenty-first-century readers that
nineteenth-century plays, comedies and farces in particular, can be fully appreciated only by reference to the actors who performed them. But the recognition
that media developments brought actors – not only their reputation but even
their physical appearance – increasingly into the public domain is an important
one. Martin Meisel supposes that the creation in 1842 of the *Illustrated London News* 'ranks among the most important cultural events of the century'.[14]
Through its sophisticated techniques, the *News* could pictorialize politics as
theatre, but its particular service to the stage was to carry the 'look' of actors
and plays into middle-class homes.

Part Five

The theatre industry:
1843–1901

Chapter 13

The material circumstance

A lazy habit of thinking of the Victorian age as all of a piece – and a mighty stuffy piece at that – has done as much damage to our reading of cultural history as it has to our understanding of ethics and politics. The habit can be usefully troubled by a consideration of the variety of work published in the critical year of 1859, the year of Charles Darwin's *On the Origin of Species by Natural Selection*, after which biblically dependent Christians had either to abandon their faith or convince themselves that the heavens still declared the glory of God, and telescopes magnified it. Darwin's study was **not** immediately recognized as a watershed in human history, being far outsold by Samuel Smiles's contemporaneous *Self-Help: With Illustrations of Character and Conduct*. It was Smiles's celebration of the benefits of self-interest that Tom Taylor's opportunistic attorney, Dodgson, echoed for Haymarket audiences of *The Contested Election* in June 1859: 'The general good being the sum of individual goods, every man is only to do what is best for himself in order that the country may obtain what is best for all.' Taylor was less impressed by Smiles than he was by John Stuart Mill's radical essay *On Liberty* (1859). In the same year he might also have bought first editions of George Eliot's *Adam Bede*, Charles Dickens's *A Tale of Two Cities*, George Meredith's shocking *The Ordeal of Richard Feverel* and Edward Fitzgerald's pagan *Rubáiyát of Omar Khayyám*. He may have been among the 10,000 buyers of the first four of Alfred, Lord Tennyson's *Idylls of the King* (1859) in the first week of publication.

There was nothing monochrome about nineteenth-century Britain, and we do well to bear in mind G. M. Young's famous distinction between the early Victorian 'age of production' and the late Victorian 'age of finance' and his equally famous claim that 'of all decades in our history, a wise man would choose the eighteen-fifties to be young in'.[1] We are looking at the theatre that developed during a period of profound debate and cultural contestation, of regular scientific and technological advance, unprecedented prosperity and visible deprivation. For the first time, parliament was under pressure to concern itself with the welfare of all the queen's subjects, at home and abroad. The emancipation of slaves in British territories was completed

(1838), the Divorce Act (1857) was a partial acknowledgement that bad marriages were better terminated, the demand for universal education found its first tentative response in the Education Act (1870), and the Married Women's Property Act (1881) went some way towards righting a manifest iniquity. It was an age that made mistakes and made corrections, too. We need not be surprised by a stage that mistook and corrected in comparable measure.

Table of events referred to in Part Five	
1843	Theatres Regulation Act
1845	First year of Irish potato famine
1846	Repeal of the Corn Laws
1848	Revolutions in Europe. Chartist march in London
1851	The Great Exhibition
1854–6	Britain allied with Turkey in the Crimean War
1857	Divorce Act. Sepoy uprising in India
1858	Irish Republican Brotherhood founded
1859	Charles Darwin's *On the Origin of Species* and Samuel Smiles's *Self-Help* published
1863	Thomas Cook's first European tours
1867	Fenian uprisings in Ireland
1870	Education Act
1875	First recorded use of the word 'typewriter'
1877	Queen Victoria proclaimed Empress of India
1881	Married Women's Property Act
1886	Defeat of Gladstone's first Irish Home Rule Bill
1889–95	Terrorist bombs in London
1890	Fall of Charles Stewart Parnell
1893	Defeat of Gladstone's second Irish Home Rule Bill in the House of Lords
1895	Empire of India Exhibition at Earl's Court
1899	Outbreak of Boer War
1901	Death of Queen Victoria. Accession of Edward VII

Melodrama, Methodism and Martin Tupper

Martin Tupper (1810–89) was the great purveyor (in rhyme) of bourgeois moral platitudes. 'He presented as vatic wisdom the established convictions of his readership, which responded by venerating him as a sage. But as those convictions themselves began to crumble in the 1860s, under the pressure of scientific advance and social change, so Tupper's status declined and he came to seem an embarrassing survival from a superseded past.'[2] Even so, his *Proverbial Philosophy* (first edition 1838, but thirty-eight variously augmented editions by 1860) retained its scriptural place among earnest evangelicals into the twentieth century. My Dorset grandfather (born *c.*1870) kept a copy on his sparsely populated bookshelf, next door to Smiles's *Self-Help* and up against a set of bound volumes of the *Boy's Own Paper*, a representative library of classics (with Tennyson and a cheap complete Dickens) for a lower-middle-class Methodist with his heart in the nineteenth century and money to earn. Tupper and sermons were standard means for the conveying of serious truth to the godly, and the encouragement to its preachers to temper theology with homely exhortation goes some way to explain the phenomenal nineteenth-century growth of Methodism, predominantly among urban and rural labouring families.[3] Unease about this growth was not confined to the Church of England. The vulgarity of Nonconformism is a *leitmotif* of Matthew Arnold's secular *Culture and Anarchy* (1869), and intellectual distaste can be traced back to Samuel Foote by way of William Hazlitt.

> The first Methodist on record was David. He was the first eminent person we read of who made a regular compromise between religion and morality, between faith and good works . . . The principle of Methodism is nearly allied to hypocrisy, and almost unavoidably slides into it: yet it is not the same thing; for we can hardly call any one a hypocrite, however much at variance his professions and his actions, who really wishes to be what he would be thought.
>
> William Hazlitt, 'On the Causes of Methodism', in *The Round Table* (1817)

Given the chapels' accommodation of the paradox that, while money is the root of all evil, its possession by Methodists was a good thing[4] and thrift a key to the Kingdom of Heaven, the association of Methodism and hypocrisy, however prejudiced, is understandable. More germane, though, was the assurance of salvation that it offered to those whom the government neglected.

It can be reasonably assumed that Methodism and drama were antithetical, but only at risk of losing sight of their common ground. The temptations that beset us, the frailty of our resolve, the desperate need for someone to turn to in trouble, *all* the metaphors of Methodism were acted out in Victorian melodrama. The salvationary hymns sung with such un-Anglican enthusiasm in chapels encapsulated onstage action:

> How oft in the conflict, when pressed by the foe,
> I have fled to my refuge and breathed out my woe:
> How often, when trials, like sea-billows roll,
> Have I hidden in Thee, oh Thou Rock of my soul.[5]

Choosing to preach an antitheatrical sermon during one of his British missions in the 1870s, the American evangelist T. De Witt Talmage came up with a parable that is also, ironically, a melodramatic scenario.

> One went forth from a bright Christian home. There was no reason why she
> should forsake it; but induced by unclean novelette literature and by
> theatre-going, she started off, and sat down at the banquet of devils. Every few
> weeks she would come back to her father's house, and hang up her hat and
> shawl in the old place, as though she expected to stay; but in a few hours, as
> though hounded by an inexorable fate, she would take down again the hat and
> the shawl, and start out. When they called her back she slammed the door in
> their faces, and cried, 'Oh mother! it's too late!'
>
> T. De Witt Talmage, *Sports That Kill*
> (London: James Blackwood & Co., n.d.)

The languages are indistinguishable, and there is the same reaching out for
a response rather than working to perfect the artefact. The vast majority of
nineteenth-century melodramas, certainly prior to Dion Boucicault's sophis-
tication of the genre, operate within the homiletic tradition. An artisan family
could absorb the same kinds of moral truth from the pulpit or from the stage.
There must have been some that tried both.[6]

Christianity, trade and industry

The doctrine of Samuel Smiles (1812–1904) was more to the taste of Victorian
capitalists than the doctrine of the New Testament. Having studied and practised medicine in Scotland, Smiles turned first to journalism and then to the
railways after moving to England. He was assistant secretary to the Leeds and
Thirsk Railway (1845–54) and company secretary for the South Eastern Railway
(1854–66). He was also the first biographer of George Stephenson (1857),
whose successful trials of the Rocket at Rainhill in 1829 had provided the initial impetus for the first railway boom (1837–40). The image of the engineer
as Victorian hero owes as much to Smiles, whose *Lives of the Engineers* ran
to three volumes (1861–2), as to Isambard Kingdom Brunel (1806–59).[7] In
Tom Robertson's *Progress* (1869) the ancestral abbey home of the Mompes-
sons is threatened by the progressive plans of a railway engineer, an issue on
which Robertson, characteristically nervous of a decisive response to the social
problems he highlighted, seeks a safe compromise. He knew that the threat to
the old order brought about during the 'age of production' was not universally welcomed. Asked his view of railway trains at the 1830 opening of the
Liverpool-Manchester line, the Duke of Wellington (a guest of honour) grum-
bled that 'They encourage the lower classes to travel about.' He could not have
predicted the distant destinations available after the third peak of rail-laying
(1860–6), nor the new mobility of the labour force that would construct and

run the railway network. The old hierarchy of local communities was being destroyed by new incomes and new incomers.

It was not the engineering feats themselves, but the financial chicanery and speculation they fed that most troubled Christian apologists for material progress. By 1850 fifteen railway companies accounted for 62 per cent of paid-up capital in Britain. They were the largest firms listed on the Stock Exchange, rich pickings for fraudsters and ripe for scandal. The industry was rocked in 1863–4 when a leading engineer, Daniel Gooch (1816–89), manager of the Swindon works of the Great Western Railway and chairman of the Ruabon Coal Company in north Wales, was accused of favouring Ruabon coal on behalf of the GWR. Gooch, a staunch Anglican active in church affairs, defended himself robustly, but was forced to resign.[8] Whether or not Taylor (1817–80) and Augustus Dubourg (1830–1910) had the Gooch scandal in mind when writing *New Men and Old Acres* (1869) is unrecorded, but their comedy, produced in the same year as Robertson's *Progress*, provides a pertinent commentary on the tension between inherited privilege, new money and Christian morality.

The matter at issue is the ancient estate of Cleve Abbey, property of the now impoverished Vavasour family since the Norman conquest of 1066. Marmaduke Vavasour reluctantly recognizes the need to sell to 'some mushroom moneymaker', and the man at hand is their *nouveau riche* neighbour.

'The present representative of the family is Benjamin Bunter Esquire, honourably known in connection with extensive public works, and financial operations in all parts of the world.' That's very neatly put. 'He is the only son of the late eminent Nonconformist divine, the Rev. Boanerges Bunter, of Ball's Pond, Islington.' Ah, how proud the old man would have been, if he could have read all that, in the coal and 'tatur shed where he worked all the week, afore taking the pulpit at the Sniggs Rents Ebenezer.

> Tom Taylor and Augustus Dubourg, *New Men and Old Acres* (1869), Act 3

Unlike Gooch, Bunter is a Methodist, one who can square his sharp practice in business with his chapel attendance: 'Give a man ways and means and Cheristian [*sic*] principles, and there aren't many things that'll stop him' (Act 3). It is Bunter's financial adviser, a German called Blasenbalg (= 'bladderskin'), who discovers lodes of iron on the Vavasour estate, and who instructs Bunter in the new world of postindustrial economics.

Do you remember vot you vos yourself? A poor, crawling, commonplace contractor, mit no idea beyond a lucky job and a paying profit – no higher

> standpoint than de brute forces of hard work and hard money. Who taught you
> financing? Who revealed to you de modern philosopher's stone – a bill-stamp. De
> alchemy dat transmutes fools' hopes into wise men's profits, and condenses de
> puffs of a prospectus into golden showers.
>
> Tom Taylor and Augustus Dubourg, *New Men and Old Acres* (1869), Act 3

Blasenberg spells out the transition from the 'age of production' to the 'age of finance', but Bunter is a ready pupil. Without breaking the law, though at some odds with most people's 'Cheristian' principles, he conceals the discovery of the ironstone from Vavasour in order to purchase the estate at way below its market value.[9] But *New Men and Old Acres* is a comedy: Bunter, though certainly faulty in Hazlitt's terms and 'Philistine' in Arnold's, is not a melodrama villain. When his plans are foiled by Samuel Brown, his acceptance of defeat, and of Blasenberg's 'German' duplicity, is surprisingly ungrudging. Brown is a Liverpool merchant who represents honest trade. He values money only for the 'nobler uses' to which it can be put – 'To relieve suffering and to comfort sorrow – to feed the lamp of learning, and to strengthen the hand of art – to foster into fruit the seeds of promise that neglect might kill – and to crown with comfort the head grown gray in worthy service' (Act 2). Brown's reward is the hand of Vavasour's sprightly daughter, a marriage that is obversely matched by that of the Ruskin-obsessed Fanny Bunter to the penniless (and largely witless) Etonian, Bertie Fitz-Urse. The falling aristocracy and the rising plutocracy were often enough meeting in the middle by 1869.

Railways and theatres

By the last quarter of the nineteenth century, not only individual actors but whole companies were touring the country by rail, the most ambitious of them in chartered trains with extra coaches for the carriage of scenery, costumes and special effects. Provincial centres were linked with London as they had never been, to the inevitable detriment of the old stock companies that could no longer mount metropolitan 'hit' plays to their own specifications, and without fear of invidious comparison. Audience access to London's theatres was improved by the suburban and underground networks,[10] but the railway cult also infiltrated the stage itself, not only in metaphor[11] but also in visible form. Railway stations were sites of fascination for the Victorians, places in which social distinctions were blurred. William Frith's large painting of Paddington (*The Railway Station*, 1862) features upwards of a hundred human figures between the dog on the extreme left and the detectives apprehending a criminal on the extreme right.

Figure 28 The railway sensation featured in this poster for Augustin Daly's *Under the Gaslight*.

As a portrait of London on the bustle in the 1860s, it brought thousands to a small gallery in the Haymarket during the month of its public exhibition. At the Princess's Theatre in 1882, it was Euston that spectators saw in *The Silver King*, with 'passengers of all classes' crossing the stage. The authors, Henry Arthur Jones and Henry Herman, kept the crucial train-crash off stage, but Boucicault had been more demanding at the same theatre fourteen years earlier. The 'sensation scene' of his *After Dark* (1868) required the hero to be tied to the rails of the Metropolitan Line, with 'tunnels converging in perspective to the stage' and a train approaching. It was a scene shamelessly stolen from the New York production of Augustin Daly's *Under the Gaslight* (1867), but it was London's first sight of a theatrical train. In 1882 Drury Lane staged a double train-crash in *Pluck*.[12] 'What next?' asked *Vanity Fair*. 'Shall we dramatise the deluge or the apocalypse?' Drury Lane, so recently the jealous guardian of the national drama, was now trading in technological trickery. The quality of the play there mattered less than Bruce 'Sensation' Smith's staging of the boat-train's departure from Waterloo for *Flood Tide* (1903) and of the villain's scaling moving carriages to uncouple a horsebox for *The Whip* (1909).[13] In *The Whip* the eponymous horse was rescued in the nick of time, but the horsebox was shattered by the next train, which slewed onto its side, gushing steam. It was not long before film took over this kind of sensation from the stage, but that was still distant when *After Dark* was thrilling packed houses.

The Great Exhibition: 1851

As a symbol of economic recovery from 'the hungry '40's', the Crystal Palace which housed the Great Exhibition was as near perfect as any of the exhibits it housed. But the duality of nineteenth-century England, ineradicably identified by Robert Louis Stevenson in *The Strange Case of Dr. Jekyll and Mr. Hyde* (1886), is aptly located in 1851 by the serialization that year of Dickens's *Bleak House*, a building as dark and gloomy as the Crystal Palace was light and airy. The choice of so implicitly adversarial a title may not have been accidental. Dickens had been a member of the Central Working Classes Committee, established by the Bishop of Oxford, Samuel Wilberforce ('Soapy' Sam), to confirm that the nation was patriotically united behind an enterprise that would advertise Britain's leadership of the industrial world, and was not best pleased when the committee was disbanded after failing to reach any kind of compromise between its extremes of Conservative protectionism and working-class radicalism. Chartism, though less overtly threatening – its claws partly drawn by Methodism's opposition to violence and subversion – was not yet a spent force.[14] As recently as 6 May 1848, Prince Albert – the public face of the Great Exhibition – had written to his German mentor, Baron Stockmar, 'We have Chartist riots every night, which result in numbers of broken heads. The organization of these people is incredible. They have secret signals, and correspond from town to town by means of carrier pigeons.'[15] Conspiracy theory was alive and well in the royal family in 1848 – the year of revolutions in Europe – and there were soldiers on London's streets for the last major Chartist demonstration.[16]

In the event, the Great Exhibition was an extraordinarily triumphant, and even more extraordinarily popular, celebration of Britain's leadership of the industrialized world. Its origins lay in the campaign for free trade, which had become irresistible once Sir Robert Peel, leader of the traditionally protectionist Conservative party, had seen the wisdom of repealing the Corn Laws (1846), thus lowering at a stroke the cost of bread in a decade when the poor were starving. The working partnership of Peel and Prince Albert was crucial during the planning stages of the Exhibition, and Peel's death after a fall from his horse a year before its opening added sentiment to the sense of occasion. His flexible intelligence had done much to bring Liberals (the old Whigs) and Conservatives (the old Tories) closer, though there were still diehard protectionists in his party and diehard free-traders in opposition. For the span of the Exhibition (1 May to 15 October 1851), though, the free-traders held the field. Until then, Albert had been generally viewed as a foreign interloper – he and the queen communicated with each other in German, and even Victoria's command of her subjects was fragile – but his astuteness in the lead-up to the Exhibition, which included a previously unheard-of royal trip to York to address a fundraising banquet, and the leadership he showed during it made the British monarchy a major beneficiary of the great event, even a sharer in the spirit of consensus initiated by Peel and eventually inherited by Gladstone. The innovatory internationalism of the Great Exhibition owed much to Albert, and there was great significance in its bringing other countries to the attention of the six million British islanders who came to the Crystal Palace. Those who entered Hyde Park from the Kensington Road would pass through a British section, seeing in the distance 162 metres of railtrack and two British locomotives, but to reach them they would pass India in one transept and China, Turkey and Tunis in the other. Germany was well represented, France and America more circumspectly, but there were exhibits from countries whose very names were unknown to many visitors. It felt like a stocktaking of human progress thus far, and seemed to herald a new era of world peace, with 'liberal' Britain showing the way to 'reactionary' Europe.

There was little the London theatres could offer to rival the spectacle of the Crystal Palace, though they relished the influx of visitors in search of entertainment. James Robinson Planché was asked to advise on heraldry and historical costume for the queen's costume ball and Samuel Phelps seized the patriotic spirit by staging *Henry V* at Sadler's Wells. Beyond uncertain evidence of prolonged runs of popular plays at some of the nineteen playhouses operating in the city in 1851, records of the theatre's immediate response to the Great Exhibition are sparse. In the longer term, though, it felt the effects of the nation's new self-confidence. Richard Schoch sees 1851 as the starting date for a renewed assertiveness: 'From the new perspective of the Crystal Palace, a dream of social order founded on respectability at last seemed possible. And leisure pursuits, one of the prized benefits of economic prosperity, were a prime area for achieving and advancing social harmony and intellectual enlightenment.'[17]

Thinking about foreigners

It is a convenient rule of thumb, when reading or watching nineteenth-century plays, that no foreigner is to be trusted, and in that respect, even after the Great Exhibition, theatre was in line with the majority of the population and a disturbing number of their political leaders. Imperial adventurers, fuelled by a confusing mixture of naked profiteering and missionary zeal, were certainly stimulated by the 1851 experience. Some carried guns, some Bibles, to far-off places, none more enticing than India, whose theatrical treatment will serve here to represent British responses to the baffling behaviour of 'Johnny foreigner'.

The sepoy uprising of 1857, quickly labelled the 'Indian mutiny', shocked a nation that had, for a century, taken for granted the benevolence of its administration of that strife-ridden – though intriguing and certainly profitable – subcontinent. Most of all it shocked the 1,700 stockholders of the East India Company, which was still in formal control of British interests in India. Only savages, it was argued, could have perpetrated the atrocity of the Cawnpore massacre of 200 European women and children – after raping them, it was darkly rumoured – and Nana Sahib, the native commander who was said to have ordered it, was the oriental devil incarnate.[18] Cawnpore and the prolonged siege of the British residency in Lucknow were the *causes célèbres* of the western media. Boucicault, flush with the success of his 'contemporaneous melodrama' *The Poor of New York* (1857), was in America when news of the relief of Lucknow broke, and he seems to have relied on a single press report for the local detail of *Jessie Brown; or, The Relief of Lucknow* (1858). The play is a swashbuckling melodrama in which a handful of British soldiers and a working-class Scottish girl outscheme and outfight Nana Sahib and his hordes before the nick-of-time bagpipes of General Havelock's relieving force scatter the savages. Boucicault himself played the murderous Nana Sahib, partly because he had difficulty in finding an American actor willing to brave the hostility of a New York audience.

In the immediate aftermath of Cawnpore and Lucknow, it was easy for Boucicault to portray Indians as either ignorant cowards or soulless serpents and the British as the gallant few. There were, after all, 250,000 sepoys and only 45,000 British in the East India Company's army, a ratio adjusted to two to one when the Crown ousted the Company in 1858.[19] The eventual quelling of the sepoys and subsequent establishment of the Raj went some way to assuaging British outrage. Sufficiently, anyway, for Taylor to skirt round xenophobia in *The Overland Route* (1860), which colourfully presents a group of British escapees from the 'mutiny' on board the Peninsular and Oriental steamship *Simoom*. But in *Not Guilty* (1869), Watts Phillips (1825–74) returned to the Boucicault formula. This is an action-packed melodrama incorporating details of fraud and false identity from a recent criminal trial and carrying its hero, villain and comic men and (one fat) comic woman from Southampton via Dartmoor Prison to a mythical Bhurtpoor on the banks of the Jumna in 1857 before returning them to Southampton for its sensational denouement. In Bhurtpoor, against 'fearful odds' of 'a hundred to one', there is a 'grand fight – a tussle between bull-dog and wild cat; and as usual the bull-dog has the best of it'. Jack Snipes, one of the two comic men, dislikes India – as any right-thinking Englishman should: 'Do you take me for a tiger, or what's worse,

Figure 29. Edward Armitage's *Retribution* (1858) is an outraged patriot's response to Cawnpore. Over the slaughtered bodies of an English mother and child, Britannia has seized the Indian tiger by the throat and is about to run it through.

for one o' these gamboge coloured ragamuffins, who are rampaging about the country, a warring with babies and women.' The sepoys are 'copper-coloured scum', and the gallant British can take comfort from their commanding officer's reassurance: 'Baulk the tiger in his first spring and you may beat him back into the jungle with your knotted handkerchiefs.'

The Delhi durbar of 1 January 1877 in celebration of the queen's proclamation as Empress of India marked an important shift in official British perceptions. The title was cherished by Victoria. Her employment, in old age, of the unreliable Abdul Karim, whom she created Indian Secretary in 1892, was a source of amusement and scandal in equal measure. ('These Injuns are too much for me', noted her Private Secretary Sir Henry Ponsonby.) The ceremonies of the Moghul Empire were reinstated under the aegis of the Raj, and it became the business of government to emphasize the stateliness and decorum of the Indian way of life. A high point came in 1895 with the Empire of India Exhibition at Earl's Court.

The impresario of this spectacular event was Imre Kiralfy (1845–1919), a Hungarian immigrant who had started his career in entertainment as a dancer but who had become interested in pageantry after visiting the Parisian Universal Exhibition in 1867. Having staged a number of dance-based spectaculars in America, he transferred *Nero; or, The Fall of Rome* (1889) to London's Olympia stadium, following it up there with a large-scale production of *Venice, the Bride of the Sea* (1891), to accompany the Venice in London Exhibition featuring canals, bridges and a glass factory. *America* followed in 1893, profitably staged at Chicago's huge Auditorium Theatre to coincide with the World's Columbian Exposition. Kiralfy was now rich enough to acquire a twenty-one-year lease on the Earl's Court exhibition grounds, which he radically redesigned to accommodate a new theatre, the Empress, intended to be the largest in the world. Roofed in a single span of 67 metres – second in London only to that of the most fantastic of all fantastic Victorian railway stations, St Pancras – and 36 metres high at its apex, the Empress had a proscenium-arched stage 96 metres wide and 30.5 metres deep. In addition, it was fronted by a hydraulically operable arena 23 metres deep, which could cover or reveal a concrete water tank. The capacity was 6,000. Kiralfy's Earl's Court was a new kind of pleasure garden, with a lake, three bridges (one covered), a giant ferris wheel with forty carriages, a 'Ducal Hall', a 'Queen's Palace' for indoor exhibitions, a massive (155 × 58 metres) outdoor exhibition space, a colonnaded 'Imperial Court' and an 'Indian City' – a mosque, houses, shops and theatres clustered together to focus the Indian style on which the architecture of the reconstructed 24-acre site was based. The old pleasure gardens, at best peripherally concerned with enlightening visitors, had closed – Ranelagh in 1803, Vauxhall in 1859, Cremorne in 1878. Kiralfy's Earl's Court was imperialist propaganda in architectural form, but the Empire of India Exhibition was undeniably educational, and so popular that it ran for a second season in 1896. At its centre, inaugurating the Empress theatre, was Kiralfy's 'Historical Spectacular Play', *India*, a four-part pageant with a cast of a thousand patchily covering the story of the subcontinent from 1024 to its 'Grand Apotheosis, Victoria. 1895'.[20]

The transformation of the land of 'copper-coloured scum' into the 'jewel in the crown' was a parable of empire, as slippery as most parables are. It was never absolute – there was still a murderous Raja in William Archer's *The Green Goddess* (1921), for example – but late Victorian plays such as Henry Arthur Jones's *Carnac Sahib* (1899) and Gilbert Murray's *Carlyon Sahib* (1899) are less likely to contrast blameless Europeans with black-hearted Indians.

Racism, though, remained the birthright of the patriot, and anti-Semitism a sign of good breeding. (Only a lamentable upbringing could explain the future Edward VII's friendship with the Rothschild brothers.[21]) Foreigners might have funny ways, they might even be funny, like Gilbert's Japanese in *The Mikado* (1885), or they might be sinister, like Svengali in *Trilby* (1895), Paul Potter's adaptation of George du Maurier's sexually contorted novel. The one thing they could not hope to be was 'British', a defect that went some way towards explaining their tendency to jealous vindictiveness.

The Irish problem

For five successive years (1845–9) blight destroyed the Irish potato harvest, depriving the rural population of its staple diet and the island of its most reliable export. It was Ireland's plight that finally convinced Peel of the need to repeal the Corn Laws (1846), but mass emigration – to England, Scotland, Australia and, in great numbers, America – continued. Unskilled labourers found employment where they could, most notoriously as railway navigators ('navvies'). Unshaven Irishmen, dangerous in drink, lurk in dark corners of Victorian crime melodramas, ignorant representatives of an angry people. The death of Daniel O'Connell in 1847 deprived the independence movement of its most charismatic spokesman but played into the hands of lesser leaders who, unlike O'Connell, preached violent resistance to British rule. Fired by the European revolutions of 1848, an armed group of about twenty Young Irelanders rose up in County Tipperary, only to be routed by the local constabulary in what came to be known as the Battle of Widow MacCormack's Cabbage Patch. As if in anticipation of Frith's painting, their leader, William O'Brien MP, was arrested at Thurles railway station. It was a fiasco, but it was also a portent. The Irish Republican Brotherhood was founded in 1858, linked with the secret society of Fenians which had its organizational centre among Irish immigrants in America. The bungled Fenian uprisings in Ireland in 1867 might have fed the old comedy stereotype of the blundering 'Paddy', had it not been for their aftermath in Manchester. It was there, in September 1867, that two captured Fenians were rescued from an unescorted prison van by a party of rebels, one of whom shot dead an uncooperative police sergeant. The charge in any court would have been manslaughter, but the guilty man and the two rescued Fenians were never found. Instead, the English executed three of the rescue party whom they had managed to track down. There are statues of Larkin, Allen and O'Brien, the 'Manchester Martyrs', in various parts of Ireland.[22] In the House of Commons ten years later, the Chief Secretary for

Ireland referred to the 'Manchester murderers', and the member for County Meath rose in protest: 'I wish to say as publicly and as directly as I can that I do not believe, and never shall believe, that any murder was committed at Manchester.' Charles Stewart Parnell (1846–91) had announced himself to the nation.

The failure of successive governments to deal with the Irish problem was a failure of understanding. As Parnell had insisted in his maiden speech in 1875, Ireland was not 'a geographical fragment' but a nation, with its own history and its own mythology. Even Gladstone, defeated parliamentary champion of Home Rule, misread the Irish text, not only splitting the Liberal party but also cutting himself off from Parnell at a time when their alliance could have changed the course of history. Both men sought change by constitutional, not violent, means, and Gladstone came to recognize that the key issue was ownership of the land. They were on the road to reconciliation when 'Mrs Grundy' stepped in. The fatal parting of the ways had nothing to do with politics: Parnell's fall in 1890 followed his being named as co-respondent in a divorce case. He had been Kitty O'Shea's acknowledged lover for ten years. The debt that misdemeanour owes to respectability was a constant theme in the serious drama of the period, and this ruinous relationship between a spirited woman and a public man was shadowed in the society plays of Arthur Wing Pinero and Henry Arthur Jones, the leading professional dramatists of the *fin de siècle*.

The founding of the Gaelic League in 1893 heralded a nonpolitical alternative to the promotion of the Irish cause: the revival of the Irish language and the recovery and promotion of national folklore. Through the friendship of the League's first president, Douglas Hyde (1860–1949), and Lady Augusta Gregory (1852–1932), the Dublin theatre became involved in Hyde's deanglicization project. Lady Gregory's vision of an Irish Literary Theatre, flamboyantly adopted by W. B. Yeats (1865–1939), was partly realized after the amateur company that she and Yeats had fostered found a permanent home in the Abbey Theatre in 1904, but the necessity for compromise was reflected in Lady Gregory's own translations into English of Hyde's Irish plays. The Abbey's is a twentieth-century story, but the problems it faced are partly explained by the portraits of Ireland and the Irish painted on the colourful stage of the English nineteenth century.

In the popular image theatrical Ireland was populated by beautiful colleens who could only with difficulty be dissuaded from singing, stout-hearted muscular boys (or 'bhoys') to defend their virtue and comically cheerful peasants with a weakness for drink and an inability to complete a sentence without saying 'begorrah', not to mention the jolly old priest with a not very secret store of poteen in the sacristy and surprising dexterity with a shillelagh when the going gets too tough for the hero. It was an image which George Colman the Younger's *John Bull* (1803) had exploited and which George Bernard Shaw was grappling to destroy as late as 1904, in *John Bull's Other Island*, and it was in this fantasy land that the Dublin-born Edmund Falconer (*né* O'Rourke, 1814–79) set his Irish plays: *Peep o' Day; or, Savourneen Deelish* (1861), *The O'Flahertys; or, The Difficulties of Identifying an Irishman* (1864), *Galway Go Bragh; or, Love, Fun and Fighting* (1865), *Eileen Oge* (1871), and *Agra-ma-chree* (1875). Only the first of these – and then in America rather than London – had any durable success. Except as librettist for fellow-Dubliner Michael Balfe (1808–70), Falconer struggled for the recognition that has conclusively eluded him,[23] but he created the role of the crippled Danny Mann in one of the best Irish romantic dramas, Boucicault's *The Colleen Bawn* (1860). The plum part of Myles-na-Coppaleen was bagged by Boucicault himself.

Myles is a variation on the comic man of melodrama – a garrulous rogue who pits his wits against the law in the service of true justice, and does so (this is Boucicault's innovation) as an essential contribution to the central narrative. *The Colleen Bawn* is a crafted melodrama, in which even the by-play of Myles's jocular flirtation with Sheelah (no longer simply the comic woman) is designed to strengthen the hold of a plot which grips. The problem that faced the Irish Literary Theatre, as it faced Shaw, was that Boucicault had fashioned a compelling drama out of the material of fantasy.

> Dion Boucicault, when he invented Myles, was not holding the mirror up to nature, but blarneying the British public precisely as the Irish car-driver, when he is 'cute' enough, blarneys the English tourist. To an Irishman who has any sort of social conscience, the conception of Ireland as a romantic picture, in which the background is formed by the lakes of Killarney by moonlight, and a round tower or so, whilst every male figure is 'a broth of a bhoy', and every female one a colleen in a crimson Connemara cloak is exasperating.
>
> George Bernard Shaw, reviewing a revival of *The Colleen Bawn* (1896)

The Dublin-born Boucicault could play the Irish patriot when it suited him, as it quite often did during his self-promotional years in American cities saturated with Irish immigrants. *Belle Lamar* (1874) opened in New York and *Robert Emmet* (1884), an embroidered version of Emmet's doomed 1803 attempt to capture Dublin from the English, in Chicago. Had *The Shaughraun* (1874), the finest of his Irish melodramas, opened in London rather than New York, the specified Fenianism of its nominal hero, Robert Ffolliott, would have been censored. The *real* hero is Conn the shaughraun, 'the soul of every fair, the life of every funeral, the first fiddle at all weddings and patterns' – the comic man located at the centre and played, of course, by Boucicault. The long journey from Conn to Christy Mahon in J. M. Synge's *The Playboy of the Western World* (1907) began in England's Ireland. The proposition that it ended in Ireland's Ireland was hotly disputed by some of the rioters when Synge's play opened at the Abbey. They, at least, were happier with Boucicault's version. Gladstone's failure to establish home rule and a Dublin parliament is easily understood. After centuries of English (mis)government, Irish consensus was a mirage.

Women who did, and women who didn't

At the height of the bicycle craze, the bestselling novelist Marie Corelli (1855–1924) took it upon herself to remind her devoted readership that neither Dante's Beatrice nor Petrarch's Laura would ever have stooped to wearing bloomers.[24] She was only one of a number of prominent women whose reactionary pronouncements lent support to patronizing patriarchy. The middle-class trope of the incorruptible 'angel in the house' folding her wings over her vulnerable children and clasping an ever-erring husband in a forgiving embrace served simultaneously to elevate and disempower women. The archetypal Victorian expression of it is less Coventry Patmore's *The Angel in the House* (1854–62) than Tennyson's *Enoch Arden* (1863), almost unreadably sentimental now but bringing its author at the time a popularity that no other English poet has ever achieved. It is an unrealized melodrama, in which a lost husband, believed dead, returns to glimpse the cosiness of his wife and her second family through a window of her new home – and moves on. Marriage generally meant multiple motherhood and a secure place in a social circle determined by the husband.

The exceptions – among whom actresses figured prominently – are almost always more interesting than the rule. Ellen Terry (1847–1928) weathered a divorce from the admired painter George Frederick Watts, who was more than three times her age when they married in 1864, a liaison with the architect and occasional scene-designer Edward Godwin which produced two illegitimate children, and two broken marriages to men much younger than herself, on the way to a socially untroubled old age and, in 1925, the accolade of a Dameship of the British Empire. Something about her demeanour, its uncomplicated charm perhaps, persuaded contemporaries that she was not so much immoral as a bit unorthodox. Most of her fictional counterparts were punished much more severely for doing much less, and the right of women to decide for themselves could certainly have done without the perfidious support of a self-trumpeting male advocate like Grant Allen (1848–99). Allen's sensational novel *The Woman Who Did* (1895) purports to celebrate the 'stainless soul' of Herminia Barton, who dares to have a child out of wedlock because she shares the radical views of her lover. The fatal blow to her self-esteem, just as it is the fatal blow to Paula Tanqueray in Pinero's moral blockbuster of a drama *The Second Mrs Tanqueray* (1893), is her daughter's rejection of her. For Herminia, as for Paula Tanqueray, the only escape is through suicide. Just beneath the surface of the superficially sympathetic portrayals of errant women in almost all the male-authored 'problem' plays that were a particular feature of the theatre during the last two decades of the nineteenth century lurks an atavistic sexism. Unlike Pinero and Henry Arthur Jones, though, Grant Allen – champion of the rights of women – is crass enough to declare himself.

> The man must needs retain for many years to come the personal hegemony he has usurped over the woman; and the woman who once accepts him as lover or husband must give way in the end, even in matters of principle, to his virile self-assertion. She would be less a woman, and he less a man, were any other result possible. Deep down in the very roots of the idea of sex we come on that prime antithesis – the male, active and aggressive; the female, sedentary, passive and receptive.
>
> Grant Allen, *The Woman Who Did* (1895)

Had Edith Craig (1869–1947) turned on her mother as Dolores Barton and Ellean Tanqueray turn on theirs, might Ellen Terry, too, have killed herself?

If the idea is preposterous, so must be the 'serious' plays and novels of the period, Mrs Henry Wood's much-dramatized *East Lynne* (1861) included, that seek their social resolution in the death of the woman with a past. Quite intelligent people were, it seems, persuaded that carnal desire, however burdensome, was natural in men, but that even love, when infected with carnality, was a social disease in women. One of the most admired episodes in the whole of Victorian drama – Act 3 of Henry Arthur Jones's *Mrs Dane's Defence* (1900) – involved the unmasking of the woman who claims to be Lucy Dane by Sir Daniel Carteret, adoptive father of her would-be husband. Carteret is neither a bully nor a martinet, but he is every inch a *man*, and the sexually tortured Jones speaks through him in his later summing up of the case for the prosecution.

> Do, for heaven's sake, let us get rid of all this sentimental cant and sophistry about this woman business. A man demands the treasure of a woman's purest love. It's what he buys and pays for with the strength of his arm and the sweat of his brow. It's the condition on which he makes her his wife and fights the world for her and his children. It's his fiercest instinct, and he does well to guard it; for it's the very mainspring of a nation's health and soundness.
>
> Henry Arthur Jones, *Mrs. Dane's Defence* (1900), Act 4

Between the woman who said 'yes' and the woman who did not, Victorian drama set an unbridgeable gulf.

There was some slackening of the patriarchal hold on positions of power as the century approached its end, but it required an uncommonly resolute woman to take advantage of it.[25] At no time since 1660 did women playwrights feature so meagrely as during the reign of Queen Victoria. The prospect of a good marriage (and not *too* many children), with the new safeguard provided by the Married Women's Property Act (1881), was expected to satisfy all but the neurasthenic (a debility generally associated with sexual disorder – too much sex or, more often, none at all was the presumed source, much whispered about in single-sex gatherings), and there was no British playwright before Shaw to argue a serious case for the equality of the sexes. Shaw's *Mrs Warren's Profession*, written in 1893 as a counterblast to *The Second Mrs Tanqueray*, was not licensed for public performance until 1925. 'I want to be something so much worthier than the doll in the doll's house,' protests Bella Wilfer in Dickens's *Our Mutual Friend* (1864–5). Twenty-five years later, when Henrik Ibsen's *A Doll's House* was first performed in England, nobody thought of Dickens. Uppermost in almost all the (male) reviewers' minds was the decadent Norwegian's assault on the sacred institution of marriage. It would be eye-opening to explore the marital histories of those reviewers in this heyday of the double standard.

A technical coda

The availability of typewriters after 1875 was an aid to actors, since their learning of parts – still measured by the number of 'sides' they occupied – became less dependent on scribal legibility, and the duplication of dialogue scenes could replace the old system of 'cues only'. Gilbert was the first playwright to distribute printed versions of his complete 'manuscript' to his actors, but he had been encouraged to pay close attention to the detail of stage production by the example of Tom Robertson (1829–71). In Robertson's *School* (1869) the definition provided by limelight is exploited in an exquisite dialogue of dawning love between Lord Beaufoy and Bella Marks.

BEAUFOY: What long shadows the moonlight flings. See – there I am.
BELLA: But so tall – so high.
BEAUFOY: And there are you.
BELLA: But not so tall as you are.
BEAUFOY: And yet you're nearer the skies – see! (*moving*) Now we're far apart.
         (*The moonlight throws long shadows from right to left*)

> BELLA: And now – (*moving*) – we're joined together. Wonderful things, shadows, are they not?
>
> BEAUFOY: Yes, when they lie before us.
>
> BELLA: I often wonder what they're for – what they mean?
>
> BEAUFOY: No one can tell, except poets, and painters, and lovers; and they know all things, and what they don't know they feel. See, we are divided again.
>
> BELLA: No. (*placing her hand on the jug*) The jug unites us.
>
> > Tom Robertson, *School* (1869), Act 3

But the fascination with theatrical gadgetry, as in the twenty-first century with new technologies, had its drawbacks. At least twenty-five theatrical patents were issued in 1887 (the first year of the patent explosion), and the number rose year by year thereafter.[26] New limelight techniques, improved optical illusions, mechanisms for flying or suspending actors, appliances for representing horse races, anything that might help blur the distinction between the fictional and the real. Production costs rose in line with an expectation that costumes and properties should, wherever possible, be what they purported to be. The costly tea-set in the fashionably furnished drawing room should be a costly tea-set in a fashionably furnished drawing room. It was a trend, begun in the nineteenth century, that dictated the operational terms of smart theatres all over Britain for a hundred years.

> Once the idea of a stage-property had suggested itself there was no end to the number of accessories that the actor found he required, until finally the art of acting was degraded to the practice of dressing up in real diamonds in order to be drowned – and why not really drowned? we feel obliged to ask – in hundreds of gallons of real water.
>
> > Leon Moussinac, *The New Movement in the Theatre* (1931)

With the installation of electricity in the Savoy in 1881, the London stage announced its readiness for the twentieth century.

Chapter 14

The drama

Dion Boucicault sold *London Assurance* (1841) to the Vestris/Mathews management for £300:

> Three years later I offered a new play to a principal London theatre. The manager offered me £100 for it. In reply to my objection to the smallness of the sum he remarked, 'I can go to Paris and select a first-class comedy; having seen it performed, I feel certain of its effect. To get this comedy translated will cost me £25. Why should I give you £300 or £500 for your comedy, of the success of which I cannot feel so assured?'[1]

The theatrical slump of the 1830s continued through the 1840s, and was sufficient to persuade so instinctive a dramatist as Charles Dickens to place his financial faith in the novel. The position improved significantly over the second half of the nineteenth century, however, particularly for playwrights shrewd enough to sign up with literary agents. Working through English's Dramatic Agency, W. S. Gilbert had earned £2,200 from *The Palace of Truth* (1870) by 1876. The International Copyright Act of 1851 strengthened the arm of agents, though international pilfering remained widespread until the Berne Convention of 1886 and the American Copyright Bill of 1891 discouraged it more effectively.

Equally significant was the precedent of Boucicault's opting for a profit-share, rather than £50 per week, during the run of *The Colleen Bawn* at the Adelphi (1860), though only a confident playwright would have taken such a risk. Boucicault, never short of confidence, established two companies to tour the play to the provinces during its London run, and may have made as much as £23,000 in the 1860–1 theatrical year. Only late in the century did publishers – other than those of flimsy acting editions (Dick's, Lacy's, French's, Webster's) – begin to dignify modern plays with book-binding, thus conferring on them an implicit status as literature and attracting the interest of established novelists and poets. Charles Reade (1814–84), who would achieve Bulwer-like fame with his boisterous historical novel *The Cloister and the Hearth* (1861), began by writing plays and then turning them into novels, and went on to write novels with a view to turning them into plays, and the lure of the stage was later felt by Robert Louis Stevenson, Alfred, Lord Tennyson, Thomas Hardy and even – to his mortification when *Guy Domville* (1895) was hissed by a first-night audience at the fashionable St James's – Henry James.[2]

Elaborate stage directions mark a recognition that plays were for reading as well as viewing. They are there in Tom Robertson, whose *Principal Dramatic Works* were published in two volumes in 1889,[3] but only to affirm the theatrical provenance of the stage 'business'. A new world has been entered between Oscar Wilde's second drawing-room comedy, *A Woman of No Importance* (1893), and his third, *An Ideal Husband* (1895). We are on the way to the opulence of George Bernard Shaw's sermons to the reader.

> *Enter LORD GORING in evening dress with a buttonhole. He is wearing a silk hat and Inverness cape. White-gloved, he carries a Louis Seize cane. His are all the delicate fopperies of Fashion. One sees that he stands in immediate relation to modern life, makes it indeed, and so masters it. He is the first well-dressed philosopher in the history of thought.*
>
> Oscar Wilde, *An Ideal Husband* (1895), opening of Act 3

The use of stage directions to supply comment or information beyond the natural range of an actor would not have occurred to Robertson. It signifies the eagerness of the 'new' drama to gain access to the discursive territory of novels and essays. With the abolition of the patent monopoly, playwrights felt less bound by the old categories of tragedy, comedy and so on, down to the lowly 'burletta', and the old assumption that highbrow plays (tragedies or comedies) must occupy five acts was quickly abandoned. As a distinct genre, in fact, 'modern' tragedy was ineffectual in the Victorian theatre. By mid-century an author could indicate that his play was predominantly 'serious' rather than 'funny' by calling it a 'drama'. It was through their choice of themes – after the style of Edward Bulwer's *Money* (1840) – rather than of genres that playwrights declared their claims on critical attention.

'Mr Hawtree's grandfather was in trade': the misalliance *motif*

The crossing, or not crossing, of class boundaries was an issue that no British nineteenth-century writer could leave alone for long. It was so securely in the national bloodstream that even the poacher would doff his cap to the squire.[4] The puzzle is that not one of the countless plays featuring the clash of classes offers any serious resolution of the contradiction at the heart of the debate: it was evidently possible to believe simultaneously that people should stick to their own class *and* that 'Kind hearts are more than coronets, / And simple faith than Norman blood.' The provenance of this much-quoted Tennysonian tag was, even at the time, generally forgotten. 'Lady Clara Vere de Vere' (*c*.1830) is a short poem encasing a domestic tragedy: young Laurence, a commoner, has cut his own throat after being first enticed and then spurned by Lady Clara.

> Lady Clara Vere de Vere,
>   There stands a spectre in your hall:
> The guilt of blood is at your door:
>   You changed a wholesome heart to gall.
> You held your course without remorse,
>   To make him trust his modest worth,
> And, last, you fix'd a vacant stare,
>   And slew him with your noble birth.
>   Alfred, Lord Tennyson, 'Lady Clara Vere de Vere' (*c*.1830)

It was one thing – not advisable even in a dramatic character, but oddly admirable just the same – for a noble youth to be 'chums' with a school-master, or for a young lady to share secrets with a governess, but marriage was a different matter. Either the prospect or the aftermath of misalliance, treated with increasing seriousness from about 1880 when melodrama was yielding ground to the social 'problem' play, was so regular a dramatic subject that it droops, in retrospect, into a tedious insignificance until its witty reappraisal in the hands of Shaw.[5]

It was, though, a live issue then, particularly in the theatre where authentic gossip linked actresses and aristocracy. Had not Harriet Mellon (1777–1837) married the Duke of St Albans when she was fifty? Louisa Nisbett (1812–58) returned to the stage as Lady Boothby after her second widowhood, and the beautiful Helen Faucit (1814–98), once William Charles Macready's leading lady but for many years a star in her own right, was Lady Theodore Martin after 1880, when her husband was knighted on the strength of his adulatory biography of Prince Albert. Much seamier was the marriage (in 1871) of Kate Walsh, a variety 'artiste' rather than an actress, to the Earl of Euston. When the Earl sought a declaration of nullity on the ground that, in 1871, she was still married to a man called Smith, he lost the case after it emerged that Smith's first wife was still alive when he 'married' Kate Walsh. There were others, too. In 1884 the eccentric Marquis of Ailesbury married a ballerina whose stage-name was Dolly Tester, and in the same year – most sensationally of all – Kate Vaughan (*c*.1852–1903), bright star of the Gaiety quartet of burlesque performers (1876–83) and originator of the mildly erotic 'skirt dance', married the nephew of the great Duke of Wellington. The aristocrat at the stage door was not a mere music-hall joke: three musical comedy actresses married into the peerage in 1901, the year of the queen's death. Misalliance was almost as much an offstage as an onstage feature of the Victorian theatre, and that must have added piquancy to an otherwise routine dish.

H. J. Byron's *Our Boys* (1875), the first London play to record a thousand consecutive performances, shows what playwrights could get away with if they chose to laugh off the problems of class division.[6] Like Brandon Thomas's *Charley's Aunt* (1892), which broke its long-run record, *Our Boys* is what might now be called a 'feel good' play, in which a baronet and a 'butterman' (manufacturer and/or vendor of dairy products) find themselves in unlikely alliance for no better reasons than that each loves his son ('our boys' having formed an equally unlikely friendship while travelling in Europe) and that they, like everyone in the play, are so fundamentally *nice*. Some social levelling may have been a by-product of the European tours organized by Thomas Cook (1808–92)[7] from 1863, since they carried the British middle classes for the first time to places still frequented by their social superiors, but Byron (1835–84) has made no attempt to explain what has brought the effete Talbot Champneys and the vigorous Charles Middlewick together. On the contrary, contrast being the lifeblood of traditional comedy, he has made them as incompatible as their respective fathers. Nor is there any particular reason *within* the play why Middlewick should pair up with the girl the baronet has designed for his son and Champneys with the spirited but penniless dependant. The complications are formulaic, not intrinsic, and there are straightforward reasons for that. The most prolific of mid-Victorian playwrights, Byron wrote potboilers for money, and he wrote them to serve the preference of particular theatres and audiences: burlesques and pantomimes for the fun-seeking regulars at the Strand and the Gaiety, heavy melodramas for the Holborn Theatre Royal (*Blow for Blow*, 1868) and the Queen's (*The Lancashire Lass*, 1867), comedies for the Haymarket, nothing to suggest social insight. He was a kindly man, self-indulgent but not selfish, who liked writing funny lines ('I never let concealment, like a worm in the bud, feed on my damson cheese, as Milton says': *Old Soldiers* (1873), Act 3) and whose chief contribution was his sustaining of the punning tradition brilliantly exemplified by the poet and journalist Thomas Hood (1799–1845). It would not have occurred to him to wonder what would have happened if the baronet of *Our Boys* had to introduce the butterman to his society friends.

It was Byron who brought together, in what proved to be a momentous partnership, Robertson and the burlesque actress Marie Wilton (1839–1921), now in 1865 on the road to respectability as manageress of the old Queen's theatre, newly refurbished and renamed – with permission – the Prince of Wales's. It was a small house (capacity *c*.500) with an evil reputation, and despite Wilton's energetic optimism, combined with her catchy fondness for interior chintz, the polite audience she craved was not easily attracted. Her legs, regularly on display in burlesque travesty roles, and her sex appeal had excited the predominantly male habitués of the Strand: now, bent on a change of image, she wanted to play to postprandial families from Bloomsbury or St John's Wood. It was a sequence of long-run comedies by Robertson that sealed it for her: *Society* (1865), *Ours* (1866), *Caste* (1867), *Play* (1868), *School* (1869) and *M.P.* (1870). Posterity has been unwilling to confirm the view that these plays heralded a revolution in British drama, but their out-of-the-blue popularity created a different target audience, one which would serve not only Henry Arthur Jones and Arthur Wing Pinero but also Wilde and Shaw. *Caste* is the one that offers to tackle the misalliance theme most directly.

Robertson was born into the provincial theatre: his parents were actors on the Lincoln circuit, managed by his uncle. By 1848 Lincoln was sharing in the decline of the old stock companies, buckling under competition from national tours, and Robertson moved to London in search of work as a 'utility' (bits and bobs) actor, prompter, stage-manager, author, adapter or translator of plays, theatrical factotum, journalist, whatever. His ideas were unremarkable and his intelligence shaped by convention, but he had a distinctive interest in the onstage relationship of actors and their material environment: lighting, stage properties (not only their appearance but also the sound they might make), scenery (including doors, whose opening to admit the 'wrong' person – or the 'right' one – will change the direction of the narrative). Robertson's stage directions are remarkable: his plots are not. *Caste* is built around the contrasting courtships and marriages of the two (contrasting) daughters of a drunken layabout. Polly Eccles (Marie Wilton's lively part) is paired with Sam Gerridge, a gas-fitter who knows his place, Esther with George d'Alroy, a serving officer with an ancient pedigree and a formidable mother (school of Lady Bracknell in *The Importance of Being Earnest* (1895)) in the Marquise de St Maur. D'Alroy has fallen for Esther after seeing her dance at an unnamed theatre (possibly the Strand), thus contravening what his 'swell' friend Captain Hawtree calls the 'inexorable law of caste': 'The social law, so becoming and so good, that commands like to mate with like, and forbids a giraffe to fall in love with a squirrel'.[8] The Marquise, of course, agrees ('There is blood – and blood, my son. Let Radicals say what they will'), proud of a lineage that dates back to the fourteenth-century *Chroniques* of Froissart. For her, Hawtree is a *parvenu* whose grandfather was 'something in the City – soap, I think, perhaps pickles', whereas her husband 'always is paralysed at this time of year; it is in the family. The paralysis is not personal, but hereditary'. (Like Wilde's Lady Bracknell, the Marquise contrives to appeal to us by the sheer excess of her snobbery.)

There is nothing to surprise us in such entrenched views, but Robertson seems on the edge of making a point when he has Gerridge summarize them in one of the best-known Victorian railway metaphors.

> Life's a railway journey, and Mankind's a passenger – first class, second class, third class. Any person found riding in a superior class to that for which he has taken his ticket will be removed at the first station stopped at, according to the bye-laws of the company.
>
> Tom Robertson, *Caste* (1867), Act 1

But the point, if Robertson ever had one, is shrugged off by the plot. D'Alroy has married Esther before his regiment is sent off to quell the Indian 'mutiny' (for the first audiences, then, the events occurred ten years ago), and is reported killed before discovering that he has a son. His return supplies us with a Robertson moment. Instead of the conventionally histrionic entrance of the *revenant* (throwing off a cloak, usually), he comes into his wife's humble home in Lambeth carrying a milk-can which, having put his hat on the piano, he places on the table, saying, 'A fella hung this on the railings, so I brought it in.' Very soon the Marquise will be kissing her daughter-in-law, Hawtree will shake hands with Gerridge in mutual acknowledgement of fundamental decency, and D'Alroy will misquote Tennyson's 'Kind hearts and coronets' before providing the bland conclusion that 'Caste is a good thing if it's not carried too far.' Robertson is in good Victorian company – Tennyson's included – in offering facile solutions to discomforting problems.

Misalliance remains an underlying theme in most of the best, and many of the worst, plays of the late nineteenth century, *Mrs Warren's Profession* (1893) and *The Importance of Being Earnest* among them. Still writing a Victorian play seven years after the old queen's death, Pinero (1855–1934) presents the criminal destruction of a will by a decent woman as the outcome of her being ostracized by her husband's relations because of her humble origins. *The Thunderbolt* (1908) is a powerful variation on the kind of 'last will and testament' play that Bulwer had written in *Money* but it surrenders to prejudice as meekly as *Caste*. The Mortimore family are Midlands industrialists whose snobbery is based on money rather than birth, and that, at least, is Pinero's recognition of a social shift. The youngest sibling is despised partly because he earns so little as a professor of music, but more because he has married a woman whose father 'kept a grocer's shop on the corner of East Street'.[9] The rise of a plutocracy, advanced by Edward VII's friendships with the rich, may have changed the key of the 'caste' melody, but Pinero is no nearer a harmonic resolution than Robertson.[10]

Taking your breath away: the sensation scene

There can be no question that Victorian audiences were drawn to the theatre by the promise of spectacular action: train-crashes, horse races, conflagrations, deep-sea rescues – all the twentieth-century material of disaster movies – were ingeniously staged to gratify appetites that had earlier fed on Gothic extravagance. Even Henrik Ibsen, the unimpeachable champion of the theatrically plausible, was prepared to conclude his last completed play, *When We Dead Awaken* (1899), with an avalanche, almost certainly unaware that Mary Elizabeth Braddon had long beaten him to it in her creaking melodrama *Genevieve; or, The Missing Witness* (1874). Mrs Braddon (1837–1915) was one of many 'sensation' novelists to cash in on the fame of Charles Dickens: her *Lady Audley's Secret* (1862), a luridly vengeful 'woman with a past' story, was still being serialized when unsanctioned dramatized versions opened at three London theatres. Such novels were meat and drink for theatrical journeymen, and remained so into the next century. An unsolved murder, or a solved one, might spark off a melodrama: crime almost always paid in one or other of London's theatres, commonly in plays much more slovenly than Tom Taylor's *The Ticket-of-Leave Man* (1863) or George Sims's *The Lights o' London* (1881). Sims (1847–1922) in particular was alert to the wretched conditions in which the poor of London lived, and his sensation scenes, like most of his published ballads,[11] were designed to expose them. Time-locked by the superior illusions of the cinema, such scenes have little more than curiosity appeal now. Much more chilling in *The Lights o' London* is a throwaway episode (Act 4, Scene 2) in which two charitably inclined unnamed 'gentlemen' plot their contribution to a Christian mission in Africa before brushing aside the appeal of the play's victimized hero to spare a penny to save his wife from starvation. Missionary generosity was often blind to urban privation at home: a sympathetic policeman offers Harold Armytage a swig of brandy, but there is no institutional support – not even the workhouse – for the unemployed poor in London. *The Lights o' London* remained unpublished until 1995.[12] It is formulaic in its dependence on misalliance, but rich enough in sociohistorical detail to remind us of how much has been lost by the neglect of Victorian drama.

Only through an awareness of the contemporary appeal of sensation scenes can the charm of Robertson's revisionary tactics in his Prince of Wales's comedies be appreciated. *Ours* transports us from the peace of an English country home to a hut in the Crimea, '*built out of boulders and mud*' and close to the battlefront. Sensation here is evident each time the crude door is opened to release a flurry of snow into the hut, and reaches its climax when Mary Netley rolls up her sleeves to prepare a rolypoly pudding out of improvised ingredients. Look! She's using the leg of a stool as a rolling-pin and a soldier's towel as a pudding-cloth! Robertson was not the first playwright to punctuate dramatically fraught action with such contradictorily everyday activities as sipping tea or nibbling bread and butter. Taylor had done it brilliantly in his worm-that-turns play (always a surefire formula in the theatre), *Still Waters Run Deep* (1855), when Mildmay, on the edge of turning, undercuts the portentous urgings of his wife's interfering aunt.

MRS STERNHOLD:	I have a secret to confide to you – a most important secret; one I should not dare to entrust to anyone in whom I had not the most implicit confidence.
MILDMAY:	I'm much obliged to you; what is it? And as I've not breakfasted, if you will give me a cup of tea while you tell me. (*sits at table*)
MRS STERNHOLD:	(*pouring out tea*) Promise me first not to mention the subject to anyone – not even your wife.
MILDMAY:	My wife! Didn't you say it was a secret? The cream, please.
MRS STERNHOLD:	If your mother were alive, and a man had insulted her, what would you do?
MILDMAY:	The right thing, of course. Might I trouble you for the sugar basin?
MRS STERNHOLD:	You have lost your mother; so has Mrs Mildmay; but your marriage with her has given you a claim upon me, second only to that of a brother. From all I have seen of you, I feel I may expect of you a brother's devotion.
MILDMAY:	Do you? Butter, please.

Tom Taylor, *Still Waters Run Deep* (1855), Act 2, Scene 2

Robertson's 'sensational' innovation was to hold the audience's attention on the incidental everyday business to such an extent that the main action of the play became subsidiary to it. That the theatre should be *so like life* was a thrilling novelty.

Containing multitudes: the Jekyll and Hyde *motif*

There was a scholarly Yorkshireman, a philologist and schoolteacher, called Eugene Aram (1704–59), much respected in King's Lynn where he had taught since 1757; and there was a corpse up north near Knaresborough, where it had

SCENE FROM THE NEW PLAY, "OURS," AT THE PRINCE OF WALE'S THEATRE.

Figure 30. *The Illustrated London News* version of a scene from Tom Robertson's *Ours* (1866). Mary Netley has not yet set about the rolypoly pudding, but there are stars in the sky, snow in the air and a smoking chimney.

lain undiscovered from 1745 until 1758, close to the home of Aram's abandoned wife and seven children. Events so panned out that Aram was arrested in front of his King's Lynn class, transported to Knaresborough, tried in York and hanged at Knavesmire on 6 August 1759. The eighteenth century blinked and carried on, but the nineteenth century was mesmerized by the spectre of the outwardly good man who 'contained' a murderer. Thomas Hood's balladic 'The Dream of Eugene Aram' (1829) made the issue of the *Gem* in which it was published an instant bestseller. Three years later, Bulwer's novel *Eugene Aram* cashed in on public interest, and was immediately dramatized by William Moncrieff for the Surrey theatre. There were at least three other adaptations in 1832. Hood's poem was the favourite curtain-piece of Henry Irving, who in 1873 commissioned a play on Aram from his Lyceum poet, W. G. Wills (1828–91). It was an act of indirect homage to the (purloined from the French) drama that had catapulted Irving into celebrity. Leopold Lewis's *The Bells* (1871) features – to the exclusion of any interest in its other characters – a respected burgomaster who, to his own destruction, fails finally to contain the secret that he escaped from poverty into his present wealth by robbing and murdering a Polish Jew fifteen years previously. The cloaking of crime, or sin, in outward virtue is a common enough theme in nineteenth-century fiction to justify the suspicion that it was also a common Victorian fact. In the theatre, particularly when portrayed by an actor with Irving's visceral access to a tortured inner life, it had evidently the lubricious lure of the forbidden. True self-knowledge is a fearsome threat to the unrepentant sinner who has to fight off a recognition that the only route to peace is through being found out. That is the *real* horror of Stevenson's *Dr Jekyll and Mr Hyde* (1886): not that there is a drug that can transform a good man into a monster, but the doctor's discovery that the monster was inside him all the time.

Stevenson's own attempt to dramatize the double life in *Deacon Brodie* (1879) is comparatively tame, though the original William Brodie (1746–88) was a promising subject.[13] Lesser writers had greater theatrical success, particularly when the double life was merged with the *Doppelgänger* – the exact lookalike who is, but is not, you. To play both Sydney Carton and Charles Darnay in dramatizations of Dickens's *A Tale of Two Cities* (1859) was an actor's dream, inviting any would-be virtuoso into bravura performance. Sam Emery (1817–81), rarely much more than a jobbing character actor, leaped at the chance offered to him in Watts Phillips's *Not Guilty* (1869), but the doubling here is purely theatrical. There is no hint of elision between the heroic Colonel Willoughby and the indestructibly malevolent Silas Jarrett, who saves his own skin by impersonating his dead lookalike. Phillips employs the double for sensational purposes, taking the audience by surprise when Jarrett appears on one side of the stage while the colonel is still lying dead on the other.

> The COLONEL by an effort drags himself painfully up to rock, and after supporting himself for a moment with difficulty, falls to the right behind it. His head is thrown back against ground, and half his body, from waist downwards, is still in view of audience, and one arm to which still hangs the uniform, which ARNOLD has previously unbuttoned. [To manage the situation which follows, a 'super' dressed as COLONEL WILLOUGHBY stands prepared behind the rock, and falls instead of him to extreme right. The actor playing the two parts disappears by means of a trap under the stage, and re-appears almost immediately on opposite side as Silas Jarrett.]
> Watts Phillips, *Not Guilty* (1869), Act 3, Scene 3

The advantage of the *Doppelgänger*, when given its full sinister value, was that it gave the virtuoso actor an opportunity to play a good and an evil self – extreme contrast being, as ever, a source of theatrical delight. Reade's was the one of several English versions of the French *Courier de Lyons* (*c.* 1840) in which Irving chose to display his versatility as the faithful Lesurques and the villainous Dubosc: 'A wonderful touch was his blithe camaraderie in patting the horse as he murdered the postboy,' Henry Arthur Jones recalled.[14] In the hypnotic atmosphere of the Lyceum, though, a disconcerting apprehension that Irving was playing himself in *both* roles was always in the air. The evil is within!

Indecency's conspiracy of silence: theatre and sex

To take a seat in any theatre is to volunteer for voyeurism, though the measure of titillation anticipated will vary from person to person and show to show. Within the patriarchal conventions of the Victorian theatre, as acceptably to managers and playwrights as to audiences, beautiful actresses traded on their beauty and pretty actresses on their prettiness, and if sexy actresses traded on their sexuality, they were called pretty or beautiful and assumed to be innocuous until the newspapers proved otherwise. Male sex appeal was altogether more mysterious, since it was conventionally supposed that no natural woman (let alone any man) was susceptible to it, and that it was the manly will rather than the handsome face or the manly chest (and certainly no part south of that) that overpowered the womanly woman. It was according to such rules that Victorian audiences were officially expected to watch Victorian actors playing out dramas of sexual pursuit and surrender. We may be sure, but cannot prove, that a high proportion of audiences broke the theatrical rules, experiencing vicariously the stirrings of the troubled characters. So much that is surreptitious happens in the plays that they must have been designed to feed the habitual surreptitiousness of the onlookers, particularly, I suspect, the young women. As Elizabeth Robins (1862–1952) – actress, playwright, novelist, feminist, promoter of Ibsen – recognized, a middle-class girl growing into womanhood in Victorian England was caught in a trap: 'Though a woman's first business in life was to please, she had to live out her youth in fear of the results of pleasing.'[15]

This, though, is to accept one truth about Victorian society at the neglect of another, to confuse an inclination towards purity with purity itself. The Victorian middle classes knew and did a lot more than they admitted. They were happy to read between the lines, and sensed that even their world was changing as the century neared its end. Henry Arthur Jones (1851–1929), always a barometer of shifts in the sexual climate, made two bold bids to express his own confusion. In both *The Dancing Girl* (1891) and *Michael and His Lost Angel* (1896), he presents men overpowered by the sexuality of 'free' women.

The first was a tolerable success at Beerbohm Tree's Haymarket, the second failed at the Lyceum. Jones, who always though *Michael and His Lost Angel* his finest work, blamed everything but the text. But such abject masculinity as that of Michael Feversham, after his descent into carnality, was more appallingly confessional than he can have intended. 'Your skirts have swept through all the gateways of my being,' he tells Audrie Lesden *before* they become lovers, and afterwards defines the image of his sin as 'a greyish-green reptile, with spikes, and cold eyes without lids'. Even before Freud's influence was felt in England, this was too revealing for some sections of the Lyceum audience, and hostility was augmented by Jones's trespassing into religious territory. Feversham is an Oxford-educated country vicar, in the F. D. Maurice school of muscular Christians – a fighter for his own and others' moral survival in a sea of temptation. The play opens with his insistence that a young female member of his congregation should make public confession of her sexual fall, charts his own seduction by a woman of the world, and ends, after his own public confession, in a Catholic monastery to which he has retreated (the seductress tracks him down just in time to die in his arms). Contentious treatments of religion in plays were routinely banned by the Lord Chamberlain's office, and it is more surprising that *Michael and His Lost Angel* was licensed for performance than that its closing of the sexual gaps between the lines troubled a vocal minority.

Even odder, though, is Jones's own attitude to the play. His parents had been strict Baptists and his upbringing joyless.

> Dancing, card-playing and theatre going were vices. Lying was a sin to be promptly punished by a severe thrashing. I have never been able to tell a lie without feeling the greatest discomfort and reluctance.
> Henry Arthur Jones, 'In the Days of My Youth' (1923)

During his youthful training as a draper (later a commercial traveller in drapery), he concealed his visits to the theatre from his family. More than thirty before *The Silver King* (1882) brought him any success as a dramatist, he was famous for twenty years, during which, without quite lying, he generally put his faith in the audience, writing as he believed they would have written had they his application. And yet he was sure they were wrong about *Michael and His Lost Angel*. Why? Because this time he believed he had told the truth – written on his own behalf rather than that of his public. Perhaps he had. He was a ferociously opinionated man, who wished to be a good one. But the sadder truth is that *Michael and His Lost Angel* is likely to make a twenty-first-century reader cringe with embarrassment for Jones. Like many of the moralizing plays of the late Victorian era, it justifies the words that Wilde put into Lord Darling-ton's mouth in *Lady Windermere's Fan* (1892): 'I am afraid that good people do a great deal of harm in this world. Certainly the greatest harm they do is that they make badness of such extraordinary importance.' Three years later, the good people would find Wilde's badness important enough to merit a gaol sentence.

Daughters and ducats: the Silas Marner *motif*

Shylock's anguished mourning for the simultaneous loss of his daughter and his ducats resonated for Victorian audiences through a succession of stunning productions of *The Merchant of Venice*. In her short novel *Silas Marner* (1861), George Eliot reconfigures the episode. The miser Silas, robbed of his gold, *finds* a baby girl and is transformed by his growing love for her. Gilbert acknowledged, but understated, his debt to *Silas Marner* in the composition of *Dan'l Druce, Blacksmith* (1876), an uncharacteristically crude melodrama given a largely spurious historical setting spanning the English Civil Wars and the restoration of Charles II. He knew well enough that it was second-rate work, but he knew as well as Sheridan Knowles, Dickens and Alfred, Lord Tennyson that tender-hearted Victorian audiences lapped up stories of heart-rending parental care. Mrs Henry Wood's *East Lynne* (1861) was published in the same year as *Silas Marner*. Even without the benefit of dramatization – and it has been more often dramatized than any other novel – its tear-jerking treatment of a mother's mute love for her dying son would probably have made it a bestseller, but the *performance* of parenthood had a ferocious theatrical grip on the Victorian obsession with the idea of a family, and sales of *East Lynne* soared.

In *East Lynne* it is her adulterous past that prevents Lady Isabel from admit-ting her motherhood – Wilde's Mrs Erlynne (as the choice of name wryly indicates) in *Lady Windermere's Fan* (1892) is similarly silenced – but it was the embodied clash between money and parental love that gave the Silas Marner *motif* its sociotheatrical bite. There is nothing extraordinary about Palgrave Simpson's *Daddy Hardacre* (1859), nothing, that is, except the performance of the title role, the miser who loves his daughter and is robbed by her, by Fred-erick Robson (1821–64). It is very likely that Eliot saw the production at the Olympic – her partner, George Henry Lewes, was a friend of Simpson (1807–87) and an admirer of Robson. If so, Robson's Hardacre was an as yet unacknowl-edged source for *Silas Marner*. As an actor, Robson was certainly an inspiration to Dickens.[16]

To be or not to be Ibsen

Ibsen's arrival among English dramatists was as disconcerting as that of an adult stranger at an adolescents' party in the middle of a game of 'postman's knock'. It forced some of them to realize that they ought to be more grown up, but most of them to insist that it was *their* party and Ibsen hadn't been invited. What was unacceptable about *A Doll's House* (1879) was not that Nora walked out on her husband, not even that she walked out on her husband *and children*, but that the play *ended* there after giving the audience every chance to sympathize with her. English plays – the versions of *East Lynne* and Henry Arthur Jones's *The Case of Rebellious Susan* (1894) are relevant examples – might portray a wife's desertion, but not without also underlining the consequences. So strong was the resistance to Ibsen, and above all to *Ghosts* (1881), which dared to haul the skeleton of inherited syphilis out of its cupboard,[17] that he had generally to be smuggled into the theatre by way of ill-subsidized matinée performances or 'private' productions 'for members only'. It was, of course, as futile for the theatre to try to exclude him as for the art world to try outlawing French Impressionism. Not only *A Doll's House* and *Ghosts* were staged during the Ibsen year of 1891, but also *Hedda Gabler* (1890), *Rosmersholm* (1880) and *The Lady from the Sea* (1888): and, as if that were not enough, a fluent music and drama critic called, but not yet widely known as, George Bernard Shaw (1856–1950) published, in October, his own dramatic manifesto, *The Quintessence of Ibsenism*.

The full impact of Shaw's plays was not felt until the twentieth century: the impact of Ibsen was felt in the nineteenth even by those who denied it. Clement Scott warned readers of the *Daily Telegraph* (14 March 1891), in his review of the Independent Theatre's production of *Ghosts*, that the play was 'an open drain . . . a loathsome sore', and its staging 'a dirty act done publicly'. A wiser critic, who had attended the same performance, felt differently.

> One wonders whether these hysterical protestants have ever read anything, observed anything, pondered anything. Have they no eyes for what stares them in the face: the plain, simple fact that *Ghosts* is a great spiritual drama?
> A. B. Walkley, in the *Star*, 14 March 1891

When Shaw set himself to becoming a playwright, he did not so much reject the time-worn conventions of Victorian drama as recycle them for his own un-Victorian ends.[18] Much as he admired Ibsen, he was too much a jester to copy him.

The serious dramas of Pinero, from *The Profligate* (1889), through *The Second Mrs Tanqueray* (1893) and *The Notorious Mrs Ebbsmith* (1895), to *His House in Order* (1906) and *Mid-Channel* (1909), represent the peculiarly British dilution of Ibsen that was felt to be necessary (perhaps, in view of censorial vigilance, *was* necessary) before social criticism could be served up in West End theatres. As in the plays of Henry Arthur Jones, sex is the problem: cope with that, and you can cope with anything. That Ibsen was concerned to probe the abuses of power and the consequent laceration of the human spirit seems to have been noticed by few British playwrights other than Shaw. The American actress Elizabeth Robins, perhaps through playing Hedda Gabler in 1891, understood Ibsen in ways that were beyond Pinero. For all its clumsiness, *Alan's Wife* (1893), which she wrote with Florence Bell, is the maturest, most Ibsenite play to have been staged (privately) in the nineteenth century.

An alternative approach to social criticism – through mockery rather than excoriation – is best represented by Gilbert (with or without Sullivan) and Wilde (1854–1900). The most enjoyable, perhaps the best Victorian drama belongs here, recording the century's often forgotten sense of fun. Farceurs such as John Maddison Morton (1811–91) and Joseph Stirling Coyne (1803–68) are part of the unbroken tradition that preserves the legitimacy of a 'good night out'. But farce has often a subversive aspect. Pinero's most assured work – the trio of farces for the Court Theatre – shows pillars of the community tumbling into indignity: a magistrate (*The Magistrate*, 1885), an admiral and a headmistress (*The Schoolmistress*, 1886), a vicar (*Dandy Dick*, 1887). The fact that so many Victorian dramatists were also contributors to *Punch* (founded in 1841) is significant: laughter and astringent observation were in alignment.

Gilbert's genius in the *Bab Ballads* and his best plays was to apply logic to paradox and absurdity. Act 2 of *The Palace of Truth* is one of the funniest *sustained* passages of humour in the history of drama – perhaps to the detriment of the savage point Gilbert is making: that customary politeness hides the utter selfishness of people with social and political authority. *Tom Cobb* (1875) covers some of the same ground as Bertolt Brecht's *Man Is Man* (1926), its naïve hero browbeaten into surrendering his own identity to the self-interest of his 'friends'. Brecht's mild Galy Gay becomes a human fighting-machine, docile Tom Cobb a major-general. Arthur Sullivan (1842–1900), who took art seriously, could never come to terms with Gilbert, who took frivolity seriously. Their incompatibility, expressive of a deep fissure in Victorian culture, is central to the abiding appeal of the Savoy Operas. Gilbert's masterpiece is *Engaged* (1877), a play which gives the fullest scope to his ability to phrase insincerity as if it were sincerity, thus alerting receptive members of his audience to the difference between manners and meaning. That Gilbert was a brilliant writer is too little recognized, but a reading of *Engaged* can leave no doubt that it was Wilde's primary source for *The Importance of Being Earnest*.

Gilbert was defiant enough to deny the right of people who felt no temptation to condemn those who succumbed to it. With good reason, Wilde agreed. Both men tried, through humour, to break the chain that linked the personal pursuit of virtue to the passing of public judgement, and neither trusted the appearance of sincerity. 'Taking sides is the beginning of sincerity, and earnestness follows shortly afterwards,' Lord Illingworth warns in Wilde's *A Woman of No Importance*. It was the importance of *not* being earnest that Gilbertian satire stressed and that is the message of Wilde's greatest play. His earliest society dramas are overloaded with witty paradoxes which have no bearing on their contrived plots. That is not to say that *Lady Windermere's Fan* and *A Woman of No Importance* are poor plays, but they left Wilde open to the unusually cruel burlesque of Charles Brookfield's *The Poet and the Puppets* (1892). Brookfield (1857–1913) charges Wilde with plagiarism and with filching his laugh-lines from Joe Miller's joke books.[19] More significantly, though, he implies that he falsified himself. When the actor Charles Hawtrey (1858–1923), mimicking Wilde, summons a fairy to help him with his play, the fairy warns him that 'I don't much believe in you.' The burlesque was the beginning of a sad story. Hawtrey and Brookfield were in the cast of Wilde's third and best society comedy, *An Ideal Husband*, at the same time as they were amassing evidence and gathering witnesses of Wilde's homosexual activity for the Marquis of Queensberry.[20] It is the great virtue of *The Importance of Being Earnest* to enact paradoxes rather than spout them. The paradox that Wilde came to recognize was that earnestness did for him in the end.

Trelawny of the Wells: a retrospect

Trelawny of the Wells (1898) is Pinero's affectionate portrait of the 'old' theatre at the point of its adaptation, through Robertson and Wilton, to the 'modern' era. It ends as the rehearsal of Tom Wrench's play (*Life: A Comedy*) is about to begin. We know what it will be like, the speeches short and with 'such ordinary words in them', and the stage with 'windows on the one side doors on the other – just where they should be, architecturally. And locks on the door, *real locks*, to work; and handles – to turn!' 'There's not a speech in it,' complains old Telfer, for whom the mid-century shift in offstage conversational style towards the brisk and understated has passed unnoticed, 'not a real *speech*; nothing to dig your teeth into.' Poor Telfer, actor-manager of the Wells before the reformation, is reduced to playing 'an old, stagey, out-of-date actor'. 'Will you – be able – to get near it, James?' asks his sympathetic wife in one of the play's many touching moments.

From the perspective of 1898, what was new in Wilton's Prince of Wales's was already old. Pinero writes in the confidence that his modern audience at the Court will agree that the drama has advanced since then, assimilating Robertsonian innovation and going beyond. There were, though, more lingering traces of the old tradition than Pinero supposed. Despite the example set by Gilbert, most theatres continued to distribute a new play in 'sides', for the actors to learn before rehearsal began. And every theatre had its pit orchestra, and a backstage call for 'overture and beginners'. At the Haymarket, for *A Woman of No Importance* and *An Ideal Husband*, the musical director was Mr Carl Ambruster. If there were music cues, they are not announced in the published texts, but the established dominant-seventh for surprise and diminished-seventh for shock would not have been out of place. Pinero's dislike of incidental music was exceptional: 'I can't see that anything of this sort is required,' he told George Alexander when *The Second Mrs Tanqueray* was in preparation. 'Don't you think "incidental" scraping vulgarises a piece that doesn't belong to either "the kettle-on-the-hob" or "the Blood-on-the-Breadknife" order of play?'[21] Even so, the fall of the curtain at the end of each act of *The Second Mrs Tanqueray* demands an orchestral response, in the case of the last three to accompany an onstage tableau.

The greatest change was in the audience. The installation of electricity facilitated the darkening of the auditorium before the performance began. In the little Prince of Wales's, Wilton had replaced the four rows of pit benches with individual stalls, and the innovation was soon copied. The combined effect was to make attendance at the play less communal, less boisterous, and this aided West End theatres in their quest for a fashionable audience. Not that the quest was always successful. There had been a falling off of middle-class attendance in the 1850s and 1860s at playhouses from which the working classes already felt excluded (they had their own theatres in the East End, and a monopoly on music halls). Irving's tenure of the Lyceum from 1871 did something to reassure the middle classes: the Savoy Operas of Gilbert and Sullivan in the 1880s did more. By the end of the century, different theatres were targeting different audiences and being rewarded by loyalty, though never without the risk of giving offence. And the avant-garde was being championed by club performances from J. T. Grein's Independent Theatre (1891–8) and the Stage Society (founded 1899). There was even a private performance of *The Cenci* (1819), sponsored by the Shelley Society in 1886. The urge to counter retrospect with prospect has almost always taken a grip on public consciousness as the end of a century approaches or as a new century begins. In the theatre this urge expressed itself through a growing impatience with the constraints imposed on British drama by a system of censorship that continued to inhibit free enquiry. If the 1890s brought Wilde's dramatic career to a sad end, the decade witnessed also the first plays of two highly original, if profoundly contrasting, playwrights. From 1895 to 1898 Shaw was able to declare his modernity in the explosive reviews he wrote for the *Saturday Review*, as well as in *Widowers' Houses* (1892), *Arms and the Man* (1894), *Candida* (1897), *The Devil's Disciple* (1897) and *You Never Can Tell* (1899). More enigmatically – enigma was not Shaw's mode – J. M. Barrie (1860–1937) was beginning to find his theatrical feet. Properly understood, *Peter Pan* (1904) is a wry retrospect on a theatre that might yet grow up, even if Peter Pan wouldn't.

Chapter 15

Actors and acting

When Henry Irving (1838–1905) was knighted in 1895, Queen Victoria acknowledged on behalf of the nation the respectability of acting, or so it could be said. More generally, though, she was confirming the respectability of success. Irving had been effectively the actor-manager of the Lyceum since 1871, during which time it had achieved the status of a national theatre. Victorian respect for (insistence on) hierarchy made inevitable the hegemony of actor-managers. They determined the repertoire and style of the theatres they ran, sometimes even gave their names to them: the great farceur J. L. Toole (1830–1906) opened Toole's in 1882, Edward Terry (1844–1912), on the profit of his burlesque fame as one of the Gaiety quartet, built Terry's in 1887, Charles Wyndham (1837–1919) made enough money as actor-manager of the Criterion to build Wyndham's in 1899 and the New Theatre (later the Albery, after his wife's first husband) in 1903. These were middle-class men on the rise. Toole was a favourite of the Prince of Wales, Terry a Freemason who was Grand Treasurer of all England in 1889, and Wyndham was knighted in 1902, third in a long line of actor-managers (Marie Wilton's husband, Squire Bancroft (1841–1926), was the second in 1897) to receive the accolade.

More than ever, the theatre was also an area in which women asserted their independence. There is work to be done on Fanny Josephs (*fl.*1860–80),[1] who managed the Holborn Theatre Royal in the late 1860s after a brief career in burlesque, and on Marie Litton (1847–84), who managed a succession of London and provincial theatres through the 1870s. Lydia Thompson (1836–1908) splendidly defied propriety by heading a burlesque troupe, even taking it on a pioneering tour of America, Australia and India, which lasted from 1868 to 1874, and in the course of which she was tried and fined for horse-whipping the censorious editor of the *Chicago Times*. Sarah Thorne (1836–99) was not only the most prominent provincial manager of her time, but also an admired trainer of actors, and Elizabeth Robins and Janet Achurch (1864–1916) were outstanding promoters of Henrik Ibsen's plays. To be an actor-manager became the routine aspiration of anyone who achieved stardom. The peaks and troughs are sensitively recorded in Leonard Merrick's theatrical novel, *The Actor-Manager* (1898).

Actor training

Irving made no secret of his belief that there was no training like practice in a well-disciplined theatre, but the spirit of the age was not entirely with him. If acting was to earn its professional status, should it not, like the law and even painting, have an educational profile? Gustave Garcia's *The Actor's Art* (1888), typically of instructional handbooks, assumes that the art is to conceal the art, and that '*to be natural* is the first consideration for an actor', while outlining a series of highly artificial 'practices' and 'studies' as stepping stones to naturalness. This is entirely in line with the prospectus for Sarah Thorne's School of Acting (opened 1885), with its promise of training in 'voice production, gesture and mime, dialects and accents, make-up, the portrayal of characters, the value of pace and the value of pauses'. Britain in the nineteenth century introduced no new system of physical or emotional preparation for the arduous business of becoming someone else for a while, and neither Garcia nor Thorne makes any reference to the idea of ensemble. That is not to say that ensemble acting was unknown in the Victorian theatre. It had been there in embryo at Madame Vestris's Olympic, and was a feature of the Wilton/Robertson comedies at the Prince of Wales's. John Hare (1844–1921) had been one of the company there, and carried the ensemble principle into his own distinguished actor-management (he would be duly knighted in 1907). But training schools like Thorne's were set up to attract pupils from the middle classes, and pupils from the middle classes had visions of stardom. Garcia was professor of singing at the London Academy of Music (established 1861), and omitted the concluding three words of the Academy's name, 'and Dramatic Art', from his title page because music was what mattered there. The founding of a Royal Academy of Dramatic Art in 1904, then, was significant, but its significance was more symbolic than practical. It dignified a profession it did little to change.

Still writing for actors

The nineteenth century was the first to produce a significant body of unperformed plays, though very few that have exerted much of a claim on posterity. Pragmatic dramatists continued to take their cues from actors, tailoring plays for outstanding individuals or creating characters appropriate to flourishing

Figure 31. Aubrey Beardsley's drawing of Mrs Patrick Campbell authenticates her claim to have invented the dreamy eyelid.

companies. The system was not foolproof. Henry Arthur Jones had written *Michael and His Lost Angel* (1896) with Irving and Ellen Terry in mind for the two dominant roles, and it is possible that the ferocity of the one and charm of the other would have carried it. As it was, though, Irving and Terry were on an American tour, and the title roles were handed on to the genteel Johnston Forbes-Robertson (1853–1937, knighted 1913) and the arch-temptress Mrs Patrick Campbell (1865–1940). To make matters worse, Jones and Campbell quarrelled, and she walked out on the production three days before its opening. Terry's sister Marion took over, but the play was already doomed. Its story of a good man lured into fornication by lust and driven to the brink of madness when he discovers that his mistress is married was a test too far for Forbes-Robertson, a good man who was in the early stages of a fraught affair with the married Campbell. Using the excuse of hostility from sections of the Lyceum audience, Jones closed the production after eleven nights. He was on more secure ground when supplying Wyndham with well-crafted society dramas for a Criterion audience that had come to expect no less.

Wyndham and George Alexander (1858–1918, knighted 1911), actor-manager of the St James's from 1890 until his death, had generally the pick of dramas set in the upper echelons of society, and they catered for audiences that liked to be thought fashionable. Wyndham, whom Shaw considered the only man for the title role of *The Philanderer* (1898), was the better actor, but Alexander's steadiness – his ability to keep a straight face amid comic chaos – made him an ideal Jack Worthing in *The Importance of Being Earnest* (1895).

> I had written a part which nobody but Charles Wyndham could act, in a play which was impossible at his theatre.
>
> George Bernard. Shaw, preface to *The Philanderer* (1898)
>
> [Alexander] was in the middle of a scene with Ethel Irving when he stopped and stood with that doleful, harassed look which used to overspread his face when the bottom was dropping out of his world. From the stalls, I asked him what was the trouble. He replied: 'We're in the centre of the stage.' I was a little staggered, for I had never thought of actor-managers as people liable to be distressed upon finding themselves in that position. As a rule they drift by some process of magnetism inevitably towards it. But he explained. 'You see, we play to rather sophisticated audiences here, and if I'm in the centre of the stage they'll say, "There of course is the actor-manager," and the illusion of your play's gone.'
>
> A. E. W. Mason, *Sir George Alexander and the St. James' Theatre* (1935)

Wyndham modelled suavity (London assurance) for his age, and he and Alexander honoured the tradition of gentlemanly acting that dated back to the

Restoration by way of such recent luminaries as Charles Mathews the Younger and would be continued into the twentieth century by Gerald du Maurier (1873–1934, knighted 1922). If you can keep your head when all around you are losing theirs, you'll be a Man, my son: Kipling's famous 'If' was well exemplified by Wyndham and Alexander, who were prominent at a time when London was being scatter-bombed by elusive terrorists: were they Fenians or anarchists? Between 1889 and 1895, attempts were made to blow up Westminster Hall, the House of Commons, three railway stations, the Tower of London, London Bridge, Nelson's Column and the Royal Observatory. Calmness and worldly wisdom like Wyndham's provided a very British antidote to fanaticism.

The Irving phenomenon was different. Lyceum audiences were rarely out of touch with pathology when their revered – and slightly feared – actor-manager was on form. George Bernard Shaw was understandably antagonized by the Lyceum's repertoire of 'modern' plays, already old before they were born, but Irving's interest was in theatre first and drama as its servant. He had none of Alexander's hesitancy about taking centre-stage, not least because that was what his audience wanted. His was a pictorial vision, and great historical canvases always had a central focus. He owed it to his public to be remarkable, and modern dress reduced him. The roles that best expressed him were those that displayed a tormented man – either heroically villainous or heroically virtuous, or both[2] – struggling titanically against circumstance. The Victorian image of the divided self, a source of both horror and illicit pleasure, was embodied by Irving's Mathias in *The Bells* (1871) and his thrilling doubling of Lesurques and Dubosc in *The Lyons Mail* (1877). In that sense, even in a production whose setting and costume were historically Venetian, his Shylock was Victorian. But so, in a less flattering sense, were his attitudes to the socially critical modern drama. Irving was superbly equipped to play Solness in Henrik Ibsen's *The Master Builder* (1893) or the riven Rosmer in *Rosmersholm* (1886). In 1897 Terry tried reading *John Gabriel Borkman* (1896) to him – he took over from her after two acts – but his notebook response was 'Threadworms and leeches are an interesting study; but they have no interest to me.'[3] Instead, and to the immediate detriment of British theatre, he devoted his unrivalled stagecraft to the mothballing of magnificence, shaping theatrical magic out of the raw material of Alfred, Lord Tennyson's poetic tragedy *Becket* (1893), and bemusing audiences into a belief that the verse plays of W. G. Wills were great drama.

He was utterly unlike anyone else: he could give importance and a noble melancholy to any sort of drivel that was put into his mouth; and it was this

> melancholy, bound up with an impish humor [*sic*], which forced the spectator to single him out as a leading figure with an inevitability that I never saw again in any other actor until it rose from Irving's grave in the person of a nameless cinema actor who afterwards became famous as Charlie Chaplin.
>
> Shaw's preface to *Ellen Terry and Bernard Shaw: A Correspondence* (1931)

Shaw rightly resented Irving's control over Terry's career, but his deeper regret was that 'a new drama inhered in this man', and was wilfully stifled.

The decorative and the dangerous

When Aubrey Beardsley's drawing of Mrs Patrick Campbell as Paula Tanqueray appeared in the first volume of the controversial *Yellow Book* (1894), it tended to confirm the actress's reputation as a woman who had seen and done too much. If her decision to act under her married name was intended to discourage gossip, it failed. There was plenty to feed it. Her father, John Tanner,[4] had money, and her mother was the daughter of an Italian count. They had sent her to Paris to complete her education, and indulged her wish to attend the Guildhall School of Music, but all links with them were severed when, already pregnant at eighteen, she secretly married Patrick Campbell (he was twenty) in 1884. By the time she made her professional debut in 1888, she had a second daughter and her husband was working in South Africa (he was killed there in the Boer War in 1900). She stood on the wrong side of the moral dividing line, sharing nothing with the ultra-respectable Madge Kendal (1848–1935), Tom Robertson's youngest sister in a widely spread Victorian family, except the role of Paula Tanqueray. That Victorian society should so clearly distinguish between the original Mrs Tanqueray and her most famous successor is evidence of the conventional rigidity with which women were judged. Mrs Kendal, despite playing the stage's notorious 'woman with a past', remained a madonna; Mrs Campbell confirmed herself a magdalene. The image of the opposing female 'types' – the temptress Eve and the nurturing Mary, mother of Jesus – was regularly, though not invariably, imposed on actresses. Playing against type as Paula Tanqueray, Kendal convinced audiences that there was innocence at the heart of this fallen woman; playing against type as Mélisande in an English version of Maurice Maeterlinck's breathy *Pelléas et Mélisande* (1898), Campbell was received as innocence concealing corruption, Jekyll and Hyde in female form.

> Her strange beauty and mysterious eyes full of brooding sadness were of great
> help to her . . . 'My eyes are really nothing in particular,' she once observed to
> me. 'God gave me boot buttons, but I invented the dreamy eyelid, and that
> makes all the difference.'
>
>   W. Graham Robertson, *Time Was* (1931)

The pairing of contrasting women, archetypally in the Becky Sharp and Amelia
Sedley of William Thackeray's *Vanity Fair* (1847–8), was echoed almost *ad
nauseam* in Victorian drama. At some risk to their own reputations, strong
actresses wisely preferred wicked Beckys to insipid Amelias, but there was a
living to be made out of either.

Campbell held her own with most of the actor-managers she worked for, and
when she had had enough went into management on her own account, with
mixed fortune. Womanly women – madonnas – were better protected. The
American Gertrude Elliott (1874–1950) was nursed into the London theatre
by Forbes-Robertson, who married her on the rebound from Campbell. Like
her more famous sister Maxine (1871–1940), she was more often required to
be beautiful than to do anything startling. They were among the hundreds of
(mostly forgotten) actresses and hundreds more chorines whose main function
was to keep in step and decorate the stage. However it was disguised, the male
response to the female presence in the Victorian theatre generally invoked the
line between the dangerous and the decorative. Exceptionally, the indefinable
Ellen Terry was allowed to straddle it. In 1895, when the two leading foreign stars
Eleonora Duse (1858–1924) and Sarah Bernhardt (1844–1923) were in open
competition on the London stage,[5] Terry was said to combine the qualities of
both the lymphatic madonna Duse and the flamboyant magdalene Bernhardt:
not a divided self, but a whole one in two parts.

Victorian Shakespeare

Shakespeare remained the measure of greatness, as much in Manchester or
Margate as in London.[6] The most extraordinary response to the 1843 abolition
of the patent monopoly was that of Samuel Phelps (1804–78) at the 'low'
playhouse of Sadler's Wells. During his eighteen years of management there
(1844–62), he staged and took leading roles in thirty-one of Shakespeare's
plays, including the impossible *Antony and Cleopatra* in 1849 – impossible on
the pictorial stage because of its multiple locations – and the unloved *Pericles*
in 1854 and *Love's Labour's Lost* in 1857. Phelps was a solid actor and a serious
Shakespearean, resistant to the making of 'points' and ready to restore the Fool
to *King Lear* and clear away some of the wilder accretions to the texts – like the

witches' songs and ballets in *Macbeth*. Phelps's belief that Shakespeare's plays should be performed within reach of every class of people was in tune with the educational spirit of the age. It is legitimate to admire his enterprise without greatly warming to it.

The same is true of the elaborately mounted productions of Charles Kean (1811–68). Torn from the start between living off and living down the reputation of his father Edmund, Kean was temperamentally closer to William Charles Macready, whose career-long struggle to prove theatre respectable he emulated. There is a depressing aura of propriety about almost all his initiatives, not least his spotless marriage to the angelic Ellen Tree (1806–80), who regularly acted with him for more than thirty years. The Keans came as a package, particularly in their meticulously planned tours of the provinces, the colonies (Australia in 1863–4) and America, and the keynote of their productions was not charisma but correctness. It was a sensible way to remind audiences that he was not his clap-happy father. Kean's Drury Lane Hamlet (1838) had signalled his breakaway. The young Queen Victoria was excited by it, following his subsequent career with an interest capped in 1848 by his appointment as director of royal theatricals at Windsor Castle, a sinecure which meant much more to him than to her.

It is on his management (1850–9) of the modestly sized Princess's theatre in Oxford Street that his Shakespearean reputation is based. Under his artistic supervision seventeen of the plays were staged, in a repertoire that balanced Shakespeare and melodrama (Dion Boucicault was house dramatist for a while), and that set the fashion for long runs, a luxury that Phelps could never afford at the much larger Sadler's Wells (capacity *c*.2,500). Because he intended each new production to settle for at least a month, Kean could afford to indulge the interest in historical accuracy that he shared with painters and an influential section of theatregoers. His place in histories of Shakespearean production is assured by scenery and costume. Antiquarianism had been active in the theatre since John Philip Kemble's tenure of Covent Garden. The latter's younger brother Charles (1775–1854) had famously employed James Robinson Planché to provide historically accurate costumes for *King John* (1824).

This present Monday, January 19, 1824, will be revived Shakespeare's Tragedy of King John with an attention to Costume never equalled on the English Stage. Every Character will appear in the precise HABIT OF THE PERIOD, the whole of the Dresses and Decorations being executed from indisputable Authorities, such as Monumental Effigies, Seals, Illumined Mss., &c.

Covent Garden playbill (1824)

Macready, too, had done his best, within the limits of his fragile budget, to sustain the contested marriage of scholarship and performance. But it was Charles Kean who made antiquarianism spectacular. Souvenir programmes at the Princess's were history lessons, products of his own researches. He used theatre to embellish scholarship – with a stage of modest depth and width, he asked his stage-carpenters to build up levels, his scene-painters to reproduce the past and his musical directors to enhance the action at each dramatic climax. The outcome was an inflated realism that had a profound effect on Shakespearean productions for the rest of the century. Kean's career reached an appropriate climax in 1857, when he was elected a fellow of the Royal Society of Antiquarians, but it was a year of mixed fortune: his directorate of the Windsor Castle theatricals was terminated, the queen having taken a dim view of a letter from his wife soliciting a knighthood for him. In a curtain speech on his last night as actor-manager of the Princess's, he reviewed his achievement with justifiable pride, but his lingering decade as a touring actor would be soured with bitterness.

> In this little theatre, where £200 is considered a large receipt and £250 an extraordinary one, I expended in one season alone little short of £50,000. I have given employment, i.e. weekly payment, to nearly 550 persons, and £10,000 has been expended on improvements and enlargements.
> Charles Kean, speaking on 29 August 1859

It would take nearly forty years of social readjustment before Britain was ready to reward an actor with a knighthood.

Irving was, in some ways, Kean's successor: he, too, was a devotee of spectacular staging and a demanding overseer of every aspect of the performance, and he, too, alternated Shakespeare with the kind of melodrama in which both men were more consistently at ease. But in Lyceum Shakespeare antiquarianism played second fiddle to theatricality, and Irving was a far finer actor. Inflated realism, in his case, embraced psychology: he was the theatrical father of A. C. Bradley's seminal *Shakespearean Tragedy* (1904), with its scholarly emphasis on character. Of more enduring theatrical influence than the pictorial Shakespeare of Kean and Irving, though of marginal importance at the time, was a minority interest in the return to the simple staging of the Elizabethan era. The success of the concert readings of Fanny Kemble (1809–93) may have contributed to this movement. Niece of John Philip Kemble and Sarah Siddons, she was personally the most impressive and independent of the Kemble dynasty, confident of holding an audience while she read a whole play. But the first of her London performances in 1848 was predated by an eccentric experiment at the normally

Figure 32. The *Illustrated London News* representation of Charles Kean's *The Winter's Tale* at the Princess's Theatre in 1856. Kean chose to transfer Act 1 from Sicilia to an archaeologically researched Syracuse in 330BC, where Leontes was entertaining his royal guest in the banqueting hall of his palace. 'Thirty-six resplendently handsome young girls, representing youths in complete warlike panoply, entered, and performed the evolutions of the far-famed Pyrrhic dance.' (J. W. Cole, *The Life and Times of Charles Kean*, 1860)

conventional Haymarket. It was once again Planché who took the initiative in proposing to present *The Taming of the Shrew* on an approximation of an Elizabethan platform stage.[7] The 1844 production was given a mixed reception by reviewers, some critical of its historical shortcomings, some bewildered that such bareness could ever be considered a theatrical asset. Shakespeare would surely have preferred the resources of the Victorian theatre. The actor-manager Ben Webster (1797–1882) was patted on the head, and Planché carried on writing extravaganzas for the Haymarket. The missionary of the Elizabethan revival had not yet been born.

William Poel (1852–1934) was the kind of zealot around whom embattled religious cults are formed.[8] Oscar Wilde would have recognized him as one of the dangerous people whose insistence on taking sides was the prelude to earnestness. His earliest theatrical hero was the Italian Tommaso Salvini (1829–1915), whose Othello at Drury Lane in 1875 he admired for its close attention to the text.[9] Irving, by contrast, was anathema – everything sacrificed to effect. After a provincial apprenticeship as a utility actor, he formed a company, which he called 'The Elizabethans', to tour costume recitals of classic plays to any venue that would receive them. He was already convinced that the genius of Shakespeare was swamped by theatrical artifice, and that the true quality of the poetry would be revealed only if the scenic disguise were stripped away. The *sound* of Shakespeare was always his primary concern. Through contact with F. J. Furnivall, president of the New Shakspere Society and one of the great Victorian eccentrics,[10] in 1881 Poel secured St George's Hall in London for an unprecedented performance of the First ('Bad') Quarto of *Hamlet*, with himself in the title role. In retrospect, this production, on a stage backed by curtains but otherwise bare, is a landmark. At the time it was scarcely even a curiosity. But the ability to recognize the claim to revival of a reviled travesty of a great tragedy confirms Poel as the pioneer of a necessary reappraisal of Shakespeare. His perseverance is as remarkable as his insight. Appointed as an unofficial instructor to the Shakespeare Reading Society, the creation of students at University College, London, he supervised staged readings in which he developed his theory of 'tuned tones' as the differential basis of Shakespearean character, and directed the Society's 1893 production of *Measure for Measure*. His preference for amateur enthusiasm over professional complacence was validated by the energetic conversion of the Royalty Theatre's stage into a simulacrum of the Fortune (the only Elizabethan theatre for which detailed contemporary documentation survives). Poel went on to found the Elizabethan Stage Society (1894–1905), whose productions included a *Twelfth Night* with actors selected according to vocal pitch (Malvolio a baritone, Sir Andrew Aguecheek falsetto) and authentic music on authentic instruments provided by Arnold Dolmetsch and – his sole uncontroversial success – *Everyman* (1901).

Poel was just as much an antiquarian as Charles Kean, but they pulled in opposed directions. The New Globe, a wasteland for Kean, would have been Poel's playground. He remained an outsider to the end, though acknowledged as a mentor by such twentieth-century innovators as Granville Barker and Nugent Monck, and a detail of his biography completes an intriguing triptych on the subject of theatrical knights. Kean sought one in 1857, Irving received one in 1895, and Poel declined one in 1929 – because he had no wish to share an honour with people whose idea of theatre he despised.

Notes

1 The material circumstance

1. John Dryden, *The Vindication of The Duke of Guise* (London, 1683), p. 42.
2. By Sir William Barclay.
3. Rather than stamping out rumours that he was Shakespeare's love-child, Davenant may have started them.
4. Matthew Medbourne, a competent member of the Duke's Company and a professed Catholic, was incriminated by Titus Oates, arrested on 26 November 1678 and died in Newgate Prison in 1679 or 1680.
5. So far as has been confirmed, and unsurprisingly in the religious ethos of Scotland, these breakaway actors sank without trace.
6. Curtis A. Price, 'The Critical Decade for English Music Drama, 1700–1710', *Harvard Library Bulletin*, 26 (1978).
7. Dryden, Thomas Shadwell and John Crowne joined forces to publish their scathing *Notes and Observations on 'The Empress of Morocco'*, and Settle's angry response, *Notes and Observations on the 'Empress of Morocco' Revised*, kept tongues wagging through the first half of 1674.
8. Entry on Purcell in *The New Dictionary of National Biography* (Oxford: Oxford University Press, 2004).
9. The ban (23 February 1689) on the use of stringed instruments in the Chapel Royal declares the musical flavour of the new court.
10. John Dryden, 'Absalom and Achitophel', l.417.
11. Derek Hughes, 'Theatre, Politics and Morality', in Joseph Donohue (ed.), *The Cambridge History of British Theatre*, 3 vols. (Cambridge: Cambridge University Press, 2004), II, p. 92.

2 The drama

1. For a succinct commentary on the historical reception of plays from the period, see Robert Markley, 'The Canon and its Critics', in Deborah Payne Fisk (ed.), *The Cambridge Companion to English Restoration Theatre* (Cambridge: Cambridge University Press, 2000).

2. Jocelyn Powell, 'George Etherege and the Form of a Comedy', in John Russell Brown and Bernard Harris (eds.), *Restoration Theatre* (London: Edward Arnold, 1965), p. 60.
3. Most notoriously, Etherege was one of the company at Epsom in June 1676 when the Earl of Rochester's assault on the watch resulted in the death of a bystander; and in December 1677 his friend Fleetwood Shepherd was 'run with a sword under the eye endeavouring to part Buckley and Etheridge squabbling in a tavern'.
4. Derek Hughes, 'Restoration and Settlement: 1660 and 1688', in Fisk (ed.), *The Cambridge Companion to English Restoration Theatre*, pp. 127–41.
5. V. de Sola Pinto, *Enthusiast in Wit* (rev. edn.; London: Routledge and Kegan Paul, 1962), p. 60.

3 Actors and acting

1. Buckingham fell out of royal favour in 1677, and was briefly imprisoned in the Tower of London. At some personal risk, Wycherley circulated a poem in Buckingham's defence.
2. Edward Langhans, *Restoration Promptbooks* (Carbondale: Southern Illinois University Press, 1981), p. xxiii.
3. Elizabeth Howe, *The First English Actresses* (Cambridge: Cambridge University Press, 1992), p. 24.
4. Kirsten Pullen, *Actresses and Whores* (Cambridge: Cambridge University Press, 2005), pp. 22–54.
5. The inconclusive evidence for this is the frontispiece to volume 6 of Nicholas Rowe's 1709 edition of the *Works of Shakespeare.*
6. Roach, *The Player's Passion* (Ann Arbor: University of Michigan Press, 1993), p. 56.
7. Joseph Roach, 'The Performance', in Deborah Payne Fisk (ed.), *The Cambridge Companion to English Restoration Theatre* (Cambridge: Cambridge University Press, 2000), pp. 19–39.
8. According to the intermittently reliable Colley Cibber, John Dryden was an incompetent reader of his own plays, Nathaniel Lee so proficient as to make the moody Michael Mohun throw down his part in despair.
9. Charles Gildon, *The Life of Thomas Betterton* (London, 1710), p. 15.
10. Tiffany Stern's *Rehearsal from Shakespeare to Sheridan* (Oxford: Clarendon Press, 2000) is an eye-opening investigation of historical theatre practices.
11. According to Anthony Aston, Lord Halifax was one of a group of bibulous noblemen who contributed 200 guineas each to Anne Bracegirdle, as a reward for her virtue.
12. Cibber, *An Apology for His Life* (London, 1740), p. 77.
13. Ibid., p. 109.
14. This is, incidentally, one of many scenes from the period in which the action, on a fully lit stage, is supposed to take place in the dark.
15. Cibber, *An Apology*, p. 81.

4 The material circumstance

1. The pedantically learned Rymer's observations are most fully expressed in *The Tragedies of the Last Age Consider'd and Examin'd by the Practice of the Ancients, and by the Common Sense of All Ages* (1677).
2. In the fifty years between its premiere and 1773, *The Conscious Lovers* was performed, on the London stage alone, more than 300 times.
3. In the *Tatler* 8 Steele had recommended 'the apt Use of a Theater, as the most agreeable and easie Method of making a Polite and Moral Gentry'.
4. Paintings of family groups and friends in conversation together proliferated in the first half of the century, and remained a moneymaking proposition for artists until near the century's end.
5. Pat Rogers in Rogers (ed.), *The Eighteenth Century* (London: Methuen, 1978), p. 9.
6. The *Spectator* 125 contains a neat Addisonian parable on the perils of faction. *Cato* provides ammunition for Pope's jibe (in his biting portrait of Addison as 'Atticus' in the 'Epistle to Dr. Arbuthnot') that Addison was 'willing to wound, and yet afraid to strike'.
7. The old canard that Rich was illiterate is unsustainable, though he was certainly clumsy with words. His collection of paintings has drawn less comment than his collection of cats.
8. It might be argued that Cibber was taking belated revenge on the non-juring Jeremy Collier, whose *Short View* (1698) had dictated his own career as a playwright.
9. The chief patron of the Opera of the Nobility was Frederick, Prince of Wales, of whom more anon.
10. The figures are drawn from Maxine Berg, 'Consumption in Eighteenth- and Early Nineteenth-Century Britain', in Roderick Floud and Paul Johnson (eds.), *The Cambridge Economic History of Modern Britain*, 3 vols. (Cambridge: Cambridge University Press, 2004), I, pp. 365–6.
11. Doubts about the provenance of the House of Hanover lingered well into the nineteenth century. I was amused to read an account of the wonderfully voluble society hostess Lady Jersey's outburst at Woburn Abbey, as late as 1825, when her loyalty to the Whigs was wavering. Seizing Lord William Russell by the collar, she exclaimed, 'Why should we have Germans to reign over us?'
12. As the named dedicatee of *The Non-Juror* and *The Conscious Lovers*, he rewarded Cibber with £200 and Steele with £500, but the gifts had more to do with politics than theatre.
13. The fullest account is in Vincent J. Liesenfeld, *The Licensing Act of 1737* (Madison: University of Wisconsin Press, 1984), but Liesenfeld underrates George II's involvement. See Peter Thomson, 'Fielding, Walpole, George II and the Liberty of the Theatre', in *Literature and History*, 3rd series, 2.1 (Spring 1993), pp. 42–67.
14. Judith Milhous, 'Theatre Companies and Regulation', in Joseph Donohue (ed.), *The Cambridge History of British Theatre*, 3 vols. (Cambridge: Cambridge University Press, 2004), II, pp. 108–25 (p. 125).

5 The drama

1. Rowe's barrister father left him with an annuity of £300 and chambers in the Middle Temple. He was called to the bar in 1696, but rarely practised, and had his first play, *The Ambitious Stepmother*, staged by Betterton and the Lincoln's Inn Fields company in 1700.
2. The term 'she-tragedy' is first recorded in the epilogue to Rowe's *Jane Shore* (1714).
3. I find it hard to forgive a syllabus that pushed Richardson at me as an undergraduate, and was pleased to reread Malcolm Kelsall's angry reference to 'the antiseptic clinic of that castrator and voyeur, Samuel Richardson' in his essay in Kenneth Richards and Peter Thomson (eds.), *The Eighteenth-Century English Stage* (London: Methuen, 1972), p. 26.
4. A status comparable with that of Poet Laureate, the appointment held by Rowe until his death in 1718.
5. Hogarth's twelve-plate sequence 'Industry and Idleness' (1747) is weighty evidence of this eighteenth-century theme.
6. The prose, it has to be said, is often cadenced in iambic pentameters and aspires to the poetic in such a way as to draw embarrassing attention to itself. There are few plays more likely to make the modern reader cringe.
7. Colley Cibber, *Letter from Mr. Cibber to Mr. Pope* (London, 1742), p. 33.
8. In Act 3 Sir Charles advises the lovesick Lord Morelove to 'whip out your handkerchief, and in point blank verse desire her, one way or other, to make an end of the business'.
9. It was her third marriage, in 1707, that gave her the surname by which she is known. Joseph Centlivre was Queen Anne's 'Yeoman of the Mouth' – a palace cook.
10. Charles Elliot (1749–90) specialized in medical books, in which he outsold London's booksellers, but he was alert enough to buy out the remainder of the second edition of the *Encyclopaedia Britannica*. Robert Burns bought his copy from Elliot's shop, where he might well have seen James Boswell browsing.
11. Doggett's *The Country Wake*, particularly in its one-act form as *Hob*, was enduringly popular, as was Bullock's three-act *The Woman's Revenge*. Had he lived longer, Bullock, who wrote at least seven plays in a two-year burst of productivity, might now be known as a playwright. It was he who wrote for John Rich *The Per-Juror* as the Lincoln's Inn Fields riposte to the Drury Lane crowd-puller, Cibber's *The Non-Juror*.

6 Actors and acting

1. Richard Hurd, *Letters on Chivalry and Romance* (London, 1762), p. 120.
2. Laurence Olivier's preservation of the Cibberian 'Off with his head! So much for Buckingham' in his film version of *Richard III* is a magnificent modern showman's recognition of a show-biz predecessor.

3. Cibber's virulently anti-Catholic version of Shakespeare's play carried the title *Papal Tyranny in the Reign of King John.*

4. Stourbridge Fair (near Cambridge) ran for over a month, from late August through September.

5. The vivid description of Bartholomew Fair in Parts X and XI of *The London Spy* is demotic writing at its finest.

6. See N. W. Bawcutt (ed.), *The Control and Censorship of Caroline Drama* (Oxford: Clarendon Press, 1996), p. 269.

7. Herbert squeezed licensing fees wherever he could: in May 1664, for example, he extracted a licensing fee from Joseph Chidley 'to sell balsam, draw teeth and cut corns'.

8. Britain's first Grand Lodge was established in London in 1717. If there has yet been a study of Freemasonry's relationship with the British theatre, I do not know of it.

7 The material circumstance

1. Paul Langford, *A Polite and Commercial People: England 1727–1783* (Oxford: Clarendon Press, 1999), p. 49.

2. Ibid., p. 698.

3. Both 'God Save the King' and 'Rule Britannia' were composed in response to Dettingen.

4. In protest against the East India Company's reduction of the price for tea, a party of colonists emptied three boatloads of tea into the sea, anticipating by sixteen months the formal outbreak of war.

5. Religious conflict raised the political temperature. Right into the twentieth century, Preston had the highest proportion of Catholics of any large town in England.

6. Charles James Fox (1749–1806) was the cleverest politician, but not the most politic, of the late eighteenth century. His principled opposition to the American war had a grandeur that he never quite lived up to, partly because, like Burgoyne, he was an obsessive gambler and philanderer, and partly because he was outmanoeuvred by the bloodless William Pitt the Younger (1759–1806).

7. Smith published *An Inquiry into the Nature and Causes of the Wealth of Nations* in two volumes in 1776, but it is usually the third edition of 1784, expanded to three volumes, that is taken to be definitive. The citation here is from the 1784 edition, I, p. 265.

8. London's population rose from roughly 500,000 in 1700 to roughly 900,000 in 1800.

9. Over the years, Boswell assembled a vast 'associational' wardrobe so that he could dress himself appropriately for a big occasion. To meet Jean Jacques Rousseau, for example, he wore lincoln green.

10. Nineteen such 'nabobs' were returned to parliament in the general election of 1768.

11. It was posthumously published as *A Trip to Calais* in 1778.

12. Sadler's Wells had, in fact, been beaten to it by productions celebrating the storming of the Bastille at the Royal Grove (later Astley's Amphitheatre) and the Royal Circus.

13. Winston's notebooks contain information on 280 theatres: *The Theatric Tourist* is limited to 24 of them.

14. Tate Wilkinson, *The Wandering Patentee; or, A History of the Yorkshire Theatres, from 1770 to the present Time*, 4 vols. (York, 1795).

15. See Chapter 8, note 15.

16. I have explored some of the common ground in 'Methodism and Melodrama', in Christopher McCullough (ed.), *Theatre Praxis* (Basingstoke: Macmillan, 1998), pp. 174–92, but the seeker after historical truth will find richer food for thought in E. P. Thompson, *The Making of the English Working Class* (London: Victor Gollancz, 1963).

8 The drama

1. Tate Wilkinson, *The Wandering Patentee; or, A History of the Yorkshire Theatres, from 1770 to the present Time*, 4 vols. (York, 1795), II, pp. 196–7.

2. James Thomson, 'Spring' (1728), l.908.

3. He was a distant relative and friend of the Scottish philosopher and historian David Hume (1711–76), whose intellectual status was uncontested.

4. Dr Johnson, who disliked Thomas Sheridan, asked him for evidence of the play's quality, and Sheridan cited the line, 'Who rule o'er freemen, should themselves be free.' 'Who drives fat oxen, should himself be fat' was Johnson's put-down. Brooke's libertarianism had caused the Lord Chamberlain to ban the performance of his tragedy *Gustavus Vasa* at Drury Lane in 1738. The laconic conclusion of the *Biographia Dramatica*'s entry on Brooke relates to the argument with which my previous chapter concluded: 'Before his death [in 1783], we have heard that he became a Methodist.'

5. Drury Lane playbill, 17 February 1753.

6. Lawrence Sterne, *A Sentimental Journey* (1768). Quoted here from the World's Classics edition (London: Oxford University Press, 1928), p. 21.

7. This preposterous book incorporates a dog of feeling, appropriately named Trusty, which 'gave a short howl and died' when its master was evicted by an *unfeeling* landlord.

8. *The Memoirs of Richard Cumberland* (London, 1806), pp. 141–2.

9. Despite the parliamentary passage of a Jewish Naturalization Act (1753), Jews were widely mistrusted, and regularly caricatured as grasping usurers. Popular pressure ensured that the Act was repealed within a year. In context, Cumberland's play, full of Shakespearean echoes, is a brave challenge to prejudice.

10. Sheridan was not to know that his body would be laid to rest in Poets' Corner, Westminster Abbey – next to Cumberland's.

11. Introductory comments to *The West Indian* in Inchbald's *The British Theatre*, 25 vols. (London, 1808), XVIII.

12. Dr Johnson's voluble friend Mrs Thrale suspected that Cumberland, despite the evidence of a wife and several children, was homosexual. See *Thraliana*, ed. K. C. Balderston (1951), pp. 135, 969.

13. George Colman the Younger, *Random Records*, 2 vols. (London, 1830), II, p. 137.

14. Douglas Jerrold's two-act comedy *Doves in a Cage* (1835) is the product of the author's researching of Fleet marriages. I know of no other play that treats the subject so alertly.

15. As a matter of curious interest, Tate Wilkinson's father claimed exemption as Savoy Chaplain on the grounds that the Savoy Chapel was under royal patronage. Having married 353 couples in 1754 and 1,190 in 1755, he was brought to court and found guilty. Fortunately, the death penalty had by then been reduced to fourteen years' transportation. Unfortunately, the convict ship on which he was sailing to America ran into storms off Portsmouth and he was drowned.

16. Runaway Gretna Green marriages, even of minors, remained legally valid in England until 1856.

17. This was in May 1965. I have no record of the cast or company, but remember that when the audience laughed the noise was deafening in the tiny auditorium. No actor could have hoped to speak over laughter in a Georgian provincial playhouse. In fact, actors must surely have felt socially bound to acknowledge it.

18. This is Mr Sterling's version of Hogarth's serpentine line of beauty. The twentieth-century update is Mae West's definition of a curve as 'the loveliest distance between two points'.

19. Cowley's subsequent plays were staged at Covent Garden.

20. The identification of the author as Philip Francis (1740–1818) is, even now, uncertain.

21. Bishop Benjamin Hoadly (1676–1761) compounded his Unitarian views by questioning the apostolic credentials of the Church of England, sparking a dispute that led to the suspension of Convocation in 1717.

22. See Jacky Bratton, *New Readings in Theatre History* (Cambridge: Cambridge University Press, 2003), p. 153.

23. The fierce drubbing administered to Murphy in Charles Churchill's *Rosciad* (1761) was one among many.

9 Actors and acting

1. Richard Cumberland, *Memoirs* (London, 1806), pp. 59–60.

2. See David M. Little and George M. Kahrl (eds.), *The Letters of David Garrick*, 3 vols. (Cambridge, MA: Harvard University Press, 1963), I, p. 67.

3. Diderot was also the channel through whom the bourgeois tragedies of George Lillo and Edward Moore gained an influence on the development of French drama.

4. Little and Kahrl (eds.), *Letters of David Garrick*, II, p. 478.
5. J. T. Kirkman, *Memoirs of the Life of Charles Macklin*, 2 vols. (London, 1799), vol.1, p. 66.
6. Little and Kahrl (eds.) *Letters of David Garrick*, II, pp. 435–6.
7. Ibid., p. 765.
8. Garrick had been instrumental in bringing Torré to England in 1771, not long after he had prepared the fireworks for the marriage of Louis XVI and Marie Antoinette, and Drury Lane subsequently benefited from some of his pyrotechnical innovations.
9. Hayman's second wife was the widow of Charles Fleetwood, for whom Hayman had painted scenes at Drury Lane. She had by then retired from the stage.
10. By September 1746 Garrick was already confessing to John Hoadly that 'I have been lately alarm'd with some Encroachments of my Belly upon the Line of Grace & Beauty' (Little and Kahrl (eds.), *Letters of David Garrick*, I, p. 86).
11. The politics of clowning, from Aristophanes to Groucho Marx (and later Marxists!), are the subject of two fine books by Joel Schechter: *Durov's Pig* (New York: Theatre Communications Group, 1985) and *Satiric Impersonations* (Carbondale and Edwardsville: Southern Illinois University Press, 1994).
12. The marriage had taken place in secret in December 1785. By the terms of George III's Royal Marriages Act (1772), it was illegal, since the Prince was not yet twenty-five; by the terms of the Act of Settlement (1701), it disqualified him from succeeding to the throne. However, it was sanctioned by Anglican and Catholic authority, so that Mrs Fitzherbert's connivance, rather than a formal escape-clause, was needed to allow the future George IV to make his bigamous and calamitous marriage to Caroline of Brunswick. From 1794, when her royal husband became embroiled with Lady Jersey, until her death in 1837, Mrs Fitzherbert lived in virtual sequestration.
13. I have never met a FitzClarence – several of them were shuffled off to Canada – but anyone bearing that name is a descendant.
14. The Irish Lola Montez (1818–61) was for a while the beloved mistress of King Ludwig I of Bavaria. She died in poverty on Long Island, New York.
15. William Hazlitt (ed.), *Memoirs of Thomas Holcroft*, World's Classics (Oxford: Oxford University Press, 1926), p. 228.

10 The material circumstance

1. By 1800 virtually all the fit male population was enrolled in some kind of military organization, those not in the army ranged in 'home guard' troops.
2. Cobbett's *Political Register*, a political weekly, avoided newspaper tax because it was a single-sheet publication. He made of it a rurally slanted and unashamedly opinionated voice of reform.
3. *The Black Book* appeared in book form in 1820. Wade published a supplement in 1823, and revised editions in 1831, 1832 and 1835.

4. Reynolds, like his friend Thomas Morton, combined playwriting with a passion for cricket. They were early members of the MCC.

5. The publishing in newspapers of lists of those attending the opera was at its height from the 1780s through the 1820s, and was not completely discontinued until the 1860s.

6. Gillian Russell, *The Theatres of War* (Oxford: Clarendon Press, 1995), pp. 95–121, and George Taylor, *The French Revolution and the London Stage* (Cambridge: Cambridge University Press, 2000).

7. When George III watched *Pizarro* on 5 June 1799, it was the first time that he had attended Sheridan's Drury Lane for four years. It was a Whig theatre, so far as he was concerned, and he was a Tory.

8. I have read only J. T. Haines's *The Factory Boy* (1840), Dion Boucicault's contraction of Mrs Gaskell's novel *Mary Barton* as *The Long Strike* (1866), George Fenn's *The Foreman of the Works* (1886) and Arthur Moss's *The Workman's Foe* (c.1900). There must, of course, be others.

9. E. P. Thompson's contrasting of the 'new' science of political economy (post Adam Smith) with the 'old' moral economy is significant here. See his essay in *Past and Present* 50 (February 1971).

10. Carlile would serve his second term of imprisonment from early in 1831 to 1833, but refused to be silenced. His life story is an extraordinary one.

11. Cobbett published its three acts in successive issues of the *Political Register*.

12. Malthus's *On the Principle of Population As It Affects the Future Improvement of Society* (1798) had argued that the population of Britain was on course to outgrow its means of subsistence, and that poverty and disease were necessary checks to safeguard the nation. (We should note that there was not yet any effective way of calculating population, and Malthus was a pioneer of population studies.) Francis Place and Richard Carlile campaigned for birth control as a counter to Malthus. Cobbett did not.

13. The reference is not, of course, to old-age pensioners (there were none), but to those awarded lucrative pensions by the state for political reasons.

14. Marc Baer, *Theatre and Disorder in Late Georgian London* (Oxford: Clarendon Press, 1992).

15. The young George included imitations of Kemble among his party tricks.

16. It is precisely this John Bull who is the hero of William Moncrieff's *Reform* (1832).

17. William Hazlitt's unverifiable verdict was that 'This play met with indifferent success, of which the principal cause was a supposed allusion to political subjects in some passages' (*Memoirs of Thomas Holcroft* (Oxford: Oxford University Press, 1926), p. 211).

18. Frederick Reynolds, *The Life and Times of Frederick Reynolds*, 2 vols. (London, 1827), II, p. 352.

19. On his mother's death in 1843, Bulwer added her maiden name to his surname, and he is probably better known as Bulwer-Lytton. When he was raised to the peerage in 1866, he called himself Lord Lytton. But he was Edward Bulwer throughout

the years that interest me here. For those interested in learning more about this intriguingly complex man, I recommend Michael Sadleir's twin volumes, *Bulwer and His Wife* (London: Constable, 1931) and *Blessington – d'Orsay: A Masquerade* (London: Constable, 1933), and Robert Lee Wolff's *Strange Stories* (Boston, MA: Gambit, 1971). They expose the underbelly of nineteenth-century respectability.

20. 'If you want to have anything done as well as it can be done, you must leave it to competition,' Place informed the Committee (Minute 3739).

21. Paul Sheridan has assembled information on the penny gaffs in his *Penny Theatres of Victorian London* (London: Dennis Dobson, 1981). He associates them with areas of dense population, poverty and crime.

11 The drama

1. It is most likely Elizabeth Inchbald's version of Kotzebue's *Kind der Liebe* as *Lovers' Vows* that is being rehearsed when Sir Thomas Bertram returns to Mansfield Park in Jane Austen's 1814 novel. Sir Thomas burns all the copies he can find of this, at the time and however watered down, notoriously licentious play.

2. Where *Speed the Plough* is mentioned in literary histories, it is usually for Morton's creation of 'Mrs Grundy', the archetype of the censorious Victorian matron. Mrs Grundy never appears in the play, but fear of her disapproval haunts Dame Ashfield.

3. Boucicault's memory, like many other things about him, was not particularly reliable.

4. *New York Daily Times*, 29 December 1853, p. 2.

5. From Smith's introduction to his edition of *London Assurance* (London: Adam & Charles Black, 1984), p. xxv.

6. Boucicault allowed this final speech to be spoken by Sir Harcourt Courtly – because William Farren, who created the part, wanted it. The intended speaker was the sporting countryman, Max Harkaway, to whom it is much better suited. But George Bartley, who played Max and managed the stage, yielded to the senior actor, and Boucicault presumably accepted it within the old spirit of the out-of-character epilogue.

7. William Hazlitt's flowery coda to *The Spirit of the Age* (1825) is a cameo portrait of Knowles: 'the first tragic writer of the age; in other respects he is a common man, and divides his time and his affections between his plots and his fishing-tackle'.

8. No nineteenth-century heroine is allowed to dispute the assumption that copulation with the villain is worse than death. Men have decided for her. The right to a bit of sampling in order to test the validity of the proposition belonged to life rather than fiction.

9. If *The Borderers* (1796) is anything to go by, Wordsworth learnt nothing from his visits to the theatre. Coleridge's rejigging of his *Osorio* (1797) as *Remorse* ran for twenty nights at Drury Lane in 1813, having benefited from his labours as

a translator of Schiller's *Wallenstein* trilogy. But these are minor works of major poets.

10. It was a financial speculation that motivated Keats's 1819 collaboration with Charles Brown on *Otho the Great*. Edmund Kean, he hoped, might buy it 'if he smokes the hotblooded character of Ludolph'.

11. Frederick Reynolds did so for Drury Lane in 1834.

12. Curiously, it was Joanna Baillie's doctor father who, having examined the boy Byron's club foot, prescribed for him the brace which he neglected to wear.

13. Arthur Symons in *The Academy*, 15 August 1891, p. 129.

14. Macready emended and staged two of Browning's plays, *Strafford* (1837) and *A Blot in the 'Scutcheon* (1843), but they had little chance of success. Browning's métier was the dramatic monologue, as in 'My Last Duchess' or 'Bishop Blougram's Apology', where a single voice conducts a dialogue with itself. The extraordinary serial narrative of *The Ring and the Book* is his peculiar 'take' on melodrama, as *Maud* is Tennyson's, but a treatment of the poem as melodrama does not belong here.

15. Jacky Bratton, *New Readings in Theatre History* (Cambridge: Cambridge University Press, 2003), p. 12.

16. Partially dramatized by Robert Jephson in *The Count of Narbonne* (1781).

17. Lewis achieved notoriety with the publication of his Gothic novel *The Monk* (1796), an exploitative blend of diablerie and sex. His *The Castle Spectre* (1798) is hard to read now, but it was a huge success at Drury Lane. In deference to 'the playgoing part of the public', *Biographia Dramatica* (1812) refrains from 'giving our honest opinion of its merits'.

18. William West began issuing sheets of engraved characters from popular plays in 1811, and from 1812 added proscenium arch 'fronts' with wooden stages. Cut out and mounted, the characters could 'perform' in front of scenes painted by those (mostly children) who 'staged' the play in their home 'theatres'. By 1843 West had issued 140 plays.

19. The underfloor mechanism of the vampire trap facilitated sudden appearances and disappearances.

20. Not until the 1840s did pantomime become exclusively associated with Christmas.

21. Nineteenth-century pantomime texts are not easily come by. There is, though, an anthology, authoritatively edited by Michael Booth, in volume V of *English Plays of the Nineteenth Century*, 5 vols. (Oxford: Oxford University Press, 1976).

22. In his *Recollections and Reflections*, Planché defines extravaganza as 'the whimsical treatment of a poetical subject' (new and rev. edn.; London: Sampson Low, Marston & Company, 1901, p. 268).

23. Elected to the Society of Antiquaries in 1829, and a founder member of the British Archaeological Association in 1843, Planché was appointed Rouge Croix Pursuivant at the College of Arms in 1854 and promoted to Somerset Herald in 1866.

24. Planché termed his more insistently topical pieces 'revues', but the distinction is a fine one.

25. Giles Playfair's *The Prodigy* (London: Secker & Warburg, 1967) is a good, short biography of Betty, whom Mrs Siddons dismissed as 'the baby with a woman's name'.
26. It is a terrible play, with two comic actors pretending to be Chang and Eng, but it contains enough punning to explain why its author was, for fifteen years (1841–56), the major contributor to *Punch*.

12 Actors and acting

1. For a magisterial treatment of the interrelationship between nineteenth-century drama and the visual arts, see Martin Meisel, *Realizations* (Princeton: Princeton University Press, 1983).
2. Millais's *The Order of Release* (1853) is a perfected melodrama. The 'play' has already happened – the post-Culloden release of the rebel Highlander has been purchased by his wife's surrender to the 'fate worse than death' – and the paradoxical triumph of the principle of female strength and purity is confirmed by the child and the dog.
3. Edmund Burke, *A Philosophical Enquiry into the Origin of our Ideas of the Sublime and the Beautiful* (1757).
4. Uvedale Price, *An Essay on the Picturesque*, 3 vols. (1810), I, p. 68.
5. Quoted in George Rowell (ed.), *Victorian Dramatic Criticism* (London: Methuen, 1971), p. 11.
6. I have written at greater length on the contrast between Kemble and Kean in *On Actors and Acting* (Exeter: University of Exeter Press, 2000), pp. 113–26.
7. The phrase is Hazlitt's, in his essay 'On the Spirit of Philosophy'.
8. Kean is one of very few Othellos to have outfaced their Iagos in performance.
9. Bertrand Russell included a chapter on the Byronic hero in his *History of Western Philosophy* (1945). The Brontë sisters register the impact on nineteenth-century novelists, notably through Heathcliff in *Wuthering Heights* (1847) and Mr Rochester in *Jane Eyre* (1847), and Thomas Carlyle wove the Byronic hero into the century's political philosophy.
10. Useful accounts of Vestris's remarkable career are available in William Appleton, *Madame Vestris and the London Stage* (New York: Columbia University Press, 1974), and Clifford Williams, *Madame Vestris* (London: Sidgwick and Jackson, 1973).
11. Lesser members of the seasonally engaged companies could presumably see the risk of unemployment – a word not yet in common usage – if long runs were to become the norm.
12. It is unlikely that the profession of 'playwright' would have been claimed by anyone before Henry Arthur Jones (1851–1929).
13. Hazlitt in the *London Magazine* (January 1820), p. 66.
14. Meisel, *Realizations*, p. 33.

13 The material circumstance

1. Young's *Victorian England: Portrait of an Age* (Oxford: Oxford University Press, 1936) is a supremely elegant and disconcertingly allusive long essay. The citations here are from pp. 7 and 77 of the second edition (1953).
2. Robert Dingley on Tupper, in the *New Dictionary of National Biography* (Oxford: Oxford University Press, 2004).
3. There were 825 recorded Methodist chapels in Britain in 1800, 11,007 by 1851.
4. Jesse Boot, founder of the most enduring of British chain stores, was a Methodist, often cited from the pulpit as a model worthy of emulation.
5. Stanza 3 of Hymn 499 in the *Methodist Hymn Book* (London: Methodist Conference Office, 1933); words by William Orcutt Cushing (1823–1903), set to music by Ira Sankey (1840–1908).
6. Temperance plays provide a particularly vivid example. Samuel French published a separate list of 'New Temperance Plays' in the later nineteenth century (and, for an American readership, another series of 'Ethiopian Drama', with such titles as *The Mischievous Nigger*, *The Stage-struck Darkey* and *Black Ole Bull* at 15 cents each).
7. Brunel is, I think, the only engineer other than his father to find a place in Sir Paul Harvey's wonderfully eccentric (what did the cricketer W. G. Grace do for English literature?) *Oxford Companion to English Literature* (1932) purely on the strength of his engineering.
8. Gooch was reinstated as chairman of the Great Western Railway in 1865, and knighted in 1866 for his work on the first transatlantic cable, successfully laid that year by Isambard Kingdom Brunel's *Great Eastern*.
9. Samuel Smiles had published *Industrial Biographies: Iron Workers and Tool Makers*, eulogizing individuals like Blasenberg and Bunter as exemplary heroes of progress, in 1863.
10. The Metropolitan Line, begun in 1863, was the first to be constructed underground.
11. In *Old Soldiers* (1873), Act 1, for example, H. J. Byron describes the heart of a strong-minded woman as 'a sort of Crewe Junction for the veins and arteries; a necessary, but by no means romantic institution'.
12. *Pluck; or, A Story of £50,000* was a melodrama, concocted rather than written by the manager Augustus Harris and Henry Pettit.
13. Both these plays were largely written by Cecil Raleigh, Drury Lane's house dramatist (pantomime and melodrama) at the turn of the century.
14. For brief comment on the People's Charter, see the concluding section of Chapter 10, above.
15. Quoted in Tyler Whittle, *Victoria and Albert at Home* (London: Routledge and Kegan Paul, 1980), p. 39.
16. In 1845 Friedrich Engels had published *The Condition of the Working Class in England in 1844*, and Karl Marx, financed by Engels, was working quietly in the Reading Room of the British Museum from mid-century.

17. Richard Schoch, 'Theatre and Mid-Victorian Society, 1851–1870', in Joseph Donohue (ed.), *The Cambridge History of British Theatre*, 3 vols. (Cambridge: Cambridge University Press, 2004), II, pp. 331–51.

18. Nana Sahib, who regularly played billiards with the British and attended a Masonic lodge, protested his innocence, but it would have been inconvenient to believe him.

19. John Stuart Mill, an employee of the East India Company drafted in to plead with the government for a stay of execution, argued that the Company's rule 'has been not only one of the purest in intention, but one of the most beneficent in act, ever known among mankind'.

20. For a detailed account of this Kiralfy enterprise, see Breandan Gregory, 'Staging British India', in J. S. Bratton et al. (eds.), *Acts of Supremacy: The British Empire and the Stage, 1790–1830* (Manchester: Manchester University Press, 1991), pp. 150–78.

21. It was Edmond Rothschild (1845–1934) who, having prayed at the Wailing Wall on 5 May 1887, immediately offered to buy it from the Arabs.

22. In New Zealand and Canada, too.

23. Falconer did not provide the libretto for Balfe's best-known opera, *The Bohemian Girl* (1843). Their most successful collaboration was on *The Rose of Castile* (1858).

24. Foreword to *Jane: A Social Incident* (1897).

25. I have not been able to find the precise wording of G. K. Chesterton's antifeminist quip about the thousands of women who, having exclaimed, 'We will not be dictated to!', immediately applied for jobs as stenographers, but its reference is to the spread of typewriters in the last quarter of the nineteenth century.

26. See Terence Rees and David Wilmore (eds.), *British Theatrical Patents*, 1801–1900 (London: Society for Theatre Research, 1996).

14 The drama

1. Dion Boucicault, 'The Decline of the Drama', *North American Review* CXXV (1877), p. 243.

2. Henry James's dramatic career is wonderfully reimagined in David Lodge's *Author, Author* (London: Secker & Warburg, 2004), which is simultaneously a novel and a sensitive study of James's attempt to break into the theatre of the 1890s.

3. Sheridan Knowles's *Dramatic Works* (1841–3) and the turgid *Dramatic Works* of Thomas Noon Talfourd (1852), both published by Edward Moxon (1801–58), himself a poet, were viewed as 'literature' by their authors. Chatto & Windus, though, was ahead of its time in publishing two series of *Original Plays* by Gilbert and Tom Taylor's *Historical Dramas* in the 1880s. However, it was Reade's novels, *not* his plays, that it published, as well as – in single volumes – all of Swinburne's nine tragedies (definitely 'literature' rather than 'drama', though William Poel bravely failed to prove otherwise with his 1899 production of *Locrine*). Interestingly, its 1880s lists included James Robinson Planché's *Cyclopaedia of Costume*, while the five-volume

testimonial edition of Planché's *Extravaganzas* (1879) was left to Samuel French, a low-status publisher of acting editions.

4. In the 1820s Birmingham taverns had separate doors for 'button-makers' and 'gentleman button-makers'.

5. Shaw's *Misalliance* was not staged until 1910, but his debunking of Victorian moral platitudes was well established by then.

6. During the London run of *Our Boys*, William Duck's Bath-based company took the play on a national tour which also clocked up more than a thousand performances.

7. Cook had begun his adult life as a village missionary, carrying the Baptist message around the south Midlands. He remained a fervent temperance campaigner throughout his life.

8. Hawtree's metaphor anticipates by a century the antics of Jimmy Porter and his socially superior wife in John Osborne's *Look Back in Anger* (1956), in many ways an old-fashioned 'misalliance' play, despite the impact it had at the time.

9. If grocers' daughters had been still the victims of such social exclusiveness in 1979, Margaret Thatcher would never have been Prime Minister. There, as Samuel Beckett might have said, is 'a thought to be going on with'.

10. G. M. Young's resonant claim that 'the Universities broke the fall of the aristocracy by civilizing the plutocracy' (*Victorian England: Portrait of an Age* (Oxford: Oxford University Press, 1936), p. 96) is persuasive, but not conclusive.

11. For a riveting collection of Sims's ballads, see Arthur Calder-Marshall (ed.), *Prepare to Shed Them Now: The Ballads of George R. Sims* (London: Hutchinson, 1968). I can think of no quicker way of confronting the distance we have travelled from the unabashed sentimentality of the 'average' Victorian.

12. Michael Booth (ed.), *The Lights o' London and Other Victorian Plays* (Oxford: Oxford University Press, 1995).

13. Brodie was an Edinburgh deacon (town councillor) whose fantasy life – influenced by a fascination with John Gay's *The Beggar's Opera* – took shape in reality when he masterminded a succession of daring burglaries in the city. Despite his posttrial confidence that, Macheath-like, he would be pardoned or rescued from the gallows, he was hanged, leaving a will in which he bequeathed his evil qualities to his fellow-deacons.

14. Henry Arthur Jones, *The Shadow of Henry Irving* (London: Richards, 1931), p. 44.

15. Elizabeth Robins, *Both Sides of the Curtain* (London: William Heinemann, 1940), p. 167. What might be seen as an anticipatory riposte is Mrs Chevely's in Wilde's *An Ideal Husband*: 'there is only one real tragedy in a woman's life. The fact that her past is always her lover, and her future invariably her husband.'

16. For fuller appraisal of the remarkable Robson, see Mollie Sands, *Robson of the Olympic* (London: Society for Theatre Research, 1979), and Peter Thomson, *On Actors and Acting* (Exeter University of Exeter Press, 2000), pp. 127–47.

17. Syphilis, inherited or not, was well known in middle-class England, its painful later stages disguised as the periphrastic 'general paralysis of the insane' (or GPI). It was, for example, the cause of the sudden end to the political career of Winston

Churchill's father, Randolph. The uncle nobody talked about, or the mad woman in the attic, probably had GPI. The chances of inheritance, unknown to medical science, encouraged enquiries into a family's background when marriage was mooted. Reference to syphilis was taboo precisely because people were so afraid of it. (No one ever mentioned 'cancer' when I was a boy.)

18. The argument touched on here is fully elaborated in Martin Meisel, *Shaw and the Nineteenth-Century Theater* (Princeton: Princeton University Press, 1963).

19. Joke-books under the nominal authorship of Joe Miller had been appearing at regular intervals since the 1740s. Even the original *Joe Miller's Jests* (1739) was only loosely related to the original Joe Miller (*c*.1684–1738), a comic actor and fairground entertainer.

20. In 1911 Brookfield, who had just written in the *National Review* that English drama had never recovered its former glory after *A Doll's House*, was appointed Examiner of Plays.

21. Quoted in A. E. W. Mason, *Sir George Alexander and the St. James' Theatre* (London: Macmillan, 1935), p. 81.

15 Actors and acting

1. To judge from the determined chin in the photograph of Fanny Josephs in Charles Eyre Pascoe's *The Dramatic List* (London: Hardwick and Bogue, 1879), she was nobody's fool.

2. George Rowell captures Irving's weird access to the divided self in his reference to 'the diptych of demon and saint'. See Rowell, *Theatre in the Age of Irving* (Oxford: Basil Blackwell, 1981), p. 24.

3. See Laurence Irving, *Henry Irving: The Actor and His World* (London: Faber and Faber, 1951), p. 601.

4. I am uncertain of the precise significance of George Bernard Shaw's choice of John Tanner as the hero's name in *Man and Superman* (1903), but given Shaw's sometimes problematic relationship with Mrs Pat, it is unlikely to have been coincidental. She was the first British Eliza Dolittle in *Pygmalion* (1914).

5. They were both playing Magda in Hermann Sudermann's *Heimat* (1893) and Camille in Alexandre Dumas *fils*'s *La Dame aux camélias* (1848).

6. Manchester and Margate are not randomly selected, since Manchester was the site of the Calverts' ambitious Shakespearean productions (1864–75) and Margate of Sarah Thorne's, but I mean them to be representative of provincial pride from Dublin to Glasgow and Hull to Plymouth.

7. The production is described by Jan McDonald in Kenneth Richards and Peter Thomson (eds.), *Nineteenth Century British Theatre* (London: Methuen, 1971), pp. 157–70.

8. Poel was a child when William Holman-Hunt used him as the model for Christ in *The Finding of the Saviour in the Temple* (1860).

9. Salvini spoke it in Italian, so Poel was presumably persuaded by the *sound* of close attention to the text.

10. Furnivall combined an indefatigable devotion to literary societies with a questionable commitment to the training of ladies in the craft of rowing on the Thames. He would act as cox to the ladies' eights, as a result of which Algernon Swinburne, with whom he had quarrelled, dubbed him Brothelsbank Flunkivall.

Index of plays

General index

Abbey Theatre (Dublin) 234, 236
A'Beckett, Gilbert 202
Abington, Frances 159
Absalom and Achitophel (John Dryden)
    22, 269n.10
Achurch, Janet 258
Act of Settlement (1701) 69, 83,
    276n.12
Act of Union with Ireland (1800) 167
Act of Union with Scotland (1707) 69,
    78, 136
'Actor, The' (Robert Lloyd) 151, 152
Actor-Manager, The (Leonard Merrick)
    259
actor-managers 258–9, 261–8
Actor's Art, The (Gustave Garcia) 259
Actors' Company (1695) 18–19, 29, 63,
    78
actors' status 61–4, 103–7, 152–63,
    241–3, 258–62
actresses (Restoration) 11, 53–7
Adam Bede (George Eliot) 221
Addison, Joseph 70–1, 73–5, 77, 89,
    102, 108, 151, 271n.6
Adelphi Theatre (London) 172, 182,
    198, 211, 240
afterpieces 99–101, 122, 125, 147
Ainley, Henry 58
Albert, Prince 228–9, 242
Alexander, George 256, 261–2
Allen, Grant 236–7
Almack's 171
American Copyright Bill (1891)
    240

American Declaration of
    Independence 116, 118
Amherst, J. H. 202
Anderson, James 213
Angel in the House, The (Coventry
    Patmore) 236
Anne (last Stuart monarch) 4, 28, 69,
    72, 76, 91
Apology for His Life, An (Colley
    Cibber) 41, 58, 62–3, 104
Aram, Eugene 247
Archer, William 232
Arne, Thomas 118
Arnold, Matthew 223, 226
Ashbury, Joseph 79, 112
Astley, Philip 130–1
Astley's Amphitheatre 130, 202, 213
At Homes (Charles Mathews the Elder)
    215
audiences 47–8, 49–56, 103–4, 256
Auditorium Theatre (Chicago) 232
Austen, Jane 32, 278n.1
Author, Author (David Lodge) 282n.2
Ayckbourn, Alan 31, 112

Bab Ballads (W. S. Gilbert) 254
Baillie, Joanna 194–6
Baker, Sarah 211–12
Balfe, Michael 235
ballad opera 78, 82
Bancroft, Squire 258
Bank of England 4, 48
Banks, John 61
Bannister, John (actor) 162, 163, 213

296